A CULTURAL HISTORY OF THE HOME

VOLUME 4

A Cultural History of the Home
General Editor: Amanda Flather

Volume 1
A Cultural History of the Home in Antiquity
Edited by Andrew Wallace-Hadrill and Joanne Berry

Volume 2
A Cultural History of the Home in the Medieval Age
Edited by Katherine L. French

Volume 3
A Cultural History of the Home in the Renaissance
Edited by Amanda Flather

Volume 4
A Cultural History of the Home in the Age of Enlightenment
Edited by Clive Edwards

Volume 5
A Cultural History of the Home in the Age of Empire
Edited by Jane Hamlett

Volume 6
A Cultural History of the Home in the Modern Age
Edited by Despina Stratigakos

A CULTURAL HISTORY
OF THE HOME

IN THE
AGE OF
ENLIGHTENMENT

Edited by Clive Edwards

BLOOMSBURY ACADEMIC
LONDON • NEW YORK • OXFORD • NEW DELHI • SYDNEY

BLOOMSBURY ACADEMIC
Bloomsbury Publishing Plc
50 Bedford Square, London, WC1B 3DP, UK
1385 Broadway, New York, NY 10018, USA
29 Earlsfort Terrace, Dublin 2, Ireland

BLOOMSBURY, BLOOMSBURY ACADEMIC and the Diana logo are trademarks of
Bloomsbury Publishing Plc

First published in Great Britain 2021
This edition published in Great Britain, 2024

Copyright © Bloomsbury Publishing, 2021

Clive Edwards has asserted his right under the Copyright, Designs and Patents Act, 1988,
to be identified as Editor of this work.

Cover image © Universal History Archive / Getty Images

All rights reserved. No part of this publication may be reproduced or transmitted in any form or
by any means, electronic or mechanical, including photocopying, recording, or any information
storage or retrieval system, without prior permission in writing from the publishers.

Bloomsbury Publishing Plc does not have any control over, or responsibility for, any
third-party websites referred to or in this book. All internet addresses given in this
book were correct at the time of going to press. The author and publisher regret
any inconvenience caused if addresses have changed or sites have ceased to
exist, but can accept no responsibility for any such changes.

A catalogue record for this book is available from the British Library.

A catalog record for this book is available from the Library of Congress.

ISBN: HB: 978-1-4725-8425-0
       Set: 978-1-4725-8441-0
       PB: 978-1-3504-1224-8
       Set: 978-1-3504-1235-4

Series: The Cultural Histories Series

Typeset by RefineCatch Limited, Bungay, Suffolk
Printed and bound in Great Britain

To find out more about our authors and books visit www.bloomsbury.com
and sign up for our newsletters.

CONTENTS

LIST OF ILLUSTRATIONS   vii

SERIES PREFACE   x

Introduction   1
Clive Edwards

1 The Meaning of Home   19
   Karen Lipsedge

2 Family and Household   37
   Helen Metcalfe

3 The House   63
   Stephen Hague

4 Furniture and Furnishings   85
   Clive Edwards

5 Home and Work   109
   Leonie Hannan

6 Gender and Home   131
   Ruth Larsen

7 Hospitality and Home   155
   Woodruff Smith

| 8 | Religion and the Home
Matthew Neal | 175 |

NOTES	203
BIBLIOGRAPHY	215
NOTES ON CONTRIBUTORS	237
INDEX	241

ILLUSTRATIONS

INTRODUCTION

0.1	William Hogarth, *Marriage A-La-Mode*, 1753	5
0.2	Joseph Highmore, 'Pamela', 1744	6
0.3	*The Tea Table*, c. 1710	8
0.4	The library at Syon House	9
0.5	*High-Life Below Stairs*, 1772	10

CHAPTER ONE

1.1	Francis Hayman and Hubert-Francois Gravelot, 'Mr. B. Finds Pamela Writing', 1742	22
1.2	E. Francesco Burney, Sidney Bidulph, 1786	28

CHAPTER TWO

2.1	Thomas Gainsborough, *The Cottage Door*, 1788	44
2.2	Johann Zoffany, *John, Fourteenth Lord Willoughby de Broke, and His Family*, c. 1766	45
2.3	John Hamilton Mortimer, *William Powell and his Wife, Elizabeth, and his Daughters, Ann and Elizabeth Mary*, 1786	46
2.4	John Singleton Copely, *Sir William Pepperrell and his Family*, 1778	46
2.5	Carrington Bowles, 'The Pleasures of a Married State', 1774	47

CHAPTER THREE

3.1	Old Dutch House, Long Island, New York, nineteenth century	65
3.2	Chatsworth House	67
3.3	William Hogarth, 'Beer Street', 1751	70
3.4	Versailles	72
3.5	Blenheim Palace	74
3.6	'A common Council-man of Candlestick Ward and his wife', c. 1750	79

CHAPTER FOUR

4.1	Design for a China Case, 1753	89
4.2	Panelled Room, c. 1740	93
4.3	State Bed, c. 1708	96
4.4	Furniture Designs from Kenwood House, late eighteenth century	99
4.5	'Cottage Life', c. 1750	106

CHAPTER FIVE

5.1	'An Experiment on a Bird in the Air Pump', 1769	114
5.2	Thomas Rowlandson, 'Mr. Burchell's First Visit'	117
5.3	'A Brewhouse', 1747	120
5.4	Mrs. Wyndham's Improved cross bar Lever	127

CHAPTER SIX

6.1	Thomas Rowlandson, 'Dr Syntax with a Blue Stocking Beauty'	137
6.2	Hannah Glasse, *The Art of Cookery Made Easy*, c. 1775	140
6.3	James Gillray, 'Farmer Giles & his Wife shewing off their daughter Betty to their Neighbours', 1809	144
6.4	Johann Joseph Zoffany, *Queen Charlotte with her Two Eldest Sons*, c. 1765	146
6.5	Elizabeth Brain, Woollen Canvas, 1785	151

CHAPTER SEVEN

7.1	'The Baron's Hall', 1844	156
7.2	'Virtuous Love', 1793	159
7.3	*A Family Being Served with Tea*, c. 1740s	163
7.4	'Ladies at Tea', c. 1790s	164
7.5	'A Ball at Scarborough', c. 1820	167

CHAPTER EIGHT

8.1	Wenceslas Hollar, *The Whole Duty of Man* frontispiece, 1658	178
8.2	*The Whole Duty of a Woman; or, a Guide to the Female Sex*, 1735	179
8.3	'Morning Worship', *c.* 1848	184
8.4	'The Diligent Mother', 1740	187
8.5	Michael van der Gutch, Queen Anne at Prayer	198

SERIES PREFACE

A Cultural History of the Home is an authoritative, interdisciplinary, six-volume series investigating the changing meaning of home, both as an idea and as a place to live, from ancient times until the present. Each volume follows the same basic structure and begins with an overview of the cultural, social, political and economic factors that shaped ideas and requirements of home in the period under consideration. Experts examine important aspects of the cultural history of home under eight main headings: the meaning of home; house and home; family and home; gender and home; work and home; furniture and furnishings; religion and home; hospitality and home. A single volume can be read to obtain a thorough knowledge of the period or one of the eight themes can be followed through history by reading the relevant chapter in each of the six volumes, providing an understanding of developments over the longer term.

Individual volumes in the series will cover six historical periods:

Volume 1: *A Cultural History of the Home in Antiquity* (500 BC–800 AD)
Volume 2: *A Cultural History of the Home in the Medieval Age* (800–1450)
Volume 3: *A Cultural History of the Home in the Renaissance* (1450–1650)
Volume 4: *A Cultural History of the Home in the Age of Enlightenment* (1650–1800)
Volume 5: *A Cultural History of the Home in the Age of Empire* (1800–1920)
Volume 6: *A Cultural History of the Home in the Modern Age* (1920–2000+)

Amanda Flather

Introduction

CLIVE EDWARDS

During the Enlightenment period, there was a growing distinction between the terms 'house' and 'home'. Early in the period, home might refer to the family as a social group, the household as an economic unit, or the physical structure of a house and its interior. By the later part of the period, the term home encompassed all these functions and more, including conditions of experience, emotion and representation. Definitions are never really stable and the home was a different place or idea for different people, but generally the home had become a state of belonging, of domesticity and ownership.

The Enlightenment was a widespread European (and later, American) cultural movement that developed in the late seventeenth and matured during the eighteenth century. The early Enlightenment began around 1680 whilst the mid-eighteenth century saw the heyday of the movement. The primary purpose of those who championed the movement was to use the concept of reason to change society and thus to lessen the impact of ideas based on tradition and/or faith. The scientific revolution encouraged these new ways of thinking and thus opposed superstitions, through scepticism, as scientific discoveries overturned many traditional concepts and introduced new perspectives on nature and man's place within it. These developments brought conflict with the Church, but were supported by some enlightened rulers who were keen to try out the new ideas. These included Frederick the Great of Prussia (1712–86), Joseph II of Austria (1741–90) and Catherine the Great of Russia (1729–96). However, the Enlightenment ideals of democracy eventually ran contrary to the despotic regimes and their notions of central control and concentration of power.

These new intellectual approaches were soon disseminated to cities across Europe, and then moved to some of the European colonies, especially America.

Here politicians such as Benjamin Franklin (1706–90) and Thomas Jefferson (1743–1826), amongst others, were influenced by Enlightenment ideas that were to play a major part in the advance towards the American Revolution. Although there was a lot of common ground across this wide geographic spread, there were differing approaches to the Enlightenment dependent upon regional context.

The origins of the Enlightenment are customarily found in the late seventeenth century when such thinkers including Francis Bacon (1561–1626) and Thomas Hobbes (1588–1679) in England, René Descartes (1596–1650) in France and other philosophers including Galileo Galilei (1564–1642), Gottfried Wilhelm Leibniz (1646–1716) and Johannes Kepler (1571–1630) had already established themselves. Works such as Isaac Newton's *Principia Mathematica* (1686) and John Locke's *Essay Concerning Human Understanding* (1689) were to become key texts of the period. Newton's development of calculus and optical theories supplied authoritative metaphors for Enlightenment ideals. Nature and all in it could be understood through 'laws' that were universal – and rational. Everything could be explained, categorized and defined. Whilst Newton was a key figure in the scientific revolution, Locke developed the idea that there were natural laws that controlled human behaviour, and these were to be found through reason. It is no surprise to find that the French philosophe Jean d'Alembert (1717–83), in his 'Preliminary discourse' to the great *Encyclopédie, ou Dictionnaire raisonné des sciences, des arts et des métiers*, acknowledged Bacon, Newton and Locke as the embodiment of the concepts of empiricism and the scientific method.

Human nature was a leading concern for eighteenth-century philosophers. Individual human nature was considered in terms of how to develop personal moral sensibilities, refined tastes and an understanding of beauty, all within a framework of a polite and organized society. The home was a main focus for the development and circulation of these ideas. It is important at the outset to mention that there was no generic concept of home and that although cultures had links between cities and provinces, for example, they were quite distinct entities, and within each there were multiple distinctions in terms of literary, visual and material culture.

The home can be a specific and defined physical living space, the location of domestic life, or a concept related to ideas of roots, origins and retreat. The changes that the Enlightenment encouraged, particularly in terms of human nature, created the circumstances for the concept of home to change and develop in three ways. First were the literary and cultural manifestations that included issues around attitudes to education, social order and disorder, sensibility and sexuality. Second were the roles of visual and material culture that were manifested through print, portraiture, literature, objects and products, and dress and fashion. And third were the industrial and sociological aspects that included concepts of luxury, progress, trade and technology, consumption, domesticity, and the notions of public and private spaces.

LITERARY AND CULTURAL MANIFESTATIONS

As the old domestic system gradually gave way to industrialization and urbanization, the home became less a place of work and more a family household. Other changes that impacted upon this shifting situation were the development of external workplaces, schools and asylums that impacted on the earlier nature and operation of the home. This separation of functions left many homes to become more of a site of childrearing and the location of a family unit. Indeed, Samuel Johnson (1709–84) in his *Dictionary* defined the word 'family' as 'Those who live in the same house; household' (Johnson 1755). The home as a place of living and being brought up, also often supplied a sense of belonging, of comfort and a state of being to its inhabitants.

Changes in attitudes to issues of domestic space and location also led to the search for some privacy and intimacy within the household. These transformations also helped to develop ideas of individual freedom, romantic love and domestic familial affection, as well as internal occupational relationships. Implicit in these changes is a notion that the enjoyment and protection of privacy became a shaping process as the family became more and more a self-contained unit, but one that was still acutely aware of its status and identity. Particular rooms became defined either as public or private and this was evidenced by distinctive furnishings as well as gender related characteristics in certain cases.

The home also puts on a show of personality and the accumulation of possessions. The theatre becomes a metaphor for the home. Therefore, the home acts as a stage, with its props, its front stage, back stage and private 'wings'. Each area of the home then had a particular part to play in the presentation of self. The stage metaphor also reflects the distinctions made by Erving Goffman in terms of the representation of the self as being based on a 'front' and a 'back' (1971: 1). However, by presenting one's public face as stylish and refined did not necessarily imply that that was the case in private (these thoughts were already recognized by contemporary commentators). When visiting England in 1784, La Rochefoucauld noted that

> At first I was quite astonished at all this [cleanliness] and did all that I could to make sure whether this cleanliness was natural to the English and so pervaded all their activities, or whether it was a superficial refinement. I was led to see quite clearly that it was only external: everything that you are supposed to see partakes of this most desirable quality, but the English contrive to neglect it in what you are not supposed to see.
>
> —in Saumarez Smith 1993: 308

Although this comment indicates the establishment of a public 'front' and a private 'back', the porousness of the distinction between the two types of spaces was evident. Whether it was servants passing through, business being conducted or guests attending functions, boundaries were often blurred.

Other metaphors equated the house to a body during the eighteenth century. The Jewish physician Tobias Cohen (1652–1729) juxtaposed images of the internal body works with the layout of a house as reflections of each other, whilst architects sometimes compared the house to a human body and a living organism, and for novelists like Samuel Richardson (1689–1761) the idea of the house was compatible with the (female) body.

VISUAL AND MATERIAL CULTURE

The Enlightenment of the philosophes, with their salons and lodges, was primarily a cultural movement experienced by aristocrats and the upper middle class. But further down the social hierarchy, a version of the Enlightenment reached an increasingly literate population through the development of print cultures that included not only magazines and newspapers, but also novels and books and popular almanacs that incorporated much of the new scientific and rational knowledge. In addition, the print culture also embraced imagery taken from fine art prints as well as images of satire and caricature. Many of these images depicted homes and interiors either imagined or real.

Artists of the period produced depictions of important interiors right through to images of the meanest and humblest abodes of the poor. The home as a concept became more important as the period went on, so much so that the notion of domesticity became synonymous with the English character and thus at the heart of social stability. The lack of stability was seen, for example, in the moralizing works of Hogarth, whilst the more enigmatic 'conversation piece' interiors painted by Arthur Devis (1712–87) and others were not realistic representations of particular places. These images reflect concerns about the vice of over-consumption and the vulgarity of sociability as an example of shallowness. These paintings were not showing a 'real' home interior, but a depiction of a client's familiarity with fashion, and their control in its adoption.

Moralizing in a different form is seen in other paintings such as George Morland's (1763–1804) genre scenes of the 1780s. The pair of images *The Comforts of Industry* and *The Miseries of Idleness* depicts cottage interiors that indicate the extremes of household management and family values. Here standards of housekeeping, the state of clothing and even the location of the interior offer two dramatically contrasting images of home and social order.

Preoccupation with domestic spaces and familial contexts was a hallmark of the work of the artist Jean-Baptiste Chardin (1699–1779). Chardin was a painter of the Enlightenment, being an artist who based his works on what could be observed and experienced. He painted genre pieces that reflected the domestic values of order, industriousness, education and affection through his

FIGURE 0.1: William Hogarth, *Marriage A-La-Mode*, Plate VI, 1753. © Heritage Images / Getty Images.

observation and recording of everyday home and family life. The bourgeoisie particularly enjoyed these images of enclosed and ordered safe havens, often set in the country, as they depicted the qualities of simplicity and naivety, virtue and happiness. Interestingly, adult males are not often depicted in his scenes, thus reflecting a wider understanding of the important role of women in the Enlightenment home. The entry on 'Femme' written for the *Encyclopédie, ou Dictionnaire raisonné des sciences, des arts et des métiers* clearly makes the point that Chardin was interested in depicting.

> Caught up in the duties of wife and mother, she devotes her days to the practice of unobtrusive virtues: occupied with the governing of her family, she rules over her husband through kindness, over her children through sweetness, over her domestics through goodness: her house is the abode of religious sentiment, filial piety, conjugal love, maternal tenderness, order, interior peace, gentle sleep and of health: thrifty and settled, she thereby avoids passions and needs . . .
>
> —Desmahis [1756] 2004, 6: 472–75

Eighteenth-century novels also give an insight into contemporary attitudes to the concept of home. Daniel Defoe's (1660–1731) *Journal of the Plague Year* (1722) and his idea of home as being about liberty (the dichotomy of home as both refuge and a prison) and the centre of a network of narrative spaces, that figuratively stand for the nation, is instructive in placing the idea of home in early eighteenth-century novels (Cousins and Payne 2015: 113). Twenty years later, in 1740, Samuel Richardson wrote what some have called the first modern novel. The links to the notion of house and home in the story of *Pamela; or, Virtue Rewarded*, are important to the structure of the work. The house where she first worked, which eventually became her own home, is described in detail, thus creating a new realism that reflected Enlightenment ideals. As Ian Watt points out:

> modern realism of course, begins from the position that truth can be discovered by the individual through his senses; it has its origins in Descartes and Locke and received its first full formulation by Thomas Reid in the middle of the eighteenth century.
>
> —1957: 26

FIGURE 0.2: An illustration of Samuel Richardson's 'Pamela', by Joseph Highmore, 1744. © Topical Press Agency / Stringer / Getty Images.

Eighteenth-century novels, therefore, were the first to engage with discussions of living spaces and to explore their psychological impact. From the realism of walls either as enclosures or exclusions, as protective or restraining; to spaces as havens or prisons; to rooms as either public and private, the novel made readers aware of the potential of home spaces to embrace or reject individuals.

Whilst images and texts were important in disseminating new or revised concepts of the home, other issues such as emulation, status, identity, politeness, sociability, urban living, as well as country idylls and the world of goods, were all influential on the notion of house and home.

The growth in social mobility, entertaining and being 'at home' meant that an individual's status was increasingly reflected in the home and is furnishings. This reflection had to be seen to be suitable for and in accord with their social position. In his *Elements of Architecture* of 1624, Sir Henry Wootton (1568–1639) recognized this need early on:

> Every man's proper mansion house and home, being the theatre of his hospitality, the seat of self fruition, the comfortablest part of his own life, the noblest of his son's inheritance, a kind of private princedom; nay to the possessor thereof, an epitome of the whole world: may well deserve by these attributes, according to the degree of the master, to be decently and delightfully adorned.
>
> —1624: 82

Although it seems that forms of self-consciousness (in the sense that individuals were knowingly able to express themselves) were well established by the eighteenth century, there were also 'standardized' systems of social communications. So ordinary people adopted and then adapted to their own various special needs, a system of courtly behaviour and furnishings borrowed ultimately from a protocol first developed in France and then disseminated through Amsterdam and London to provincial England and the colonies.

In 1711, the Earl of Shaftesbury summed up the effort required: 'the inward ornaments of houses, apartments, furniture, the ranging, order, and disposition of these matters. What pains! What study! Judgement! Science!' (Saumarez Smith 1993: 52). For many people the study and judgement required did not come easily, so pattern books on architecture and design established the appropriate models for particular styles.

Demand for specific goods was also derived from other changes in the home. These included the development of polite social habits, for example, tea drinking, social entertaining, reading and writing, which meant that new practical but fashionable furniture forms were required.

FIGURE 0.3: *The Tea-Table*, c. 1710, a satire of women's social discourse in the Queen Anne period. © Hulton Archive / Handout / Getty Images.

For many social groups, the importance of entertainment and the social round and the subsequent display of oneself and one's home meant that fashion had a major role to play in the maintenance of self-image. Although the fashion system was particularly influential in matters of personal dress and adornment, furniture was also affected by the changes fashion demanded. The polished surfaces with dramatically coloured and grained veneers, rare timbers from the Indies, and contrasting inlays of wood and metals all excited the visual appetite, as well as satisfying other egotistical demands.

A small but fascinating connection between the Enlightenment and decorative arts is found in the craft of coloured shell-work in the home. It links the classical symbolism of the sea with the fashionable shell-based rococo style and also the particular interest in Enlightenment natural science of which shell collection and ordering was one aspect. The fact that it was undertaken in a domestic environment indicates the potential spread of ideas for the philosophers' thoughts to the domestic interior.

FIGURE 0.4: An engraving of the library at Syon House. Designed in the late eighteenth century by Robert Adam. © Historical Picture Archive / Getty Images.

It can be argued that Neoclassical art and design was the only true visual embodiment of Enlightenment ideals. Educated men and women learned Latin and Greek and studied the poetry, art, architectures, histories and philosophies of classical Greece and Rome. This background provided Enlightenment intellectuals with a standard to work towards, and a set of principles to look at the past and encourage future developments. In addition to these aesthetic issues, the egalitarian features of the ancient Greek city-states and the Roman republic were a part of the political discussions around democracy and governance. The importance of Enlightenment Neoclassicism was that not only did it borrow directly from antique models of sculpture, architecture and decorative motifs, but also encouraged the emulation of the principles of order, unity, proportion and harmony that were seen as the crux of Classicism and rationality.

INDUSTRIAL AND SOCIOLOGICAL ASPECTS

The pre-industrial idea of a household with its many varied activities including aspects of production, education and religion, as well as the domestic arrangements added up to a community. The role of the house as a workplace

FIGURE 0.5: *High-Life Below Stairs*, 1772. Illustration from *Social Caricature in the Eighteenth Century* (London, 1905). © Print Collector / Getty Images.

as well as a dwelling gradually changed due in part to industrialization and urbanization. The old communal roles of the household were partly taken over by other agencies. The later home therefore became more of a private space that catered to the emotional, physical, moral and spatial needs of a family unit. This concept of a private space for a family was a bourgeois construction that developed during the eighteenth century. However, it must be remembered that a household was also home to non-family members including apprentices, servants and lodgers amongst others.

During the Enlightenment period, the availability and thus the consumption of goods expanded, and the nature of these material changes that equate to a growth in possessions were partly responsible for the rise of domesticity. Shopping for food, clothes, household items and luxuries became an important feature of society in the period. Inevitably, the home was a focus for these consumption practices. The portrayal of the usually urban middle-class family through their possessions is well known, and has often been seen in terms of emulation and conspicuous consumption.

Both the philosophical and practical advantages of the scientific method were further and vividly brought out in the second half of the eighteenth century with startling advances in industrial technology. The *Encyclopédie, ou Dictionnaire raisonné des sciences, des arts et des métiers* was explicitly inclusive of 'the arts', and in the eighteenth century these included technology and the mechanical arts. In his article 'Stocking-machine' in the *Encyclopédie*, lavishly illustrated in one of the supplements, Diderot showed how mechanization ingeniously multiplied human efforts and thus facilitated human comfort and convenience. In Britain, improving on James Hargreaves's spinning-jenny (1764), Richard Arkwright with his water-frame (1768) and Samuel Crompton with his mule (1779) applied technology to the mass production of cloth by steam-driven machines. Such labour-saving devices, so manifestly advantageous, illustrated the triumph of scientific method and Enlightenment rationalism. These developments of course fuelled the consumer demand for goods for self and home.

One classic example that shows how industry, trade and consumption came together is that of the work of Josiah Wedgwood (1730–95). A good example of an Enlightenment man, Wedgwood was a member of two London-based learned societies, the Royal Society and the Society of Arts, as well as the Lunar Society in Birmingham. Brought up in the world of pottery and ceramics, he began to work on his own in 1759, eventually linking with partners. Importantly, Wedgwood constantly explored the properties of materials used in the business, allowing him to develop new colour glazes and clay bodies. His experimentation and analysis, together with the systematic logging of results reflected the scientific and philosophical methods of the Enlightenment. However, this was only one part of his success. Wedgwood understood his market and clientele and developed showrooms to display and promote his 'trademark' products both in utilitarian and luxury spheres.

The effect of these developments on the home can be found in the myriad of consumer goods that were introduced, developed and promoted during the period. Examples include ceramics, textiles, papier mâché goods, brass and other metalwork, carpets, toilets, stoves and lighting.

The Enlightenment debates on luxury as an economic phenomenon were also central to moral and political issues and therefore had an impact on the home. In 1685, Nicolas Barbon (1640–98), a London-based entrepreneur and builder commented upon the beneficial economic effects of the 'Great Rebuilding', particularly in the capital. He noted how the building of great works provided employment for 'all those trades that belong to the furnishing of a house . . . as upholsterers, chair makers, etc.' Barbon was also a perceptive commentator on the acquisitive nature of people and the impact this had on trade and business. In his *A Discourse on Trade*, he pointed out that: 'if strictly examined, nothing is absolutely necessary to support life but food: for a great part of mankind go naked, and lye in huts and caves'. However, he went on to say: 'The wants of the mind are infinite, man naturally aspires, and as his mind is elevated, his senses grow more refined and more capable of delight.' He further observed that 'Fashion or the alteration of dress is a great promoter of trade, because it occasions the expense of cloaths before the old ones are worn out: it is the spirit and life of trade: it makes a circulation and gives value, by turns to all sorts of commodities: keeps the great body of trade in motion' (Barbon 1685: 32). It is these ideas that are directly reflected when the furnishing of interiors or purchase of clothes is undertaken with a view to representing something of oneself, rather than simply attending to functional needs.

Another contemporary writer, Bernard Mandeville (1670–1733), in his *Fable of the Bees,* asked the question: 'why distinguish between luxuries, necessaries and decencies and conveniences when considering goods?' He suggested that they are all mutable and variable and therefore do not need to be classified in a hierarchical way. In fact, the acquisition of material goods, particularly those associated with home-making was, in his view, like Barbon, of positive benefit to society:

> The greatest excesses of luxury are shown in buildings, furniture, equipage, and cloaths; clean linen weakens a man no more than flannel; tapestry, fine painting or good wainscot are no more unwholesome than bare walls; and a rich couch or a gilt chariot are no more enervating than the cold floor or a country cart.
>
> —Mandeville [1714] 1970: 144

Of course, the access to luxury was limited to those households that could afford these things. For others, it was often an aspiration to gentility rather than consumer goods themselves that they hoped would reflect their attitudes and position.

Although the idea that a home was, for some, a reflection of self and status as well as a conscious planning exercise, it was apparently not particularly part of the early eighteenth-century psyche. Some elites were purchasing objects based on conscious choice to display in architect-designed and planned houses, but at other levels goods were acquired locally and were based on need and use. Indeed, for many the purchase of second-hand furniture was common and the hiring of furniture pieces as required was a normal transaction.

Later in the century, some of these attitudes had changed. The elites had recognized that goods and their arrangement in a building demonstrated their particular choices and tastes that could reflect on them and their choice of style and architect. It is clear that the middle classes were also aware of these stylistic messages, but were as concerned with the self-conscious expressions of style and taste as with matters of comfort, albeit within particular stylistic parameters. This comfort would include an understanding of room differentiation and use, even if some rooms were still used for business or work. This concern would also recognize the changing roles of objects. For example, the importance of the grand bed declined, whilst that of the dining set rose. In addition, specific objects were introduced to assist in the coordination of social practices, for example the taking of tea.

The changes in the internal layouts of the new urban brick-built town houses were piecemeal and long-winded, but they were the backbone and framework for the new aspirations that in turn encouraged the demand for comfort. The development of the specialization of living spaces (to provide some privacy), the increasing importance of the hearth and fireplace (to avoid smoky fires), and the impact of glazing (to combat draughts) were all part of the developing comfort infrastructure that was well established during the seventeenth century. Apart from these improvements in the physical facilities, the idea of control over one's surroundings and a concern over politeness, respectability and cleanliness are also related to the issues of comfort, and could be seen as part of the psychological motivations in the growth of comfort as an idea and an ideal.

The way in which this new idea of comfort began to exercise the minds of the eighteenth century is confirmed by John Crowley when he points out that it was 'Anglo-American political economists, moral philosophers, scientists, humanitarian reformers, even novelists ... [who] sought to evaluate the relations of body, material culture, and environment in the name of physical comfort' (Crowley 2001: 142). Thomas Malthus's (1766–1834) work on population, published at the end of the century, considered that human happiness would be cruelly diminished if 'a good meal, a warm house, and a comfortable fireside in the evening' were not the incitements for a working person to look forward to (Malthus [1803] 1992: 211). Homes and hearths were the natural locations for this happy situation.

The themes that have been touched upon so far are all further explored in the following chapters of the book.

In Chapter 1 titled 'The Meaning of Home', Karen Lipsedge uses examples of contemporary literature to examine how the eighteenth-century home evolved. By using these fictive texts, particularly the novels of Samuel Richardson but also others, readers can see how they reveal the complicated relationship between interior spaces and the self that developed during the first half of the eighteenth century. The close examination of these sorts of texts that use domesticity as a part of the character's identity are of great value in assessing what 'home' meant to people in the period. An understanding of the meaning of home involves consideration of issues around sociability, privacy and politeness; gender, household roles and identity, and social and domestic order. This list demonstrates the growing complexity and interconnectedness within the home. Lipsedge considers the principles of organization, arrangement and decorative style of home. In particular, how novelists use houses and interiors as a hierarchy of spaces that reflect status though the various levels of access. The fictive representations of the organization, arrangement and interior decorative style of home that acted as signifiers of status through accessibility are explored in the example of Richardson's novel *Pamela*.

A major feature of the eighteenth-century home was the change from social domestic spaces to more private domestic spaces. The role of secretive closets and semi-private rooms is explored in a number of examples. The closet took on a number of metaphorical meanings that were expressed in literature. For example, the closet could be a metaphor for the mind, a sign of female vanity, a venue for all sorts of scheming and gossip, as well as more personal pursuits such as letter writing and contemplation. This idea of spaces reflecting female vanity is briefly explored through analysis of Jonathan Swift's writings about women and consumption.

The reframing of the role of men in the home is portrayed in Richardson's novel *Sir Charles Grandison* as 'Domestic Man'. This role fuses the public and the private, the domestic and the external, and set a moral tone that is reflected in the house and home. This chapter begins to provide an understanding of how and why fictive representations of home changed over the course of the eighteenth century. The spaces and objects depicted reflect contemporary authors' intent to express ideas of social cohesiveness. These literary representations give us a glimpse of how the idea of home was expressed in the eighteenth century.

Helen Metcalfe next explores the nature of the family and the household as being the social and practical centre of the home. She addresses important aspects of the home through the issues of gender, age, status and reputation. Metcalfe importantly questions the normative marital status of the family as the basis for a household. Clearly, there were a majority of normative family households consisting of husband and wife plus children. However, the eighteenth-century 'family' was often based on 'dependants' and was subject to degrees of flexibility over time. The concept of duty that then moved to love and affection as well as the issue of companionship, love and support were important aspects of the household in the period. Indeed, in bachelor households something akin to familial relations with servants were often evident. An important aspect of the family household was the management of the home and the maintaining of a family's reputation.

In Chapter 3, Stephen Hague considers the series of developments that significantly changed the design of houses in the period and how this changed the way people used and experienced domestic space. For much of the eighteenth century, the development of house construction by the nobility was the main driver of building. Nevertheless, over the course of the century, less grand domestic building grew in importance as the middle classes increased their purchasing power and position and subsequently a desire for home improvements. The principle of emulation that influenced the development of a common set of architectural principles came to be the architectural authority for all social classes. This 'Georgian' house form increasingly characterized the housing of the Western world but still allowed for regional variation and a continuation of vernacular traditions.

The discussion on common housing that Hague enters, explores the nature of houses that had small multi-use spaces that often combined domestic with working practices. Although there were hierarchies within this grouping where distinctions between, say, agricultural and mechanical artisans existed, the house still contained the basic elements of a family home. The step up from this was the concept of the 'polite threshold' where the builder favoured either aesthetic considerations (above the threshold) or functional ones below. The polite threshold was created by the form and spatial organization of houses overtly coded in terms of politeness. This ensured codes of conduct were enacted, while allowing inequalities of status and power to be maintained. It is clear that social position defined housing.

A similar development occurred in housing in cities where the process of urbanization created cramped and unhygienic conditions. On the other hand, inspired by Enlightenment ideas of structure and organization, town planning produced some extremely elegant solutions to housing. Houses for the middling sorts often encouraged the separation of work from home and again this created social distinctions.

Also, the houses of the elite were more than homes, as they acted as social, cultural or even political statements in the landscape. This multi-purpose role did not necessarily mean that the building was not also a home. An emphasis on comfort in myriad ways, the choice and use of a variety of rooms, the availability of servants and the employment of new technologies all assisted in this arrangement.

Finally, Hague considers rooms and how they were used. It is here that we see multiple crossovers with other chapters, as issues of furnishings, gender, social practices, hospitality, room use, as well as domestic working all come together.

In Clive Edwards's chapter on furniture and furnishings, the concepts of *habitus* and *figuration* that fashioned, inhabited, structured and performed the creation of domestic space are used to explore the furniture and furnishings that were bought and used. These items expressed *habitus* or the unarticulated but experienced symbols of life. The *figuration* or the networks of interdependent humans that created and sold the styles, types and materials that helped people to make sense of themselves and the world in which they lived, informed these. Supplementing these two considerations is discussion of furniture as a cultural signifier whereby people were socially defined by their furnishings.

In addition, furniture and its relation to gender has suggested that although there was differentiation in products, home furnishings was often a joint venture for married couples. Although gendered furniture products reinforced gender norms such as furniture items that apparently reflected the notion of feminine 'daintiness' and masculine 'bulk', they often simply reflected the style and function of the object.

It was during the eighteenth century that furniture and the concepts of function and comfort were fully developed, whilst the notions of fashion and taste played a role in the furnishing choices made for the home. During the period, many people were changing from being simply users to being consumers. This consumption was often associated with concepts of self-consciousness, difference and social performance and of course comfort in a broad sense. Initially, prestige goods and the associated idea of gentility expressed social status, rather than comfort in the purely physical sense. As the century progressed, physical comfort became more desirable in itself and also created a demand for convenience products.

Changes in eighteenth-century furniture, interiors and usage were part of the fashion system just like clothes. Edwards then discusses aspects of the furnishings of homes to give a flavour of how domestic space was fashioned and structured and how domesticity was performed so that people could make sense of themselves and their world. This idea of performance is examined in relation to the home where the theatre is a metaphor for the home. The home acts as a stage, with its props, its front stage, back stage and private 'wings'. In this analogy, each area of the home had a particular part to play in the presentation of self. Furniture in particular rooms acted as part of the setting. Edwards considers these rooms/spaces in turn, examining the types of furniture found there and how it worked. Of course these are generalizations, as each interior was different in both time and space and subject to the continuing vagaries of taste.

In her chapter on home and work, Leonie Hannan provides a fascinating snapshot of domestic spaces, busy with consumables, equipment and people – performing diverse and often complex tasks. Whilst many of these operations were ordinary in the sense that they were necessary, daily activities, when taken together, the actions of the brewhouse, stillroom or kitchen, the dairy, the laundry or the garden create a fertile context for investigation of the eighteenth-century home. Whilst domestic work is the main discussion, the connotation of work in other ways is instructive. For example, many of the wealthier households of this period engaged with work of a different kind. People chose to write or lecture about the work they undertook in experiments to learned societies and journals. They conducted their investigations with no more equipment than the average domestic space could offer them. Nonetheless, they were driven to enquire, to make some record of their observations, and to offer them up in service to the nation. These fragments of evidence begin to build a picture of eighteenth-century society that saw a broad population concern itself with intellectual labour and to do so by employing their minds and hands from the comfort of their own home. Other work that is beyond this essay is that linked to the domestic or putting-out system, which allowed people to undertake paid work in their own spaces. In her chapter, Hannan concentrates on unpaid or servant labour related to the home itself.

Hannan next introduces the network of household materials, equipment and techniques that work in the home engaged with. By using commonplace and routine documents such as recipes books, diaries and household accounts, she explores the myriad interaction between materials, equipment, tools and techniques that went into the work of running a home. The work of not only undertaking the tasks but managing them is highlighted. Instances of breweries and stillrooms are fascinating exemplars.

Hannan then explores how home economy met with innovation. She considers how the practice of working at home encouraged the development of innovations to improve the nature, speed or precision of a multitude of tasks. 'Working from home' was clearly distinct from 'working in the home'. The chapter makes clear that the home was an important location for all sorts of work, much behind the scenes, but other more cerebral forms were evident in the most important rooms as well. Hannan considers the home as a networked and vibrant set of spaces that allow connections between domestic labour with its own particular expertise as well as more cerebral intellectual endeavours to become visible.

The next chapter, by Ruth Larsen, is titled 'Gender and Home'. Many writers in Europe and North America in the eighteenth century believed that women had an important function within society, and this was usually based in the familial and domestic. This is unsurprising, as the home can act as a 'setting through which basic forms of social relations and social institutions are constituted and reproduced'. Thus, it is clear that the home developed its status as a centre for social interactions over the period until by the early nineteenth century it was an established norm. In this sense, the home both shaped and echoed concepts of masculinity and femininity in the period.

Larsen looks at the issue of gender through a range of approaches. These include assessment of the 'public' and the 'private' aspects of gender in the home; the apparent idealization of the domestic sphere; the role of gender in establishing the polite and sentimental home; gender and the managing and making of homes; and finally the natures of different forms of "homemaking". The chapter also considers Enlightenment discourses on home and domesticity and how they connected to gender, often using the records of specific individuals in order to understand their experiences.

The issue of hospitality and its relation to the home is considered by Woodruff Smith. He traces how the concept of hospitality gradually changes through the period from required enactments to becoming incorporated into and given meaning by the notions of respectability that defined a large part of what the home signified. Early modern hospitality and its relation to the home was initially based on concepts of duty and charity that were sometimes seen as reflecting domestic status. This gradually led to the idea of respectability, as consumption patterns grew and a middle class of homemakers developed. Smith explores this crucial concept and its relationship with issues including morality, gentility, civility and politeness. The preparation and consumption of tea was one of the defining rituals of the period and it is a perfect representation of respectable hospitality. The taking of tea was a sign of civility and welcome to guests and its ubiquity in visual and textual references confirms its importance as a social practice. Smith continues his analysis of tea and hospitality more generally in his discussion of period novels where the many permutations of hospitality can be drawn out as reflections of its role in eighteenth-century life.

Matthew Neal's chapter titled 'Religion and Home' draws upon eighteenth-century conduct literature such as *The Whole Duty of Man*, *The Whole Duty of Women* and *Discourses on Domestic Duties* and, through a close analysis of the advice given there, explains how a home should be run in line with religious teachings. It is also clear that these qualities offer advantages that extend beyond the home. It was not lost on many that a settled and happy home life was a microcosm of a happy nation.

The texts studied here see home as the first and best place for learning the lessons appropriate to a happy national life. Accordingly, the domestic space is one to be valued. Readers were encouraged to ensure that both the public (outside) and private (inside) self were in permanent accord. Interestingly, it was pointed out that sin could flourish as easily as virtue in the conditions of these spaces of human proximity.

The texts' 'dos and don'ts' provide a peaceable version of authority that was planned to achieve domestic harmony and political stability by following God's path. Neal reminds us that far from retreating in the Enlightenment period, religion remains at the centre of everyday life. The degree of consonance between these texts' vision of and the precepts of 'polite' and 'enlightened' living offers a salutary reminder of how little the achievement of stability in the eighteenth century owed to the retreat of religion. These Christian influences on the home include it as a space for peace and reconciliation; a place of orderliness and harmony; a place for authoritarian expressions of love over fear; an indicator of neighbourliness and hospitality; and a place to exercise discretion in matters of household management. Neal shows how spiritual best practice was redefined in the light of considerations of order, neighbourliness, and kinship and love. The authors examined by Neal offer a vision of home and home-life that united the notions of God and good living.

Taken together, all these chapters offer an extensive overview of the idea and reality of home in the Enlightenment period.

CHAPTER ONE

The Meaning of Home

KAREN LIPSEDGE

Today, fictional references to the home may seem unremarkable. But, in the eighteenth century, a reference to the home in a literary text would have been of note, in part, signalling the increased distinction between the *house* as a place of work and economic production and the *home* as an identifiable and distinct architectural structure that provided the family with a private place of retreat, comfort and succour.

From the late seventeenth century, a new type of domestic interior emerged: a home that was not only distinguished more clearly from work, but also imbued with and defined by what historians now recognize as a new 'culture of domesticity'.[1] 'Domesticity' is an elusive term. Yet, there are key characteristics that differentiate domestic from non-domestic spaces in the eighteenth century. For instance, a domestic space – a home – was conceived of as an identifiable and distinct architectural structure that provided the family with a separate retreat away from the public sphere. Judith Lewis highlights 'comfortable' and 'intimacy', as typified by body posture and furniture design, as a key factor in defining 'home'.[2] Equally significant is the notion of the intimate or private home, which highlights the idea of the domestic interior as a removed space where family members could receive respite from the demands of sociability.

The culture of domesticity relates directly to the transformation of the eighteenth-century home in terms of its structure, design and function, as well as its material culture. In the first half of the eighteenth century, developments in domestic architecture, material culture and concepts of self contributed to the evolution of an idea of home that was spatially and ideologically distinct from other architectural spaces. The home, in all its forms, was a locus for a range of human activities. These notions of the comfortable and private home increasingly characterized domestic space in the eighteenth-century British world, and the culture of domesticity with which it was associated. To understand what constitutes the home as well as the ways of life it facilitated, this chapter brings together literary analysis, architectural and socio-historical commentary to argue that the concept of home in the eighteenth century is related directly to key social, historical and cultural developments at this time. Eighteenth-century literary texts give us insight into the concept of home, and its varied meanings. They also provide insight into domestic ways of life, and the relationship between the inhabitants and their living space, as well as each other.

The first half of eighteenth century marks an important shift in the material culture of the home. It also marks the birth of new forms of literary and visual texts, namely, the novel and the conversation piece, which afforded a greater emphasis to the home as a setting for visual and literary texts. References to the home in literary texts is not new but, in contrast to earlier forms of prose fiction, such as François Rabelais' series of chivalric romances *Pantagruel* (1532) and Aphra Behn's *Oroonoko; or, the Royal Slave* (1688), the eighteenth-century novel focused on the individual's everyday life and activities. It was characterized by a degree of realism; a semblance of reality evidenced by the author's depiction of a recognizable and contemporary time, place and space, such as new and fashionable public leisure spaces like Vauxhall pleasure gardens in London (1729) and the Grand Pump Room in Bath (1706). In novels of the period, increased attention was also devoted to the protagonist's home, thereby exposing the interiors of élite and the rising middling classes and making visible a richly detailed setting for the fictional character's domestic dramas. In its focus on the domestic life of individuals, the novel gave the reader access to the emotional and psychological dimensions and meanings of home.

Fictional characters' homes and the objects within them appear in the earliest works of prose fiction, such as John Bunyan's *The Pilgrim's Progress* (1678) and Daniel Defoe's *Moll Flanders* (1722). It was only by the 1740s that the impact of this new culture of domesticity was apparent in the type of interiors depicted in contemporary prose fiction and the visual arts. Indeed, from the mid-eighteenth century, domesticity became a defining characteristic of British novels.[3] With the increased focus on domesticity in novels of our period came the expression of a new relationship between the home and its inhabitants. It is a relationship in which the concept of home begins to signal a certain set of values centred around the family, and in which these domestic values become an essential part of one's identity; as evidenced most clearly in the epistolary novels of Samuel Richardson (1689–1761): *Pamela; or, Virtue Rewarded* (1740), *Clarissa; or, the History of a Young Lady* (1747–48) and *The History of Sir Charles Grandison* (1753).

In Richardson's novels and, to a lesser extent, those of his contemporaries, interiors are often described by modern scholars as scantily furnished, especially when compared with the relatively detailed depictions of interiors found in nineteenth-century novels. Yet, by drawing the reader's attention to how a chair was upholstered and carved, the room in which it was located, and how the chair was used by a protagonist, for instance, eighteenth-century novels provide the reader with the detail needed to be able to construct gradually a clearer visual image of the interior in which a character is living. Due to his use of an epistolary genre, Richardson's novels also transport the reader into the fictional world of the protagonist, giving him or her access to the protagonist's thoughts and feelings as well as their relationship to interior space. Consequently, the reader not only has a deeper understanding of the characters and their home, but the visual quality of Richardson's novels is also enhanced.[4]

Illustrations of the period take their cue from the descriptive qualities Richardson employs in his novel. For example, *Pamela*'s visual quality is accentuated in the twenty-nine engravings commissioned by Richardson and published as part of the book in 1742. It is believed that the subjects for these engravings were chosen by Richardson, and that his aim was to choose those scenes in the novel which, when recreated visually, would elevate the character of his heroine, thereby underscoring Pamela's innate dignity, morality and virtue. Richardson's aim explains why 'over half [of the designs] depict the "high life" of Pamela' and represent her not as a 'person of inferior social position', but 'as a refined lady in elegant surroundings'.[5] The images depict a series of interactions between the characters, which are set within the domestic spaces evoked in the novel.

The scene depicted in Figure 1.1 illustrates the confrontation between Pamela and Mr. B. over a letter she has written to her mother. Visual evidence of Pamela's virtue is found in her neat and modest dress and posture, which contrasts to Mr. B.'s casually aggressive wide-legged stance. Her moral character is reinforced by the room and the objects within it, which include fine panelled walls, a large window providing light, and refined furnishings such as a mirror, delicate writing table and elegant chair. Pamela's body is associated with the table and chair where she has just been writing, the fabric of her skirt still touching the seat, while Mr. B.'s figure stands out against the wall and the door through which he has presumably just entered to intercept Pamela's correspondence. With their emphasis on the interaction between the figures as well as their setting, these illustrations were closely allied to the conversation piece; 'small, informal compositions representing real people "at home" or in intimate or private surroundings'.[6] Derived from earlier Dutch and French genre scenes and group portraiture, conversation pieces developed in eighteenth-century England as a combination of those two genres, with a distinct focus on a domestic setting. Unlike a conventional portrait, which emphasizes the sitter, the conversation piece paid at least as much attention to the setting the figures occupied – both the rooms and their decoration.

The increased use of the private home as a setting for visual and literary texts is to recognize, as Steedman notes with reference to representations of fictive

FIGURE 1.1: Francis Hayman and Hubert-François Gravelot, 'Mr. B. Finds Pamela Writing', in *Pamela; or, Virtue Rewarded*. © The British Library Board. 1457.e.14 Vol. 7 (Vol. I, 1742). Plate 1 opposite page 4.

space: 'that characters in books, and plot structures and literary devices have historical existence, and can be made to do the work of historical analysis, is not to blur the boundaries between fiction and fact, and it is not a denial of "history" – whatever that denial might be'.[7] Indeed, how literary texts can provide insights into the complexity of certain aspects of English socio-history has formed the focus of recent studies. Drawing on the earlier, and perhaps still the most influential work of Watt,[8] Ruth Perry, in her study on kinship in eighteenth-century literature, argues that '[n]arrative is a universal human response to the dilemmas about the metaphysics of existence' and that '[i]n the structure and verbal qualities of a work of art, in the anxieties and pleasures pictured there, one can trace the configuration of forces operating on people'.⁹ Perry reinforces the value of literary texts when analysing the concept of home in the eighteenth century.

In the section that follows, I consider the intimate relationship between the home and its inhabitants. The remaining sections draw on this architectural and socio-historical commentary to examine how fictive depictions of home in British eighteenth-century novels shaped and were shaped by cultural ideas about the interior. To provide awareness of how the literary representations of home altered during our period, it is the novels of Richardson to which most attention is devoted, but the early works of Jonathan Swift and Frances Sheridan's first novel also receive some detailed attention, with other literary texts drawn on, albeit to an even lesser extent. By using Richardson's novels as the basis of a comparison, this chapter seeks to provide a greater understanding of how the use, function and social significance of different types of domestic spaces and domestic ways of life were represented in literary texts. It also helps to refine the meaning of home in the eighteenth century in relation to domestic sociability, privacy and politeness; gender, domestic roles and identity, and social and domestic order, all of which alert us to the evolving complexity and dynamism of home. Such an approach also underscores the importance of the British context in the development of the eighteenth-century home and its associated material culture, where the absolute lack of monarchy left room for those down the lower social scale to exercise commercial and, eventually, political power.

The eighteenth century was a period of changing attitudes towards domestic life as much as it was a time of physical change to the spaces in which daily life took place. Interior spaces reflected changing attitudes about privacy and domesticity stemming from these geographical and cultural shifts. Writers' descriptions of rooms, furnishings and objects indicate an individual's place in society, domestic and material culture, as well as one's sense of self, of inner character. Literature, as well as the arts in general, provide us with an awareness and understanding of how people lived in and used interior space. Literary representations of domestic spaces present a constructed reality often influenced by the social and historical period in which they were written. Representations do idealize, dramatize and, to some extent, fabricate the lived experience of the interior. Yet, when analysed with reference to their context, they remain valuable sources of evidence.

THE ORGANIZATION, ARRANGEMENT AND DECORATIVE STYLE OF HOME

It is important to appreciate how the space of their houses defined people, an idea illustrated by how individuals built and finished a house, and constructed, arranged and decorated their interiors. Floor plans offer a guide to how people conceptualized and used space, whilst interior appearance and the level of finish in rooms conveyed important messages about their value. Locations, access and interior finishes all helped to establish the hierarchy of spaces.

How space was arranged in a house offers key indications of how it was used, and by whom. Building size and arrangement defined domestic space and varied enormously from tiny houses inhabited by substantial numbers of people to large country houses. Building plans signalled the importance of rooms and their intended use. Indeed, most eighteenth-century houses grew out of their plans and suggested social hierarchies. The houses of middling and upper-class Britons enabled differentiation of functions, more room specialization, the accommodation of more consumer goods and furnishings, incorporated servants to do work, and removed kitchen smells and the threat of fire.

From the 1720s, English Palladianism became the new English 'National Style' of Georgian architecture. Based on the principle of 'Utility, Strength and Beauty', this new National Style was also perceived to be the ideal visual symbol of the owner's politeness: the plain, simple facade expressing his restraint and decorum. In the interior of the house, suites of between two and four rooms were arranged hierarchically around a central staircase.[10] This hierarchal organization of the interior, in which the function of each room was signalled by its location, was believed to reflect the order and harmony of the inhabitants.

According to Shaftesbury in his *Characteristics of Men, Manners, Opinions, Times* (1711), a synergy between house and inhabitants was the 'greatest perfection'.[11] Shaftesbury also refers to 'the inward ornaments of houses, apartments, furniture, the ranging, order, disposition of these matters'.[12] The decorative style of a room was determined by its function, its location and by the types of people who should and should not have access to it. Similar approaches were reflected in the organization, arrangement and decorative design of Palladian houses owned by the gentry and lesser gentry. By the second decade of the eighteenth century,[13] then, the interior, like the exterior, was 'a public vehicle for a statement of the position of the individual in society' and an architectural reflection of the social status of the inhabitants.[14] The notion of the house as an architectural reflection of the social status of the inhabitants led to concerns about rights of access to specific domestic rooms. Similar concerns are also reflected in contemporary novels of the period.

FICTIVE REPRESENTATIONS OF THE ORGANIZATION, ARRANGEMENT AND INTERIOR DECORATIVE STYLE OF HOME

In Richardson's *Clarissa* (1747–48), the radical change to the hierarchical structure of the Harlowe family at the start of the novel is highlighted through the domestic space to which Clarissa Harlowe has access.[15] As the youngest child and 'flower and ornament of the family' (*Clarissa*, 308) prior to the start of the novel, the eponymous heroine used to occupy a prominent position at the heart of the Harlowes.[16] Clarissa's family status and innate politeness were not questioned. Her lesser parlour, private closet and summer house at the Harlowes' estate, as well as her dairy house at her grandfather's estate, are all architectural symbols of her privileged status. Yet, when Clarissa refuses to marry the 'odious Solmes' (*Clarissa*, 88) for money, at the beginning of the novel James, her elder brother, becomes a 'superior' (*Clarissa*, 54) and the servant, Betty, is promoted to the position of 'gaoleress' (*Clarissa*, 366). Meanwhile, Clarissa is displaced from her pivotal position in the family, as illustrated by her extrusion to the peripheries of the Harlowes' estate in Letter 24. As she is prohibited from using the social family areas of the house, and the main part of the Dutch garden, Clarissa only has freedom of access to her upstairs apartment, the back stairs and the outermost edges of the garden. It is to these areas that Richardson devotes attention for the remainder of the first two volumes.

In *Clarissa*, Richardson uses the internal plan, organization and function of the rooms in Harlowe Place to signify the types of 'place' – be they social or familial – the heroine occupies. The paucity of the interior and exterior spaces accessible to Clarissa at the Harlowes' estate represents her demotion within the family. Through her increased reference to the boundaries between herself and her family, Richardson also highlights a change in Clarissa's perception of her home and her family. Originally, she conceived of the Harlowes as a 'united family' (*Clarissa*, 62) and Harlowe Place as an external metaphor for the family. Once she has been denied physical contact with the family, Richardson reiterates that this familial harmony is absent, and any sense of harmony and unity is dependent on Clarissa adhering to the Harlowes' wishes. Now, the best view Clarissa has of her family is from behind a garden hedge, while her primary mode of communication with them is by letter. As Clarissa is repeatedly asked to give up her keys 'to everything', she also has very little control over her upstairs apartment (*Clarissa*, 116)

It is instructive to compare Richardson's use of Clarissa's reduced access to and use of rooms within Harlowe Place as an architectural signifier of her social and familial status, with Pamela and Sidney's, as described in Richardson's and Sheridan's first novel respectively.[17] As a lady's maid, control over Pamela's access and use of rooms in the Bedfordshire and Lincolnshire estates is determined primarily by her master, Mr. B., but it is also informed by the contemporary anxiety about the blurring of social boundaries between the 'middling' and upper ranks. Meanwhile, for Sidney, it is more her status as guest at Grimston-hall, and the increased introduction of 'gendered' rooms in the 1760s, that determine her rights of access.

Central to Pamela's access to and use of rooms in the Bedfordshire estate, is the heroine's right to a 'place' of her own; one that is not only reflective of her role within the household, but also of her virtue and morality. Like Clarissa, Pamela is also praised for her unblemished virtue and is described as an 'exemplar for all [her] sex' (*Pamela*, 431). At the beginning of the novel, it is apparent that Pamela has a clear concept of her 'place' as a lady's maid within her late lady's household; both in terms of her position within the social hierarchy of the household and the types of rooms to which she is allowed access. It is only once she becomes 'the carer of Mr. B.'s linen', and then his putative mistress (*Pamela*, 43), that her 'place' becomes more ambiguous. Pamela may have greater freedom of access to a wider variety of rooms and she may have been given an assortment of her late lady's clothes.[18] Nevertheless, Pamela is still at the whim of her master. After all, for Mr. B., rooms like the clothes are merely snares with which to trap Pamela and 'triumph over her virginity'.[19]

When Pamela is taken to Mr. B.'s Lincolnshire estate, however, Richardson employs Pamela's access to and use of the closet as a site for her closet-duties, to remind the reader that Pamela's virtue is unsullied and innate, and thus deserves to be 'rewarded'. Accordingly, it is no coincidence that on Pamela's marriage to Mr. B., Richardson alludes to Joel 2:16 and the closet's association with women and their preparation for marriage by depicting Pamela praying for thanks in the closet at his Lincolnshire house (*Pamela*, 324).

Moreover, on their return to his Bedfordshire estate, Pamela writes that Mr. B. 'gave me Possession of my Lady's Dressing-room . . . &c. that were in her Apartments, and bid me call those Apartments mine. O give me, my good God, Humility and Gratitude!' (*Pamela*, 431).

Once Pamela becomes Mr. B.'s wife, her social status also becomes more defined. The types of rooms to which she now has access marks a change in Pamela's 'place' in his household, from virtuous maid to mistress, and from the labouring classes to the upper ranks. As Richardson shows at the end of *Pamela*, and stresses in *Pamela II* (1742), the eponymous heroine's social and domestic elevation is beneficial for Pamela, the household and the family.

As a novel written as a homage to the 'exemplary Goodness and distinguished Genius . . . found united in . . . the Author of *Clarissa* and *Sir Charles Grandison*',[20] it is not surprising that a woman's need for a 'place' of her own is as significant in Sheridan's *Memoirs of Miss Sidney Bidulph*. The scene on which this section focuses takes place in the 'little drawing-room' at Grimston-hall (*Memoirs*, 80). In terms of plot, this scene seems to be about Mr. Arnold's 'declaration' of love and Sidney's objection (*Memoirs*, 80). But, at its heart, is Sidney's struggle to define her 'place' as a virtuous woman with a 'will of her own' (*Memoirs*, 85). By choosing to read Horace in Latin, rather than completing a 'little piece of embroidery' (*Memoirs*, 80), Sidney appears to challenge social conceptions about appropriate feminine occupations. As she agrees to marry Mr. Arnold shortly after this scene, Sheridan also demonstrates that Sidney's challenge is contained, literally, within the architectural boundaries of social room.

Sidney's letter-journal is dated between 1703 and 1705, but the architectural design, domestic mores and fashions represented in the novel reflect those of the 1760s, including the style of the 'little drawing-room'. From the 1760s, the dining room was increasingly conceived of 'as specifically male' and the drawing room, female.[21] Sheridan's decision to locate Sidney's challenge to conformity in the drawing-room is appropriate, if not revealing, however limited that challenge may be.

At Grimston-hall, Lady Grimston's strict adherence to the rules of propriety is illustrated by the 'regularity and solemnity' with which she runs her large 'manor' (*Memoirs*, 61–62). One room where Sidney manages to find some respite from Lady Grimston's regimen is in the drawing-room. What is apparent from Sidney's account of what she refers to as the 'little drawing-room conference', is that she conceives of it as a room in which to withdraw and receive some respite from the atmosphere of austerity which seems to pervade the rest of the manor (see Section three below). What also becomes evident in this scene is that the 'little drawing-room' is on the ground floor and accessible from the garden 'by a glass door' (*Memoirs*, 81). For Sidney, 'the little drawing-room' also appears to be the ideal room in which to read Horace (in Latin). That is until Mr. Arnold, 'a gentleman who is a distant relation of Lady Grimston's' and 'of a very good family . . . entered the room' (*Memoirs*, 63, 79–80)

What develops into a proposal scene does not actually begin with a declaration of love. Instead, Mr. Arnold focuses on the way in which Sidney chooses to spend her leisure time. As Sidney explains in her letter-journal to Cecilia, her confidante and correspondent:

> I was sitting in the little drawing-room, reading, when he came in. To be sure he was sent to me by the ancient ladies, otherwise he would not have intruded; for the man is not ill-bred. The book happened to be Horace; upon his entering the room, I laid it by; he asked me politely enough, what were my studies. When I named the author, he took the book up, and opening the leaves, started, and looked me full in the face; I coloured. My charming Miss Bidulph, said he, do you prefer this to the agreeable entertainment of finishing this beautiful rose here, that seems to blush at your neglect of it? He spoke this, pointing to a little piece of embroidery that lay in a frame before me.
>
> —*Memoirs*, 80

For Mr. Arnold, it is the intricacies of embroidery rather than the works of Horace that are a more appropriate pastime for a woman of Sidney's status and breeding. After all, the successful completion of a piece of embroidery requires a woman to follow a predetermined pattern. Conversely, as Doody has noted,

[r]eading Horace (in the original) provides escape into the life of the mind, an area considered so masculine that Mr Arnold is startled. He wishes Sidney to return to what he insists must be 'the agreeable entertainment' [. .] of completing her embroidery, and he wants to keep her attention fixed on the rose, the flower of love. Love, not thought, should concern a woman.[22]

That it is love that should be Sidney's main concern is underscored in Edward Francesco Burney's 1786 untitled engraving for this scene by the predominance of roses. The 'unfinished needlework rose in its frame', as illustrated in Figure 1.2, is resting on its pedestal on a small table near to Sidney. In the background there is the 'glass door' opening out into the flower-filled garden

FIGURE 1.2: E. Francesco Burney, Untitled Engraving 'Sidney Bidulph' (1786), in *Novelist's Magazine*, vol. 22, Plate II. © Bodleian Library, University of Oxford, Fic.3963 e 45/1.

beyond, and there is what appears to be a rose bush growing out of a pot situated next to Sidney. There is also a bunch of roses on Sidney's lap which are so large that, as Doody has noted, it looks as if Sidney is 'wearing' them.[23] But, if the rose is a symbol of love, then the prevalence of roses in the illustration seems to highlight not the presence, but the absence of love between Mr. Arnold and Sidney. Indeed, as the engraving makes clear, the focus in this scene is the tension between what Sidney and Mr. Arnold conceive of as an appropriate form of female occupation – that is, reading Latin or completing embroidery. As the engraving also underlines, it is the embroidery that is the most appropriate female pastime, since it is this needlework in its frame and the table on which it stands that are situated in the centre of the image and command the viewer's attention. Mr. Arnold is depicted standing beside the embroidery, pointing at it enthusiastically. In his hand nearest to Sidney, Mr. Arnold is holding the open book. Sidney, meanwhile, sits demurely; her arms clasped on her lap in front of her and her face bowed meekly.

In Sheridan's fictional representation of the drawing-room conference, to Mr. Arnold Sidney appears to be demure; reassuring him that 'I hope I was as innocently, and as usefully employed; and I assure you I give a greater proportion of my time to my needle, than to my book' (*Memoirs*, 80). Yet, in her retorts to Cecilia in her letter-journal, Sidney is far from meek; as she writes to Cecilia, 'in downright plain English, [he said] that he loved me!' (*Memoirs*, 80). For Mr. Arnold, Sidney may appear to behave with the decorum and propriety befitting her status and breeding in 'the little drawing-room'. Indeed, it is this outward appearance to which Edward Francesco Burney's engraving draws attention. But, if Sidney is the object of Mr. Arnold's desire, then Sidney's written retorts to Cecilia encourage a reader of Sheridan's novel to believe that Sidney finds him risible.

As a room conceived of as a feminine space, ideas about appropriate forms of female occupations seem to be questioned, if not openly challenged by Sidney. Yet, any agency that Sidney may have in this drawing-room scene is limited. After having finally declared his love for Sidney, the pair are then 'seasonably interrupted . . . by the arrival' of first the dean, and then Lady Grimston and Sidney's mother (*Memoirs*, 81). The focus of attention then shifts from the conversation between Sidney and Mr. Arnold to their hand gestures, physical location and the 'things' in the room, the chairs and window; all of which zoom suddenly into focus. At this point in the novel, the reader is also alerted to the 'glass door' opening out into the garden. As Sidney recounts to Cecilia,

> I was in some confusion on their entering the room. Mr. Arnold had at that minute laid hold of one of my hands, and I had but just time to withdraw it, when the door flew open to give entrance to the two ladies and the good man: the latter lifting up both his hands, as if conscious of having done

something wrong, with a good-humoured freedom, asked pardon; but with a look that seemed to indicate, he thought apology more necessary to Mr. Arnold and me.

—*Memoirs*, 81

This change in Sheridan's rhetoric of description indicates to the reader that what was a relatively private proposal in the drawing room has now become more public. As in the novels of Richardson, Sheridan has also altered how she represents 'the little drawing-room' to highlight the consequences of such an interruption. Sidney, desperate to avoid having to declare the outcome of the 'conference', manages to escape out of the full-length window leading into the garden. But, as she is reminded shortly after leaving the drawing-room, she has not escaped her duty to 'conform to her mother's will' and marry Mr. Arnold (*Memoirs*, 85). Thus, Sidney may seem to challenge mid-eighteenth-century constructions of femininity within the drawing-room but, ultimately, her actions are ineffectual. Due to its location in 'the little drawing-room' this scene, like the novel, is all about constraint – of behaviour, of language and of women. Regardless of the absence of love between her and Mr. Arnold highlighted by this scene, Sidney realizes she is merely a 'puppet', a 'baby' and has no right to choose whom she should marry (*Memoirs*, 84–85).

What conclusions can one draw about Richardson and Sheridan's use of their heroines' 'place' to signify their differing positions in the household? Richardson and Sheridan underscore the heroines' need for a 'place' of their own. The degree to which these rooms empower these heroines is limited; as representations of idealized feminine virtue, these heroines are defined and confined by the 'will to do right'. An awareness of the contemporary notion of the drawing-room as a female space also draws attention to the limitations of women in Sheridan's *Memoirs of Miss Sidney Bidulph* and to what Doody has referred to as, 'the complexities that arise in human life whenever human beings try to do right'.[24]

FROM SOCIAL DOMESTIC SPACES TO PRIVATE DOMESTIC SPACES

In the previous section, attention was devoted to the representation of 'social' domestic spaces in *Pamela*, *Clarissa* and *The Memoirs of Sidney Bidulph*, such as 'the little drawing-room'. Sidney may conceive of 'the little drawing-room' as a 'place' of her own, but it is represented as a social room. As noted, similar observations can be made about some of the social spaces represented in Richardson's first two novels and how they are interpreted by Pamela and Clarissa. Yet, in all these novels, emphasis is also placed on the depictions, sometimes detailed, of what is conceived of at the time as private or relatively private domestic spaces, such as a private closet – a small, separate room removed from the bustle of the social rooms, where the user, often female, can engage in private prayer, letter writing and reading, alone. Indeed, in the novels of Richardson, female protagonists spend a significant amount of time in their closets. For Richardson, a heroine's ownership of a separate, private room of her own exemplifies her moral strength.

In the second half of the eighteenth century, however, Frances Burney claimed, 'What heroine existed without her own closet?' and, in a letter to Fanny Knight about the recently married Anne Austen Lefoy, Jane Austen also acknowledges the value of a closet for hiding a woman's 'secrets'.[25] Yet, in the novels of Austen and Burney, private closets are noticeably absent. Conversely, in Richardson's novels it is private rooms that dominate. This distinction can be explained with reference to changes in interior design, cultural perception and use of domestic space in the eighteenth century.

When Burney's *Evelina* was written (1778), most people no longer had a private closet, regardless of gender or social status. This difference also reflects a change in domestic mores. In the early to mid-eighteenth century, the ideal was to have a private closet in which to retire from the social rooms, and to be alone. A private closet also enabled the occupant to travel through the private recesses of his or her mind metaphorically. Hence, Richardson relished the idea of having a closet on each of the three floors of his house at Fulham.[26] By the end of the century a resident, especially a female resident, not only wanted a separate space of her own upstairs, but also one downstairs. She no longer wanted these separate spaces to be secluded, like a closet. Rather, she wanted them either to be intimate, like an upstairs dressing room, or social, like a downstairs drawing room; in other words, rooms in which she was accepted both as an individual and as a member of a social or a familial group. The fracturing of the late eighteenth-century domestic interior into masculine and feminine rooms suggests that women and men also wanted their own space, in a gendered, as opposed to co-occupied, room.

The association of private spaces, such as the closet, with private feelings is also apparent in literary texts, most evidently in Richardson's *Pamela*, where the protagonist makes unconventional use of her late lady's closet as a private place of her own. In this room, Pamela's distress and moral fortitude are enacted.

> I have been scared out of my senses; for just now, as I was folding up this letter in my late lady's dressing-room, in comes my young master. Good sirs! how was I frightened! I went to hide the letter in my bosom, and he, seeing me tremble, said smiling, 'To whom have you been writing, Pamela?' I said, in my confusion, 'Pray your honour, forgive me! Only to my father and

mother.' Well, then, let me see what a hand you write. He took it without saying more, and read it quite through, and then gave it me again; and I said, 'Pray your honour, forgive me!' Yet I know for what: . . .

—*Pamela*, 44

In the 1740s, it may have been increasingly acceptable for individuals to retreat to private rooms in search of solitude, but that does not mean it was always acceptable to do so. Contemporary discourse surrounding reading and the young, particularly women, often refers to the dangers of women reading alone in their closets.[27] However, in *Pamela* and *Clarissa*, a woman's right to retire to her closet to write, read and pray is also represented as a sign of female empowerment and defiance. With their emphasis on the private, domestic lives of the individual characters and their experiences, novels like *Pamela* gave readers access to a protagonist's psychological depths, thus transforming novel reading into a private experience. As it became more acceptable for individuals to retreat to their bedrooms to spend time alone, the novel also reinforced the idea of privacy reflected already in the increased availability of private rooms in the middling-class home.[28]

REPRESENTING WOMEN AND CONSUMPTION

When considering representations of literary texts, it is equally important to consider the representation of contemporary anxiety over material wealth, often associated with women, their bodies and their seemingly insatiable appetite for 'things'; with the connection between character and home established through a repeated reference to things and bodies, particularly women's bodies. In Jonathan Swift's 'A Description of a Morning' (1709), for instance, Moll is described as 'whirl[. . . ing] her mop with dext'rous airs', while Betty 'from her master's bed had flown / And softly stole to discompose her own'.[29] Meanwhile, in 'A Beautiful Nymph Going to Bed' (Swift 1734), we are given unbridled access to a prostitute's 'bower', when 'Corinna, pride of Drury Lane . . . returns . . . at the midnight hour'. Swift paints a gruesome portrait of a prostitute preparing herself for bed:

> Then, seated on a three-legged chair,
> Takes off her artificial hair:
> Now, picking out a crystal eye,
> She wipes it clean, and lays it by.[30]

Swift's description of Corinna and her body as objects, as cited above, strengthens the imagery used to highlight the demands placed on women to conform to contemporary conceptions of beauty, regardless of social class or age. As Wilson notes, one could read the endless accounts of 'female grossness' as an attempt 'to reform women's boudoir habits'.[31] But, through his repeated use of a woman's dressing-room as the setting for scrutiny by the reader, Swift not only underscores the connection between women, objects and behaviour, but also between women, objects and the sexualized female body. For instance, in Swift's *A Lady's Dressing Room* (1732), both Cecelia's objects and her dressing-room 'debris' are displayed indiscriminately not only to the reader, but also to Strephon who, in Cecelia's absence, has managed to gain secret access. By facilitating the viewer/reader's access to the private space of a woman's dressing-room, Swift's *A Lady's Dressing Room* also makes a woman's body, her cleansing rituals and consumption practices available for scrutiny.

REPRESENTATIONS OF MEN AND HOME

But what about men? Histories of domestic space and domesticity have tended to focus on women's consumption of these new domestic objects, thereby creating a seemingly intrinsic link between women, femininity and the eighteenth-century home.[32] It was women, for instance, who advice literature prepared for the responsibility of managing the ritual of the tea-table, and the fitting-up of the house with tasteful furnishing. Domesticity, it is argued, created women as the 'domestic managers' of a comfortable and private interior space for the family. Furthermore, it was due to their association with and use of what Shammas refers to as these new 'tools of domesticity',[33] such as the tea cup, sugar tong and tea caddy, that 'women gleaned autonomy through a new kind of home'.[34]

Yet, as important recent studies by scholars such as Harvey, Hussey, Maurer, Carter and Vickery have shown, the rise of a new culture of domesticity in the eighteenth century did not mean that men were excluded from the home, either conceptually or in practice.[35] Rather, men's role within the household was reframed in light of the increased emphasis on women's domestic autonomy, especially in periodicals of the period. Hence, if eighteenth-century advice literature represented women as in charge of the day-to-day management and provisioning of the household, then it was the husband who was depicted as responsible for overseeing and organizing his wife's household duties. Similarly, if the construction of the home as a feminized private space placed an emphasis upon a woman's domestic and nurturing role as wife and mother, then it also placed 'an emphasis upon men's affective and economic familial role' as husband and father.[36] Gradually, therefore, the home began to be conceived of as more than just a dwelling; a physical structure with material characteristics and economic features. It was also what Charles Primrose refers to in the *Vicar of Wakefield* as 'our little habitation'; a shared, family home that acquired new emotional and psychological dimensions and meanings.[37]

In his often overlooked third novel, *Sir Charles Grandison* (1753), Richardson provides a useful example of a fictional representation of the domestic role of men; using Grandison-Hall and Sir Charles to signify the benefits (both private and public) of domestic order and harmony.

At the centre of Grandison-Hall is the baronet, Sir Charles – a model of masculinity and social order who is thoroughly enmeshed within domestic space and economy. Throughout the novel, Sir Charles is described variously as 'handsome', 'great and noble' and 'with a manly politeness'.[38] Hence, it seems only appropriate that he should be in possession of an equally 'venerable, large and convenient' 'family estate' (*Sir Charles Grandison*, VI.xliv.277). In Volume VII, Richardson highlights the synonymous relationship between Grandison-Hall and Sir Charles, with the house and surrounding grounds symbolizing Richardson's prototype of a domestic patriarch (*Sir Charles Grandison*, VII.v.17–ix.47).

A man's authority in the home was founded not on his ownership alone, but also on his close involvement and investment in the daily life and 'things' of the home, as well as his command of the overall management of the household. The domestic patriarch's role as the principal manager of the household is often underlined in conduct and advice literature focusing on the well-being of the family, where household and family management tend to be presented as a 'joint endeavour', with the husband and wife assuming differing levels of domestic duties. When Harriet becomes mistress of Grandison-Hall in *Sir Charles Grandison* (1753), Richardson highlights Harriet and Sir Charles's differing levels of household duty to suggest that they conceive of 'housekeeping' as a 'shared' domestic practice from the start of their married life and recognize its importance for maintaining order and harmony in the household. Yet, Richardson also underscores that it is Sir Charles, as overseer and manager of domestic affairs and the everyday life of his estate, who holds the locus of domestic authority and order at Grandison-Hall.

One strategy that Richardson uses to reiterate Sir Charles's domestic authority at Grandison-Hall is to highlight his hero's command and control over domestic sociability. Throughout the events to celebrate Sir Charles's and Harriet's nuptials, Sir Charles oversees and controls the 'whole space' and 'every-body' (*Sir Charles Grandison*, VII.vi.34). By making his household accessible as a site of sociability to all the neighbouring gentry, Richardson also stresses that Sir Charles's central role in the household is mirrored by his equally important role in the local community. As Harriet declares ecstatically to her family of readers:

> it is my wish, . . . that you were present, and saw him, The Domestic Man, The chearful Friend, The kind Master, The enlivening Companion, The polite Neighbour, The tender Husband! Let nobody who sees Sir Charles Grandison at home, say, that the private station is not that of true happiness.
>
> —*Sir Charles Grandison*, VII.vi.35

Harriet's use of the term 'Domestic Man' underscores the connection between Sir Charles and the home, and its implications for a reading of Grandison-Hall and social and domestic hierarchy. For Harriet, Sir Charles's 'devotion to [his] home' is shown through his relationship to and responsibility for his 'family', his neighbours and local community. As land and property owner, and baronet, Sir Charles and his estate, Grandison-Hall, signify power and control. But, as Harriet makes clear, any tension between the private and the public is eradicated through Sir Charles's role as 'Domestic Man', which fuses together a man's public and private identity through his domestic engagements. As domestic patriarch, Sir Charles has a dual but complementary responsibility to those both within and without his estate. Indeed, it is because of Sir Charles's complete control and command of the household and its inhabitants, that he can unite both his public and his private role so harmoniously through the persona of 'Domestic Man'.

The image of the house dominates each of Richardson's novels. The attention he devotes to the home and the domestic lives of the family sheds light on mid-eighteenth-century social hierarchy, the consequences of social mobility and the impact the increased emphasis on the display of wealth has on domestic order and morality. In *Sir Charles Grandison*, however, he employs Sir Charles as 'Domestic Man' to show the benefits of domestic order and the obligations afforded by status, both to the family and to society.

CONCLUSION

This chapter has sought to provide an overview of the architectural and socio-historical context in which the eighteenth-century home evolved, to provide a more comprehensive understanding of the representation of home in fictive texts, primarily in the novels of Richardson. The depictions of the home in the arts of the eighteenth century are, ultimately, images of people and the myriad ways they saw themselves. I have focused on the novels of Richardson to underscore how they reflect a complex understanding of the relationship between spaces and self that developed and changed in the first half of the eighteenth century. References to some other literary texts support and enhance such a reading. Consequently, the chapter begins to provide an understanding of how and why representations changed over the course of the eighteenth century. The interiors, rooms and objects depicted reflect the desire to express social bonds through concepts such as domestic sociability, privacy and politeness; gender, domestic roles and identity, and social and domestic order. Representations, ultimately, give us a window into the contemporary understanding of what was meant by home and inhabitants' lived experiences.

CHAPTER TWO

Family and Household

HELEN METCALFE

The boundaries of the Enlightenment 'family' were not fixed, but nor were they dependent upon a model of domesticity that centred on the marital home. Households formed what has been defined as a 'semi-permeable barrier' that linked the members of the household through contractual, emotional and occupational relationships, which were not limited to relationships of blood or marriage.[1] Indeed, the composition of early-modern households was considerably more flexible than is suggested by the work of Lawrence Stone and Randolph Trumbach, for example.[2] Criticism aside, the model proposed by Stone encouraged historians to interrogate the family and the domestic household in much more depth, and there is little doubt that the sociological and demographic studies of the family between the 1960s and 1980s also provided fertile ground for histories of the family to flourish. But this 'old master narrative of family history', as Keith Wrightson aptly defined it, led to a concentration on familial size, instead of the changing composition of the family with the, perhaps, unforeseen consequence of 'enshrining' the marital household as *the* unit of study (Hartman 2007: 8, 13; Wrightson 1998: 3).

Although histories of the family have had a tendency to reinforce the idealization of the conjugal home, such research also reveals that the concepts of 'family' and 'household' were much more nuanced than Stone's conclusions would suggest. In her study of transatlantic families and their epistolary relationships Sarah Pearsall notes the fluidity of familial composition during the period. 'Defining families is a vexed issue', Pearsall observes, 'since these were relationships of sentiment and obligation, which might imply a blood or marital relationship, but might not' (2010: 28). Other critical assessments of early-modern domestic and social lives include Naomi Tadmor's monograph on the

Turner family and Joanne Begiato's research on marital breakdown, coupled with the work of Helen Berry and Elizabeth Foyster on childless married men.[3] What these works all have in common is how they reconsider Enlightenment notions and experiences of family and social relationships more broadly. As such, they implicitly call into question the normative status of marriage within families.

Studies on the history of the family have consistently engaged with and challenged Stone's findings, and have enriched our understanding of familial structures and the domestic household – with issues of gender and social status emphasizing narratives of both continuity and change.[4] Begiato, for instance, explores how attitudes towards parenting were increasingly shaped by changing ideals of sensibility and domesticity from the second half of the eighteenth century. Begiato reveals that fathers were no longer emotionally distant men within the household, and instead became active participants in the lives of their children. Amy Harris offers an equally nuanced approach to the domestic environment in her study of Georgian sibling relationships. Harris uncovers the lives of sibling relations in order to re-evaluate the complexities of equality and hierarchy within male–female attachments, and suggests that assumptions about gendered divides did not necessarily apply within sibling relationships (Bailey [Begiato] 2012; Harris 2012).

Precisely who constituted a member of the family and by extension how a household was composed has thus been subject to important revisions in recent years, most notably in the work of Tadmor and Karen Harvey. Tadmor's conclusions on household management and organization are not limited to familial structures centred on marriage (albeit her study examines the experiences of a married man). Instead, she identifies the eighteenth-century family as one that encompassed all manner of dependents such as co-resident relatives, as well as servants and apprentices. The household was based on 'boundaries of authority and of household management', and supported by a hierarchical system that could 'expand and contract and include many individuals'; not all of whom were necessarily related by ties of blood (Tadmor 2007: 19, 23–24). Kinship, for instance, was displayed by ties of marriage and blood but was also understood through affective bonds. Indeed, Tadmor has shown how the language of kinship itself created 'webs of kinship ties' that were 'employed habitually in a wide range of interpersonal relationships to claim recognition [and] propose social bonds' among related and non-related individuals (2007: 163, 165). The flexibility of household composition has also been raised in Harvey's recent study on men in the eighteenth-century home. Harvey has highlighted how 'domestic patriarchy was a system of order in the household in which different individuals may each have access to different kinds and levels of power', within which, 'regardless of emerging domestic ideals centred on a nuclear family, flexible definitions of "family" were of ongoing relevance' (2012a: 4, 105).

The continual re-evaluation of family and household in Enlightenment Britain has increased our understanding of the spiritual, socio-political and economic, gendered, material and emotional experiences of family life in the past, and includes my own research on experiences of bachelorhood in late-Georgian England.[5] Interrogating the bachelor household unsettles historical narratives that have centred on the conjugal home, and demonstrates that the absence of a wife and children did not make the households of single men incomplete. The little research that has been conducted on British bachelor households during this period has identified them as deficient and emotionally empty realms that 'did not contain a family and therefore, according to contemporary views . . . did not constitute the ideal home' (Ponsonby 2007: 132).[6] And whilst a proposal for studies on the familial experiences of 'solitary individuals' was put forward some years ago, most scholars have continued to assume that these households were 'on the "edges" of family life' (Hareven 1991a: 119).[7] Yet such a categorization not only locates bachelors outside historical assessments of the family, it also fails to consider the varieties and inherent complexities of family composition more generally.

This chapter will first provide a broad survey of the traditional view of the family and household during the long eighteenth century, and as such will focus on the households of the connubial family. It will discuss several examples of prescriptive and instructive literature, as well as introduce depictions of the family in portraiture and prints so as to evaluate the extent to which representations of the family changed in contemporary print culture as new ideas about family relationships took shape. The remainder of the chapter will reconstruct the lives of those who are often marginalized in histories of the family and household that centre on the marital home, and in so doing re-imagine the family experience from the perspective of single men instead. Bachelors' life writings reveal that men's understanding and experiences of family and household were not limited by their single status. Indeed, the accounts below challenge assessments of bachelorhood that associate these men's lifestyles with a dissolute, lonely and solitary existence.[8] Bachelor households serve as an example of a co-existing model of family composition in the eighteenth century, evidence of which here provides us with another view of familial ties and calls attention to the many faces of the family during the Enlightenment period.

THE NORMATIVE FAMILY

Despite recent scholarship on the eighteenth-century family challenging Stone's traditional model of family composition, marriage continues to be the overwhelming focus in historical and literary research of social relationships throughout the early-modern period. Tara Hamling and Catherine Richardson, for example, have sought to uncover the social significance of the household by assessing the role of domestic material culture and the use of space in *A Day at Home in Early Modern England, 1500–1700*. They have shown how the household was organized by daily, hourly and life-cycle patterns and behaviours that were shaped by prevailing prescriptions of the socio-political patriarchal ideal, which located the husband as the figurehead of the family in a series of 'interlocking spheres'. Hamling and Richardson provide a detailed analysis of the domestic material environment to reveal 'the interplay of familial, domestic, social, commercial and religious concerns that characterised daily life and interactions' in the nuclear middling household (2017: 4, 5, 7).

It has long been recognized that the power structures of the early-modern home were used as a metaphor for the state, a model that was retained and reiterated in wide-ranging political and moral discourse. This model of the home emphasized the centrality of marriage where the husband, it was suggested, occupied the pre-eminent position within this hierarchically bound familial society. It was thought that a man's participation within this familial network verified his political legitimacy, authority and independence, and signalled his maturity. In common with Hamling and Richardson, Amanda Vickery's recent study presents a predominantly normative interpretation of the gendered material culture of the home, asserting that the 'patriarchal household family of master, mistress and children, with servants and perhaps apprentices, remained a universally recognised ideal type' (2009: 291). And whilst Ruth Perry argues that the importance of kinship structured by blood relationships was on the wane in the late-Georgian period, she still isolates the normative family unit of husband, wife and children as the focus of her enquiry. In her analysis of fictional and didactic literature, Perry contends that there was a 'seismic shift' underway in the meaning of family, which 'involved a movement from an axis of kinship based on consanguineal ties or blood lineage to an axis based on conjugal and affinal ties of the married couple' (2006: 1, 2, 14).

IDEALS OF FAMILY AND HOUSEHOLD IN PRESCRIPTIVE AND INSTRUCTIVE LITERATURE

At the beginning of the eighteenth century, religious commentators applied the metaphor of the commonwealth to discuss in great detail how the observance of a strict, albeit often contradictory, hierarchical structure in the household resulted in the successful governance of the family. The author of *The House-Keeper's Guide* from 1706, for instance, combined the terms family and household, and reinforced prevailing domestic ideals when they asserted that:

> a HOUSEHOLD is as it were a *little* Commonwealth, by the *good* Government whereof God's *Glory* may be *advanc'd*, the *Commonwealth*, which consisteth of several Families, *benefited*, and all that live in that Family may *receive* much Comfort and Advantage.
>
> —Anon. 1706: 1

Should the appropriate management of the household and the performance of duties attributed by this author to each member of the family be neglected, though, they maintained that 'things will go backward, the House will come to Ruin' (Anon. 1706: 49). The writer of *The House-Keeper's Guide* took direct inspiration for this advice from much earlier instructive literature and was, in fact, recycling the words of J. Dod and R. Cleaver verbatim, whose pamphlet *A Godlie Forme of Household Government: for the Ordering of Private Families, according to the Direction of Gods Word* was published in 1612.[9] Repeating passages of guidance from Dod's and Cleaver's material did not stop there, with *The House-Keeper's Guide* reminding its readers that 'The Governours [sic] of a family, are such as have authority in the family by God's Ordinance, as the father and mother, master and mistress' (Anon. 1706: 3).[10] The notion that the family represented a microcosm of the state continued to hold sway in the opening decades of the nineteenth century. The instructive sermons of John Angell James, for instance, emphasized that the 'domestic constitution is a divine institute', and with good government the family 'resembles the civil government of a state . . . the ecclesiastical rule of a church; and it is there that the church and the state may be said to meet' (1830: 9). The weight of responsibility associated with the successful running of a household was placed explicitly at the threshold of the Enlightenment family, within which the husband and wife laid claim to an authority that was believed to be ordained by God.

The traditional nuclear family was thus located at the heart of the private domestic commonwealth, which according to social and moral commentators throughout the Enlightenment period generated notions of emotional, moral, spiritual and spatial stability. The emotional comfort derived from marriage was a popular narrative in devotional literature, but at the start of our period was phrased in contractual terms that emphasized the duties and obligations of each spouse. Richard Allestree's extraordinarily popular and lengthy exposition, *The Whole Duty of Man* (1658), instructed his readers that love was one of several duties required between man and wife – citing St. Paul as evidence ([1658] 1704: 324–25, 326–27). Although duty and obligation remained significant factors in discussions of marriage throughout the Enlightenment period, from around the middle of the eighteenth century representations of the connubial family placed much greater value in relationships bonded by love and affection.

In 1785, John Trussler published a lengthy letter to those 'in family relation' and espoused the benefits of domestic happiness and harmony which, observed Trussler, 'confirms and increases mutual affection, between the several members of a family, & hereby renders all the relative duties of life easy and pleasant' (1785: 2, 24). Trussler's letter was framed explicitly around the notion of a nuclear family where moral instruction and influence was inspired by bonds of love between family members because:

> when those who are at the head of a family, are united in sincere affection, & live together in constant harmony, their children have an amiable pattern perpetually before their eyes, which cannot fail of attracting their esteem and love ... where this union of hearts subsists between parents, it strengthens their affection for their offspring, & prompts them to unite their utmost endeavours, for their improvement & welfare. They employ their joint skill & influence, in the important work of education; and, in consequence of this, their judgement is regarded with the highest deference.
>
> —Trussler 1785: 7, 8

In contrast to Allestree's treatise, familial love was discussed as a 'sincere affection' rather than a moral and religious obligation. Familial love and mutual respect became popular themes in late-eighteenth-century instructive and prescriptive literature, and were presented in a 1796 poem, *The Fireside*, which used the familiar trope of hearth and home to convey its message. In common with Trussler's observations, the poem promoted marriage as 'a paradise below', where 'Our babes shall richest comforts bring / If tutor'd right they'll prove a spring . . . While they our wisest hours engage / They'll joy our youth, support our age . . . They'll grow in virtue every day / And thus our fondest loves repay' (Cotton 1796: 3).

Faith and duty continued to shape ideas about the family and household structure in prescriptive literature for much of the eighteenth century (with precursors dating back to the sixteenth and seventeenth centuries),[11] yet love, companionship and domestic harmony became increasingly important in discourses of marriage and familial organization. The author of 'A Map of the Island of Matrimony', for example, envisioned an island 'abounding with all imaginable Pleasures' for couples in love who 'live there in a perpetual spring' (Single 1772: 77). Whilst for the non-conformist clergyman John Angell James, the connubial family was a 'hallowed circle' that was 'united by love and sanctified by grace', and discussed in rapturous terms when he wrote that:

> A FAMILY![12] How delightful the associations we form with such a word! How pleasing the images with which it crowds the mind, and how tender the

emotions which it awakens in the heart! Who can wonder that domestic happiness should be a theme dear to poetry and that it should have called forth some of the sweetest strains of fancy and of feeling?

—Angell James 1830: iv, 7

Angell James reproduced several familiar themes in this passage that remind us of the fervour associated with dissenting preachers, but his remarks also emphasize the continued role of sensibility in sermons on family life through which the body was presented as a vessel of heightened emotional sensations, love and attachment. Such rhapsodies of love and companionship were thus a far cry from early-eighteenth-century treatises on the family, where issues of government, subjection and obedience were placed above sentiment.[13] In common with Angell James, Trussler discussed the family in terms of a 'little society' that produced feelings of awe and wonder because the 'man who is blest with tenderness and sensibility of heart' will find that his 'family will furnish the truest & most lasting pleasures' (1785: 5, 11).

VISUAL REPRESENTATIONS OF THE FAMILY IN PORTRATURE AND PRINT

As emotional ideals about family took shape, contemporary commentators looked to each other to reinforce the elevated position of the connubial household. In an idealized description of a rural cottage scene, for instance, Trussler moved his readers to 'dwell, for a while, in this happy family ... where hearts are thus united by the firmest & most pleasing of all bonds, Mutual Affection ... there, indeed, is the seat of content and happiness' (1785: 12). By depicting the family in a pastoral idyll, Trussler recalled the aesthetics of the picturesque movement, which was typical of this period, with scenes of rural retirement reproduced in images such as Thomas Gainsborough's *The Cottage Door*. This 'cult of the cottage', according to Ann Bermingham, was reproduced in art and literature, architectural design and on decorative material objects, and located the cottage as 'both a fantasy and physical embodiment of new ideas of privacy and domesticity' (2005: 38). These compositions set the family firmly within the aesthetics of sensibility, with Gainsborough's affecting landscapes awakening viewers' sensations to suggestions that domestic bliss was to be found in the comforts and pleasures of rural family life.

Gainsborough's cottage scene demonstrates how marriage was presented as the cornerstone of social cohesion and domestic happiness not only in prescriptive literature but also in prints and portraiture, which consistently depicted the normative domestic model and patriarchal ideal. Yet from around the middle decades of the eighteenth century, family portraiture changed from scenes of

FIGURE 2.1: Thomas Gainsborough, *The Cottage Door* (1778) depicts several generations of a family in rural idyll – husband and wife with their children, and an ageing parent in the background. © Cincinnati Art Museum, Ohio, / Given in honour of Mr. & Mrs. Charles F. Williams by their children / Bridgeman Images.

stiffly posed compositional groupings to intimate representations of what Kate Retford has defined as 'mutual absorption' during captured moments where sitters seem indifferent to the external gaze (2006: 1). This newly sentimentalized view of family life was frequently attributed to Joshua Reynolds by contemporary commentators, who approved of the move to informality, compatibility and affection (Retford 2006: 4). As the popularity of the genre increased, depictions of idealized familial scenes were produced for wealthy patrons by the likes of Johann Zoffany, John Hamilton Mortimer and John Singleton Copely. The families in the examples here radiate with a sense of intimacy and playfulness between the sitters, and emphasize the bonds of reciprocal love and parental warmth that, as we have seen, were echoed in contemporary literature.

Recommendations of love and affection between husband and wife were not entirely new in this period, but from around the middle of the eighteenth century took on new meaning as the development of sentimental representations

FIGURE 2.2: The portrait is of John Peyto-Verney and his wife Lady Louisa North – who is holding their daughter while their two sons play around their feet. Johann Zoffany (German, 1733–1810), *John, Fourteenth Lord Willoughby de Broke, and His Family*, c. 1766. Oil on canvas, 101.9 × 127.3 cm (40 1/8 × 50 1/8 in.), 96.PA.312. © The J. Paul Getty Museum, Los Angeles. Digital image courtesy of the Getty's Open Content Program.

of the family in print culture more widely became a highly valued expression of refined feeling and private virtue. Depictions of intimate familial groups were not limited to commissioned works of art. Carrington Bowles re-imagined the emotional rewards and comforts of the nuptial family in a 1774 print entitled 'The Pleasures of a Married State', which depicts a scene of domestic bliss where husband and wife sit surrounded by their children – all of whom, according to the inscription below, are united in 'sensibility of Love'.

Despite this print presenting an entirely fictionalized family, the perspective it promotes underscores the role of sentiment as much as it elevates the normative model of marriage. The newly framed status of tenderness and displays or descriptions of affective familial ties in print culture of this period should not be overstated, though, as this sentimental perspective on family life did not supersede the existing patriarchal ideal, which continued to favour the dictates of ancestry, inheritance and hierarchy (Retford 2006: 8, 13, 116).

FIGURE 2.3: John Hamilton Mortimer, *William Powell and his Wife, Elizabeth, and his Daughters, Ann and Elizabeth Mary*, 1768. © Courtesy of the Garrick Club, London.

FIGURE 2.4: John Singleton Copely, *Sir William Pepperrell and his Family*, 1778. © North Carolina Museum of Art, Raleigh, purchased with funds from the State of North Carolina / Bridgeman Images.

FIGURE 2.5: Carrington Bowles, 'The Pleasures of a Married State' (1774). Words under the image depicting the ideal of family life: 'In Mutual Love both rule and both obey, / Her Charms obedient to his judgement sway. / In tenderness their smiling offspring prove. / United sensibility of Love.' © The Trustees of the British Museum.

BACHELOR HOUSEHOLDS

Studies of the Enlightenment family often identify the ways in which men's socio-political identities and notions of mature manhood were in many ways both situated, and thus defined, within the household. But in seeking to isolate the home as a gender-divided, albeit socially and culturally significant space, these studies have also implicitly suggested that the home is best explored, and subsequently understood, through the lens of the conjugal familial model.

Scholarship on the history of masculinities has prioritized the 'normative' view of the eighteenth-century family and household due to an 'assumption that the conjugal family *is* the interpretative crux for any history of the family', meaning that the experiences of single men in the period have been overshadowed by those of their married counterparts (Bray 2003: 3–4).[14]

The bachelor household could, and did, contain many individuals and was frequently in flux. Unmarried female family members, such as sisters, aunts and nieces, were often reliant, for example, on the generosity of bachelor relatives for whom their roles, according to Amy Froide, included housekeeper, nurse, childminder and business assistant (2007: 74, 75). The parson James Woodforde, for example, lived with his niece, Nancy, for the majority of his residence at Weston Longville in Norfolk, whilst the cleric William Bagshaw Stevens (rather more reluctantly) resided with his sister, Susanna, and her companion Miss Prior. The celebrated painter and life-long bachelor Joshua Reynolds, lived with his sister Frances for a period of twenty-four years before she was replaced by his favourite nieces, Mary and Theophila Palmer. As will become clear, though, the types of relationships men like these shared with their female relatives were informed by wider categories of association than material assistance, and included reciprocal attachments that centred on emotional support. John Courtney, for example, enjoyed the company of his widowed mother, with whom he lived and socialized in his childhood home until her death some fourteen years later.[15] Research by Susannah Ottoway has shown that elderly women were more likely to require the material assistance of their adult children, but her findings also reveal the reciprocity of familial relationships where co-residence connected the generations through considerable emotional and financial ties by providing a source of well-being for ageing parents (2007: 155, 171). But bachelors' life writings also reveal that their households and notions of family were not limited to ties of blood because as Tamara Hareven asserts, the household 'expanded and contracted in accordance with the family's needs', which were not necessarily determined by hereditary bonds of affiliation (1991a: 105). Moreover, as Sarah Pearsall has observed in her study of transatlantic families and their epistolary relationships, 'families can be forged by birth, marriage, cohabitation, obligation, inheritance, sex, or sentiment' (2010: 28).

The importance of dependents to the constitution of a household was remarked upon by Woodforde in July 1785 when, after having called on a fellow cleric in Ellingham, Norfolk, Woodforde not only judged the size and decoration of the house but also the family composition when he observed that:

> such a House and Situation I think very far from being agreeable. Mr. Hall however is fitting of it up in a shabby Manner and at present sleeps there of nights, no Man, Maid, Horse, Dog, or any living Creature but himself there.
> —Woodforde [30 July 1788] 2001, vol. 12: 58

Woodforde's critique indicates that the role of family within the household was one of both practicality and companionship. According to his assessment, an empty house did not make a home. Moreover, the 'fitting of it up' (the house) was inadequate because it was both 'shabby' and lacked dependents – suggesting that the role of householder was understood by Woodforde to be incomplete without co-residents of some sort. The household was the central arena for the establishment of individual men's identity throughout the long eighteenth century and helped secure both manly and social status. Relationships with co-resident family members were especially important in the presentation of domestic respectability, and were under constant scrutiny from the wider community.[16]

Co-residence figured prominently in the lives of Charles and Mary Lamb, albeit interrupted by periods of convalescence for Mary who suffered with debilitating mental health problems throughout her life.[17] Mary's relapses were frequently followed by her removal from the home, and in a letter to his friend, the poet Bernard Barton, in 1827, Lamb recounted that:

> Nine weeks are completed, and Mary does not get any better. It is perfectly exhausting . . . every thing is very gloomy. But for long experience, I should fear her ever getting well . . . Here is a comfortable house but no servants. One does not make a household.
>
> —Lamb [*c.* December 1827] BL, Add MS 35256, ff. 69

Lamb's concerns in the letter alert us to some of the ways in which contemporaries understood and applied definitions of family. According to Tadmor's research on the Turner family, for instance, the number of dependents was crucial to Thomas Turner's concept of family, as his use of 'my family' was suspended during periods when only one dependent was present (2007: 25–35, esp. 33). Principally, then, the household required more than a single individual to constitute a family but as Lamb's extract also suggests, whilst the number of residents was clearly a factor in the formation of a household, this was much less important for Lamb than their identity. The extracts from Woodforde and Lamb also reveal that servants were seen as key members of the household and, as a ubiquitous occupational group in the eighteenth century, were an expected part of all but the poorest of families.[18]

The remainder of the chapter situates bachelor households within an existing historical narrative and shows that bachelors' understanding and experiences of family shared many qualities of the traditional nuptial model, and is divided into two main sections. The first section, household management and familial reputation, extends upon the work of Harvey who notes that under the umbrella of 'keeping house', men's domestic roles were related to notions of household governance and authority (2012a: 106). It reveals that in common with the households of their married counterparts, bachelors' households often became a contested environment where issues of respectability, domestic reputation and credit were under threat if the management of the family was not maintained. The chapter then moves on to consider the bonds of affective relationships in the households and families of bachelors in a section on companionship, love and support. Affective relationships were not as constrained by the boundaries of authority and governance and, as will become evident, were much more concerned with issues of companionship, solidarity, love and friendship.

HOUSEHOLD MANAGEMENT AND FAMILIAL REPUTATION

In a society where the assumption prevailed that most men would marry and oversee the household and its inhabitants, the discourse of 'oeconomy' provided an invaluable gateway towards successful independent manhood. Credited with shaping domestic authority for men, oeconomy was, observes Harvey, 'the practice of managing the economic and moral resources of the household for the maintenance of good order' (2012a: 22, 23). By combining the positive attributes of manhood with good household management skills, bachelors could, in theory at least, validate their right to govern and be citizens.

For Edward Gibbon the household and his understanding of family were based on quite broad assessments of domestic and personal requirements. Keeping a house in London was expensive, but was magnified further by the debts incurred from his father's estate, and in March 1779 Gibbon confessed to his stepmother that:

> any plan of Oeconomy must be regulated by place and circumstances. As long as I am in London and in Parliament, a house in Bentinck Street, a Coach, such a proportion of servants, cloaths [sic] living &c are almost necessaries. But they are only necessaries in that situation, and I am not ignorant that a prudent man should adapt his arrangements to his fortune.
>
> —Gibbon [21 March 1779] BL, vol. XI, Add MS 34884, ff. 178

A certain style of living was associated with life in the metropolis for a man of Gibbon's social status, but importantly for Gibbon these standards were not rigid and could be improved in another 'situation'. The inadequacies of metropolitan life without sufficient funds motivated this bachelor to find a solution that offered him both companionship and domestic respectability at a more manageable price. By December 1783, Gibbon's 'plan of oeconomy' was realized after he moved to Lausanne, Switzerland, where he resided with his close friend George Deyverdun, and in another letter to his stepmother Gibbon wrote:

How different is the prospect which I now enjoy. I find myself in a state of perfect independence and real affluence and if I continue to enjoy a tolerable state of health I cannot easily discover what event is capable of disturbing my tranquillity. Among the ingredients of happiness you will agree with me [is] ... a sincere and sensible friend, and though you are not acquainted with half his merit, you will believe that Deyverdun answers that description.
—Gibbon [27 December 1783] BL, vol. XII, Add MS 34885, ff. 16

Compared with the first extract from Gibbon, where domestic respectability was identified with societal expectations of the appropriate number of household servants and material accessories, this second extract identifies the familial household with, amongst other rewards, domestic contentment and independence, but is explicitly framed around co-resident companionship and homosocial bonds. Gibbon later defined the move to Switzerland as a form of 'domestic Government', as it offered the means to sustain a level of comfort that was unavailable to him in London at that time, the details of which he relayed to his stepmother:

the Climate and society of Lausanne, my own situation and expence [*sic*], the character of my companion and of my looser connections of both sexes ... my style of living, my house, my table &c make me a man of mark and consequence ... My whole establishment is formed upon a comfortable yet oeconomical plan: in the single articles of house rent, carriage, servants wages, Clubs and public places I save between four and five hundred a year.
—Gibbon [15 July 1785] BL, vol. XII, Add MS 34885, ff. 51

By no means did self-imposed exile result in Gibbon's exclusion from society; instead, it provided financial respite and a form of companionship that lay outside the boundaries of traditional models of the family unit. As part of a small family household, Gibbon re-established his social status and domestic respectability under new terms. Access to networks of sociability aside, Gibbon displayed articles of wealth and social standing that were only made possible through his revised expenditure and successful co-residence with Deyverdun.

Woodforde's life writings are especially rich in detail regarding the household of a bachelor, with a wide variety of related and non-related members of the family recorded throughout the pages of his diary. Over his lifetime he supervised several households, which underscores the range of familial ties available to contemporary households and how these had a place in the successful running of a household. Woodforde's nephew, Bill, for example, accompanied him to live at the parsonage in Weston Longville – an arrangement that was to last for nearly three years, shortly after which, Bill's sister Nancy moved into the house for the duration of her uncle's life. Bill and Nancy were the children of his elder brother Heighes, whose dissolute lifestyle left little time, money or inclination for parental responsibilities. It is not possible to discern from the diary whether Woodforde was moved by duty to offer a more stable home for his niece and nephew, or if the impetus was his emotional attachment to them. A diary entry in January 1780, regarding a letter from Heighes, reveals the friction between the brothers and the level of Heighes's debts, but it also reflects the responsibilities Woodforde had assigned himself:

> Had a Letter this Evening from my Brother Heighes, rather an unpleasant one, as it mentions that he is in great distress & likely to go into Limbo, as Jeanes has brought an Action for Damages on losing his late Trial of 20.10.0. ... My Brother wants me to be bound for him, which in my present Circumstances cannot as I am distressed in many ways at present, and if I do more than I have done already for him, I must want myself. I have taken his Daughter Nancy to live with me & have been kind to his son Will during his living with me for near 3 Years.
> —Woodforde [22 January 1780] 2000, vol. 9: 11

Underlying animosities and rivalries were, as they still can be, the cause of some sibling fractures, but Woodforde's relationship with Heighes is perhaps more striking in how it demonstrates the breadth of this bachelor's paternal role.[19] Despite their acrimonious relationship, this extract clearly shows that Woodforde's paternalism extended across both households, because by providing refuge for Heighes's children, Woodforde not only managed his own household, but his elder brother's too. Heighes's inability to run a successful household is suggested by his loss of direct dependents to Woodforde's charge, particularly as it awarded Woodforde indirect governance over his elder brother's household fortunes should the offer have been withdrawn. In common with Woodforde's assigned paternal responsibilities, childless married men have also been shown to assume paternal roles and exercise patriarchal authority through the education, discipline and guidance of extended family, servants and apprentices, which emphasizes how the achievement of manhood was not restricted to a singular domestic model (Berry and Foyster 2010: 182, 183).

Blood relatives were connected by both obligation and emotional attachments, with informal and flexible transactions taking place between them, supplying financial and material support, as well as moral guidance and career advice. Heads of households were identified by their capacity to govern all their dependents, and the rhetoric of fatherhood was widely understood to offer men access to various degrees of personal and social credit (Cressy 1986: 49, 68; McCormack 2007: 47, 51). So, irrespective of marital status, Woodforde's role as head of a household was further reinforced by his patronage of Heighes's children, which provided a social credit that reflected his character, increased his reputation, and alluded to his fair and honest management of the household (Muldrew 1998: 3; Tadmor 2010: 26). But, the brothers' relationship also disrupts traditional ideas about vertical familial hierarchies where birth order and marital status generally placed expectations of moral, financial and emotional support predominantly on the first born. Woodforde's single status might in fact go some way to explain the reversal of roles, which, as Amy Harris has observed, was also vital for the widowed family and children of Thomas Huntingford, whose bachelor brother George became both surrogate father and husband (2012: 69, 158, 159). Whilst the motivations of Woodforde's material and domestic support of Nancy and Bill are never explicitly disclosed, over the years their blood ties were the starting point from which Woodforde took very seriously his role in *locus parentis* – providing Nancy with, amongst other things, an annual allowance of £10 and encouraging Bill to join the navy – a profession in which he eventually succeeded.

Woodforde also lived with siblings in his earlier years as a householder and whilst the duration of their cohabitation was brief, Woodforde was just as keen to manage the household and uphold the family reputation. Before moving to Weston Longville, Woodforde held a curacy at Castle Cary, Somerset, and shared a house with his younger brother John, who was four years his junior. Woodforde was exceptionally dedicated to his role as a householder, but found the behaviour of John particularly trying. In the early years of his diary, when Woodforde was settling into the responsibilities of keeping house, there were several references to problems with his co-resident sibling, 'Brother Jack'. As Woodforde's co-resident at The Lower House (and his dependent at that time) John was the focus of several diary entries. In May 1768, he wrote: 'My Poor Father and Jack had a dispute this evening. O that Jack was but well settled in Life, what pleasure would it give us all'. Only a week later and we find that, 'Jack brought home with him from Ansford Inn after ten o'clock this Evening, instead of the Hatspen People . . . all of Ditchet, which supped and stayed till 3 in the Morning, quite low life People much beneath Jack – I really wonder Jack keeps such mean Company' (Woodforde [22 May; 29 May 1768] 1985, vol. 3: 169, 170, 171, 172). John's inappropriate and disreputable lifestyle came to a head in June 1769:

> Jack made a terrible noise at Lower House with all the folks there. I got up out of my bed and came down at twelve at night and found the house in an uproar, Jack abusing of them all in a terrible manner. Very bad work indeed of a Saturday night in a Parson's House, it disturbed me all night. N.B. We must part.[20]
> —Woodforde [17 June 1769] 1984, vol. 4: 42

Woodforde was, however, a forgiving and gentle man, and entries on John's transgressions continue to appear at length for many years to come since he was not ejected from the household.

Woodforde worried about John throughout his life, in part because John unsettled the personal and professional character Woodforde strove to convey, but also because John's conduct was deeply incompatible with the household reputation Woodforde sought to uphold. Almost every week in March and April 1771, for example, Woodforde recorded John's drunken and raucous behaviour, resulting in Woodforde's morose comment that 'it is most unhappy the life that I am at present obliged to lead'. Only days later John disturbed the household equilibrium once more: 'Jack bullied and behaved to me as usual, when so very few I believe would bear half which I do' (Woodforde [31 March; 4 April 1771] 1986, vol. 4: 209, 210). Woodforde's experiences with John provide further evidence of this bachelor's household management skills, but also reveals how the tensions of co-residence and the subsequent breakdown of familial relationships were often a result of 'a failure to adhere to those sets of unwritten rules concerning individual conduct' that maintained order within a household (Barker 2017: 197, 198).

Eighteenth-century England was governed by a prevailing model of gerontocracy within which 'the young were to serve and the old were to rule', as youth was associated with licentious behaviour and a lack of control (Thomas 1976: 207, 218). Woodforde's seniority was, in theory, assured. But co-residence with his nephew Bill, like the difficulties with his brother John, frequently tested the gerontocratic ideal (Bill was around twenty years old when he moved to Weston in 1776 with the thirty-six-year-old Woodforde). Woodforde's diary documented the discord between them and reveals that Bill's disrespectful behaviour was a constant source of conflict between the two men, with Bill's conduct a perpetual challenge to Woodforde's household authority and ability to govern. Matters finally came to a head when in August 1778 the diary recounted that 'Bill behaved very saucy again this morning at breakfast and it made me very unhappy. It will not do at all ... Had no Conversation with Bill all Day since breakfast' (Woodforde [9 August 1778] 1998, vol. 8: 62). Knowledge of Bill's 'being great' with the maid Sukey and her subsequent pregnancy was the final straw. This turn of events found him 'very restless & uneasy' and shows Woodforde's recognition that the respectability of his household was under considerable threat were Bill to remain in the house (Woodforde [26 August; 30 August 1778] 1998, vol. 8: 67, 68).

Reputation, whether domestic or individual, was crucial to Woodforde's understanding of family and his performance of household authority. The maintenance of domestic order and the display of household respectability were also of primary importance to him. Craig Muldrew has stressed the significance of a *culture* of credit in early-modern England that served as a 'public means of social communication' that circulated 'judgements about the value of other members of communities'.[21] The management of the household and its reputation was shaped by discrete social exchanges that identified hospitality and household thrift with a cultural credit that was synonymous with reputation – something contemporary eyewitnesses were only too familiar with (Muldrew 1998: 2, 148–72). Woodforde's domestic reputation was reinforced further by his profession and position in the community, which demanded a degree of propriety since the house was an important site for the display of social standing, comfort and domestic control. Moreover, models of Christian masculinity emphasized self-discipline alongside qualities such as forgiveness and benevolence, with the intention of inspiring the household and wider community; thus Bill's frequent trysts with maids and their subsequent pregnancies made for an intolerable situation (Barker 2008: 13; Gregory 1999: 90, 93, 100).

The rhetoric of 'fatherly care' that was associated with Woodforde's relations with his niece and nephew was an important feature of eighteenth-century households but was not restricted to bonds of blood, as it also 'encouraged more mutually supportive relations' between the head of a household and his servants. The management of domestic servants often involved finding a balance between persuasion and coercion, through which the preservation of order in general was hoped to be achieved. The patriarchal role included the moral guidance of servants, with correction where necessary. The ultimate sanction, of course, was the termination of employment. (Meldrum 2014: 39, 59, 68).[22] Woodforde's diary recorded several occasions when the behaviour of servants left this, otherwise tolerant, bachelor with little choice but to ask them to leave. In December 1767, for instance, Woodforde noted:

> My man Luke Barnard, acquainted me this morning that he did not like his wages, and unless I would raise them, he must leave me, which he is to do at Lady Day next . . . I am not very sorry. He is a willing fellow but indolent and too fond of Cyder.[23]
>
> —Woodforde [3 December 1767] 1985, vol. 3: 131

Another servant, William Coleman, who had joined the Weston house from Somerset, was dismissed after ten years due to his drinking and subsequent violence, although only after repeated attempts at reconciliation:

> My Servant Willm Coleman was out all the Evening till just 11 o'clock – came home in Liquor behaved very rudely and most impudently to me indeed, I told him that I was determined never more to bear with such Behaviour, and that he sh^d certainly go to Morr'.
>
> —Woodforde [12 April 1785] 1999, vol. 11: 28

A bachelor's ability to keep house, through which 'men managed goods and people over which they exercised proprietorship', can be seen as a vital stage in their social and domestic advancement – including when this involved disciplinary action (Harvey 2012a: 108). Servants, like all familial household members, had an active role in the maintenance of the reputation and social status of the householder (Meldrum 2014: 66). Reports of servants' misconduct, poor character or appearance, for example, could weigh heavily on the employer because of its potential to reflect badly upon the household more widely.

Servants were replaced, or dismissed completely, by their bachelor employers for a variety of reasons, not just poor conduct. Servants' incompetence, marriage or age were all cited as reasons for making such changes, but they also left of their own volition due to the occupation's association with life-cycle service – particularly for women whose expectations of marriage were especially high.[24] Much of Woodforde's diaries contained reflections regarding his proficiency at maintaining a household, and entries were frequently concerned with the employment, transfer and replacement of servants. Woodforde was not the only bachelor to understand the complexities of household management in relation to the number of servants within a household, particularly when constrained by a shrinking budget. Well before the move to Lausanne, Gibbon's household was reduced by a drop in his income, resulting in a much smaller domestic unit than that to which he was accustomed. 'With respect to my expenses', Gibbon wrote to his stepmother in 1771, 'they shall always be proportioned to my income and I am already preparing to discharge a Cook, a Groom, and other unnecessary Servants' (Gibbon [c. 1771] BL, vol. XI, Add MS 34884, ff. 195). Gibbon's knowledge and application of oeconomy here was in response to his individual financial circumstances, but this episode (and his subsequent move to Lausanne) also reflects some other important features of household management such as prudence, self-governance and thrift (Harvey 2012a: 23; Harvey 2009: 533, 535).

The flexibility of servants' roles in a household allowed for greater freedom of employment – with a little negotiation at times. One of Woodforde's cooks, Molly Peachman, for example, was initially refused work because 'as she did not chuse to wash Dishes, I did not like to take her' (Woodforde [16 October 1784] 2013, vol. 13: 303). Elizabeth Claxton, on the other hand, was employed as an upper servant who 'understands cookery and working at her needle well' whilst Sukey 'is to milk, &c' (Woodforde [3 June 1776] 1991, vol. 7: 51). Ever adept at household organization, Woodforde's male servant, Briton, for instance, replaced William Coleman, who for a time was relegated to garden duties without lodgings before leaving altogether, whilst Briton was hired on the basis that:

> I ordered him into Parlour directly and made him wait at Table and he did pretty well. He appears to be a good-natured willing young Fellow.
>
> —Woodforde [26 April 1785] 1999, vol. 11: 32

Woodforde's experiences of household management suggest that whilst the organization of the household contributed to the maintenance of family reputation (and was vital to the effective running of a household), familial cooperation and compromise were also important, if not equal features of bachelors' domestic management skills. The household management skills of these bachelors supports Bridget Hill's assertion that in the homes of single men, 'the full recruitment, management, and organisation of the work of their servants fell on them and not, as in the case of most married men, on their wives' (1996: 189). But their testimony also reveals that during the long eighteenth century, 'there persisted an understanding of family that was defined by household membership, rather than more narrowly by marriage and blood' (Barker 2017: 221).

COMPANIONSHIP, LOVE AND SUPPORT

The management of dependents within the household, however, was not always the most important feature of co-residence for some bachelors. Relationships with members of the household also extended to companionship, solidarity and friendship, and were often underpinned by bonds of love and affection. The significance of 'emotional communities' in the constitution and organization of the household is increasingly recognized by historians of the family. Indeed, the household is considered to be the key social unit that defined 'interactions and relationships both inside and beyond its walls', where the expression and exchange of emotions had the potential to both unite and divide families (Rosenwein 2007: 24; Rosenwein 2010; Broomhall 2008: 1, 3).

Unlike Woodforde's experience of living with his disruptive younger brother, John, Charles Lamb's household underscores the importance of sibling attachments to some unmarried men, especially those between brothers and sisters. It was a commonplace for siblings to live together and unmarried sisters, in particular, have often been considered the perpetual dependents of their 'better off' brothers. This domestic and familial model, according to Ruth Perry, was not only reproduced in society but became a staple of eighteenth-century fiction, and assigned brothers the roles of protector, advisor and regulator (2006: 111). Assessments of asymmetry between siblings are reasonable in terms of education, legal status and inheritance, but ascribing emotional roles to them is not as transparent. Indeed, Charles's testimony emphasizes a process of exchange in emotional support that, whilst accessed differently at times of individual need, actually strengthened the emotional and horizontal ties between these siblings. Companionship was an important feature of the bachelor household but assumptions that this automatically positioned the 'poor relative' in a role of subservience out of gratitude should not be made automatically.

Charles referred to Mary as his 'prop' in a letter to Dorothy Wordsworth, underlining her role in his emotional and material support, the loss of which was only emphasized further by her illness and repeated absence. Indeed, following her removal Lamb's physical symptoms resembled those induced by grief. Mary 'is at present *from home*',[25] Lamb wrote to Dorothy Wordsworth in 1805:

> I now am calm, but sadly taken down, & flat. I have every reason to suppose that this illness, like all her former ones, will be but temporary. But I cannot always feel so. Meantime she is dead to me, – and I miss a prop. All my strength is gone, and I am like a fool, bereft of her co-operation . . . so used am I to look up to her . . . She is older, & wiser, & better than me, and all my wretched imperfections I cover to myself by resolutely thinking on her goodness. She would share life & death, heaven & hell with me. She lives but for me.
>
> —Lamb [14 June 1805] 1975, vol. II: 169, ff. 178

Living together was a joint venture for these siblings and without Mary, Charles was left emotionally destitute:

> All our pleasant prospects of seeing you here are dashed. Poor Mary was taken last night with the beginning of one of her sad illnesses, which last so long. I am here in a new house with her, and without her company. What I expected to be so comfortable has opened gloomily. But I hope she will get through it and enjoy our choice. I hardly know what to write.
>
> —Lamb [1 October 1827] 1935, vol. III: 136, ff. 703

Charles's letters suggest that the Lambs' domestic arrangements were bound by a mutual support and affection for one another, but in ways that complicate a straightforward analysis of family and household. Moreover, it would be reductive to confine sibling ties and the family household to a single model of gendered roles and expectations. Mary's illness and their domestic instability reinforced Charles's paternal role, but his devotion to his sister was such that without her presence within their shared home, the household failed to exist for Lamb. The Lambs' experiences thus continue to unsettle traditional accounts of sibling co-residence that have organized brothers and sisters, in particular, into distinct hierarchies and roles within the household family.

The eighteenth-century family provided emotional support in a variety of ways and was not always confined to ties of blood. Charles's letters also suggest that during the periods of Mary's recovery, his resilience was bolstered by the companionship and co-residence of one particular maid – evidence of which was only recorded due to her death in 1800. The loss of their long-standing maid, Hetty, had in fact brought about Mary's relapse: 'Hetty died on Friday night, about 11 o Clock, after 8 days illness', lamented Charles to his friend Samuel Taylor Coleridge; 'Mary in consequence of fatigue and anxiety is fallen ill again, and I was obliged to remove her yesterday. – I am left alone', he sighed:

> in a house with nothing but Hetty's dead body to keep me company ... Tomorrow I bury her, and then I shall be quite alone, with nothing but a cat, to remind me that the house has been full of living beings like myself. – My heart is quite sunk, and I don't know where to look for relief –.
>
> —Lamb [12 May 1800] 1975, vol. I: 202, 203, ff. 67

For most of their adult life, following the death of both parents, the Lambs' household was a small unit due to their meagre income, but this extract suggests that without Mary, Charles had often looked to Hetty for support and companionship. A subsequent maid, Becky, failed to offer Lamb the same level of support that Hetty had done, and a mutual shared interest – namely Mary – did little to resolve the differences between them. Becky left of her own accord after roughly nine years' residence, and whilst it was not disclosed why, Lamb's comments about her temper suggests an incompatibility of temperaments. Following Becky's departure, Mary was once more removed from the house and Lamb's only source of solace was his correspondence: 'to make me more alone, our illtemperd maid is gone', he declared to his friend Bernard Barton:

> who with all her airs, was yet a home piece of furniture, a record of better days; the young thing that has succeeded her is good & attentive, but she is nothing – & I have no one here to talk over old matters with. Scolding and quarreling [sic] have something of familiarity & a community of interest – they imply acquaintance – they are of resentment, which is of the family of dearness.
>
> —Lamb [25 July 1829] BL, Add MS 35256, ff. 84

In Mary's absence, the co-residence of this quarrelsome servant fostered nostalgic memories for Lamb, from which he took great comfort. Despite differences of opinion, issues of discipline and authority and their subsequent bickering, Lamb equated the servant's prior knowledge with familial connections and bonds of affinity.

Companionship was an important feature of the relationships Woodforde enjoyed with Bill and Nancy during their residence. Despite the sometimes tense and soured relationship between Woodforde and Bill, a comment from Woodforde regarding Bill's removal from the household also demonstrates that this uncle and nephew shared a familial bond that extended beyond the vertical hierarchies of the household to include affective ties. Indeed, just as Lamb grieved at the loss of his sister, Woodforde displayed both physical and emotional symptoms at the prospect of his nephew's departure: 'Quite low and ill to day, no Appetite', he remarked, after concluding that 'when Bill goes away I shall have no one to converse with – quite without a Friend' (Woodforde [26 August 1778] 1998, vol. 8: 67). The diary does not disclose the topics these two men discussed, but it is clear from Woodforde's disappointment and feelings of isolation that he confided in his nephew; sharing a familial bond with Bill underpinned by feelings of love and solidarity. Likewise, the extent of Nancy's companionate role in the house, and Woodforde's enjoyment of it, was often only made visible on those occasions when she was out visiting: 'I was very dull and low this Evening', he observed, 'having no company at all, now Nancy is from Home. And not used of late to be much by myself – better soon' (Woodforde [16 January 1785] 1999, vol. 11: 5). Woodforde's fondness for his niece and the companionship she supplied was recorded succinctly six seemingly long days later: 'Very glad she is come home' (Woodforde [22 January 1785] 1999, vol. 11: 7).

CONCLUSION

Although histories of the family and household have a tendency to reinforce the idealization of the conjugal home, this chapter reveals that notions of family in this period were not fixed by explicit categories or definitions but were, instead, understood and expressed in much more flexible and mutually inclusive ways. Co-residence was a commonplace in eighteenth-century society and was characterized by households that could include extended blood relatives, such as nieces and nephews, non-related members and siblings. The authority of the main householder over his or her dependents was crucial in establishing and maintaining an ordered house, but marriage was not a necessary precursor to its success (Tadmor 2007: 37, 272).

The centrality of the conjugal unit was reinforced throughout the Enlightenment period in prescriptive and instructive literature, as well as in prints and portraiture. A great deal of emphasis was placed on the spiritual foundations of marriage and familial organization, with contemporary commentators spending considerable time discussing the role of mutual affection and parenting in the pursuit of domestic happiness. At the start of our period, although the role of love was recognized in prescriptive literature models of marital harmony were consistently framed around familial duty and obligation, subjection and hierarchy. But from around the middle of the eighteenth century the importance of affection and companionship in marriage and parenting were pushed to the fore, evidence of which can be seen in portraiture and printed source material. These models were not, however, incompatible and did not replace traditional patriarchal structures or societal anxieties that elevated the position of the nuptial family (Retford 2006: 13). Contemporary print culture tells us a great deal about the cultural construction of the family and, subsequently, the prescribed roles allotted to men and women within the household but these sources tell us much less about how family life was experienced in the past.

Locating all family members in the households of single men challenges histories of the family and household that have placed little value on bachelors' ability to establish and govern a home. This chapter has considered notions of family that crossed traditional hierarchical ties and involved relationships with siblings, extended kin and servants. Indeed, bachelors' letters and diaries confirm that servants played a vital role in their households. Contemporary advice literature and fictional accounts of relations between employer and servant in, for example, Samuel Richardson's *Pamela* (1740) and Eliza Haywood's *A Present for a Servant-Maid* (1743) reflect contemporary anxieties concerning the immorality of bachelors and associate the bachelor householder with predatory characteristics. But as has been shown here, bachelors' actual experiences with servants need to be disentangled from contemporary anxieties in order to better appreciate servants' valued service and familial place within these men's homes.

The composition of the Enlightenment household was frequently subject to change, with the status of familial relationships and roles within the household (whether these be blood relations or not as well as servants) often determined by their behaviour or the householder's needs and affective relationships with them. The status of unmarried women in bachelors' households, for example, and their heterosocial relationships have been shown to be based on much more than authority and servitude and were, instead, frequently a source of love, support and friendship. Household management included the maintenance of the domestic reputation of the household and all its inhabitants with the social and moral credit this awarded. This credit was important to the bachelor and achieved through the practice of paternalism; and their claims to householder status were as valid as those of their married counterparts – if understood and experienced under slightly different terms. Uncovering the experiences and daily concerns in bachelors' households thus complicates long-held assessments of the centrality of the conjugal unit, and reveals that scholars of the eighteenth century have been far too narrow in their focus on the normative model of family and household.

CHAPTER THREE

The House

STEPHEN HAGUE

The years between 1650 and 1800 saw a series of developments that changed significantly the design of houses and how people used and experienced domestic space. In the early part of the Enlightenment period, baroque architecture dominated Europe, with palaces and churches the great structures of the Western built environment. The eighteenth century up to the French Revolution saw the great flowering of aristocratic building, before fortunes from trade and industry began to supplant the nobility as the main drivers of house-building. Over the course of the eighteenth century, domestic building became more important and attracted greater attention as the middling classes in countries such as Britain increased their presence in political life, commerce and society.

Most people in the Western world of course lived in simple structures with relatively few rooms and little spatial differentiation. Constructed of local building materials in rural locations, their houses combined multiple uses for work and family life. Such had been the case for centuries. But houses at all levels of Western society were complex social and cultural organisms. Houses – buildings that provided shelter to inhabitants – formed the physical settings that enabled the modern conception of the home to take shape during the Age of Enlightenment. Whereas the Palace of Versailles represented the absolute monarchy of the seventeenth century, domestic space by the late-eighteenth century was perhaps best typified by the classical Georgian house inhabited by a member of the rising commercial class. The balance, order, symmetry and segregation of the classical houses of the eighteenth century reflected Enlightenment rationality.

A cultural history of housing needs to study not only the design and production of domestic architectural space, but to consider how it was used by inhabitants. Sources from throughout Western Europe trace this process, although the perspective in this chapter is weighted towards the Anglo-world of the British Isles and North America. Beginning with an account of the houses that common people inhabited throughout Western Europe and North America, it goes on to discuss urban housing, the great houses of the aristocracy and gentry, before turning to the domestic buildings of the middling sort. Finally, it examines how architects, builders and people arranged domestic space, including the changing use of rooms.

As is discussed throughout this volume, early modern houses represented the specific worldview of their inhabitants (Johnson 2010: 138). During the Enlightenment, the architecture of domestic space both reflected and shaped broader social, political, economic and technological transformations. *Improvement*, *comfort* and *taste* are crucial concepts to understand the intersection of Enlightenment ideals and domestic space. By the beginning of the nineteenth century, more people lived in better houses, with enhanced physical comforts related to heating, sanitation and light, and changed attitudes about what it meant to be comfortable. While still hierarchical in many ways, new houses built in classical styles represented a democratization of domestic spaces, but also greater rationalization, standardization and even regulation. Professional architects increasingly took over responsibility for design from craftsmen. Inside houses, room use became more specialized, and increasing prosperity resulted in spaces being filled with more possessions. In these ways, the Enlightenment house marked an important, if incomplete, shift towards modern dwellings.

COMMON HOUSING IN THE AGE OF ENLIGHTENMENT

Those with an interest in architecture are apt to overlook the simplicity of most houses. Housing for the poorest half of the population largely evades study because of the paucity of material evidence. Many of the very poorest in town or country might have no home at all, and the homeless bring into sharp relief the importance of the house as a place that came to function as a home. Squatters and temporary abodes, as well as rudimentary dwelling spaces, were certainly not uncommon. Daniel Defoe provided an early-eighteenth-century description of a cave-dwelling family in the Peak District in England (Defoe 1724: vol. 3: 47). Houses for many were rudimentary at best. And, despite the greater availability of goods and increased prosperity in the eighteenth century, most people in Western society lived a meagre existence.

What sort of house did the common person inhabit in the eighteenth century? Although no house or house type was typical, it may be useful to begin with a tour of what would have been a recognizable, even familiar, house to many in the Western world in the late-seventeenth and eighteenth centuries. A vast literature privileges larger houses built by elites, but the average eighteenth-century person lived in a small, multi-use space. Plans for most houses reflected simple layouts with few rooms, although these could be almost infinitely variable. A typical house had a hall and parlour floor plan, with a heated hall for eating, cooking and social activity, and a separate parlour that usually contained a bed. Entry was directly into the hall. In such houses, small, often enclosed, winder stairs were the norm. Sometimes only ladders enabled access to loft spaces. Chimneys and hence fireplaces most often stood on exterior walls, although this varied by region and country. Floors were of wood or even earth. Houses had few furnishings and were bare to the twenty-first-century eye. Modernization – if it took place at all – often happened incrementally in successive adaptations, rather than a single, wholesale remodelling (Hamling and Richardson 2017: 109).

There was increasingly a departure from medieval ideas about architectural order towards a distinction between 'polite' and 'rustic' forms. Politeness suggested tasteful, mannered, more informal behaviour. The Age of Enlightenment is a particularly important period for the discussion of the

FIGURE 3.1: Old Dutch House, from 1699, Long Island, New York, nineteenth century. © Duncan 1890 / Getty Images.

'polite threshold', or the distinction between houses that displayed polite characteristics and more vernacular buildings. Polite buildings were those designed by an architect or similar specialist, such as a master mason, that followed a national or international style, and favoured aesthetic considerations over functional ones. Vernacular buildings, by contrast, were the work of amateurs building according to local practice, with an emphasis on function. Vernacular buildings therefore displayed more regional variation than those that stood above 'The Polite Threshold'. There was, however, a considerable grey area in the distinction between vernacular and polite architecture, with many houses exhibiting aspects of both (Green 2010).

Vernacular houses associated with agriculture were centrepieces of working farms. Following the Great Rebuilding of the sixteenth and seventeenth centuries in the British Isles, vernacular houses proliferated, although their spread varied in time, form and material by region. In Scotland, for example, 'non-expert' people took account of climate and topography to build vernacular dwellings of locally available earth, stone and thatch. These structures were rudimentary by architectural standards of the day – rectangular structures heated by a central hearth with thatched roofs, providing a single living space that might be shared with animals – but represent a functional, common dwelling for people in the early-modern period (Maudlin 2012). The so-called I-house of the American colonies, identified in the 1930s by Frederick Kniffen, drew on English antecedents and was a simple and flexible plan well into the nineteenth century. These dwellings were two-storeys tall, one room deep and at least two rooms long, although their plans came in myriad variations and employed regional building materials. The I-house could be dressed up with ornamentation to evoke particular architectural styles and also provided a basic floor plan that occasionally included an ell or shed addition (Kniffen 1936: 179–93).

Even simpler structures exhibited a range of house plans throughout Western Europe and its colonies. Continental models often had central chimneys, whereas gable-end chimneys characterized English designs. Some poorer houses lacked a chimney altogether, having only an opening. A study of German log house construction in the Shenandoah Valley of Virginia traced German ethnic building traditions around 1800. From the late-seventeenth century, Germans, Scots-Irish and English settlers populated this area. The traditional German log house form suggested a specific German ethnic identity, but by the late-eighteenth century it merged with house types of these other ethnic groups, transforming into a design with a central passage (Glassie 1986: 412; Chappell 1986).

Households, including extended families, servants and labourers, might be accommodated in various buildings, not restricted to the house. A clear external distinction existed in vernacular houses between the upper and lower ends associated with family life and service respectively. It was not unusual for servants, household labourers or enslaved peoples to have quarters above outbuildings. Extant quarters for enslaved people can be found in the Caribbean, southern colonies of British North America, and even in the northern colonies, such as at the Isaac Royall House in Medford, Massachusetts.

The limited domestic space available to people is a striking feature of life before 1800. In England, landlords commonly carved rows of cottages out of larger farmhouses (Johnson 2010: 140). A tax on hearths, or fireplaces, introduced in 1662, provides an indication of the relative dimensions of houses. Houses inhabited by the gentry contained between eight and fifteen hearths (Cooper 1999: 349). In Wales, 'secondary' gentry families lived in houses with an average of 9.43 hearths, although the 'tertiary' gentry families owned houses averaging 5.55 hearths.[1] Most houses, however, had only one or two hearths. Likewise, houses in the American colonies were frequently only a single room, built of horizontally arrayed logs. In Montgomery County, Maryland, typical eighteenth-century houses were log-built one- or two-room dwellings, perhaps with a loft (Kelly 2011: 53–54). Two-thirds of the houses built in Delaware between 1760 and 1830 had a first floor of less than 450 square feet (Herman 1987: 15). Compare these figures to the largest country houses such as Chatsworth in Derbyshire with 79 hearths, or Coleshill in Berkshire with 56

FIGURE 3.2: A general view of Chatsworth House, the stately home of the Duke and Duchess of Devonshire in England, in 2012. © Christopher Furlong / Getty Images.

and the vast gulf in size and space between the elite and common people becomes evident.

By the end of the eighteenth century, land reforms and the idea of improvement began to change the character of the rural landscape, and rustic housing with it. Improvement, a key ideal in the eighteenth century, helped to sweep away these vernacular houses and replace them with improved cottages or two-story farmhouses. Increasingly, even elites saw cottages as a natural, organic part of the landscape. Architects began to design cottages in a range of locales, ostensibly to provide the comfort and informality associated with rural retreat. This trend was perhaps best typified by Marie Antoinette's *hamaeu de la Reine*, her faux village at Versailles. What John Summerson called the 'cult of the cottage' had several manifestations: as a romantic, organically developed dwelling, as a rational design, and a functional domicile for an agricultural labourer (Summerson 1986: 98). As a result, by 1800 the rural dwellings of labourers had achieved a level of respectability not seen in previous centuries. By this time as well, more people had migrated to urban areas, highlighting another forum of domestic architecture for consideration.

THE HOUSE IN THE CITY

Over the century and a half after 1650, urban areas grew in many places in Western Europe as populations expanded. More and more people lived in cities, making urban housing an important aspect of any account of houses and their development in this period. The majority of Britons and other Europeans still lived outside urban areas, and there were limits to urban influence. Nevertheless, growing cities demanded housing for growing populations.

Despite expanded conurbations, urban housing was geographically restricted and even such large cities as London and Paris were densely concentrated, with small villages dotted on their perimeters. By 1800, London was Western Europe's largest metropolis, with nearly one million people, and an estimated one in six people in England had experienced life in London. To accommodate this massive population, 80,000 or more houses were built there in the eighteenth century (Guillery 2004: 7–8). Domestic space for many of the poorest in Western society – and this was a significant portion of the urban population – was unstable and often transitory, with space shared in rented accommodation with others, or carved out in dwellings. For the poor in London, one room was the most they might expect.

Houses for the lower orders lacked any sense of taste or fashion, were in older areas of the metropolis, and included only a single room. As the city grew, housing stock needed to be replenished, accomplished in many poorer areas by infilling back gardens to create courts and alleys with tiny houses for the labouring poor or below (White 2012: 6). Much housing 'ranged from wretched to non-existent'. Street names like Rotten Row, Foul Lane, Dark Entry and Piss Alley, as well as descriptions of houses as 'very meanly built and Inhabited', 'Sorry built with old Timber Houses, and as ill Inhabited', and 'old sorry Timber Houses' convey a sense of the quality and nature of urban housing in Europe's largest city (Guillery 2004: 27). The proximity of 'bog-houses' or 'houses of office' – those oft-forgotten little houses necessary for nature's call – added to the stench and squalor of the metropolis. The famous prints by William Hogarth, *Beer Street* and *Gin Lane*, illustrate the range of buildings and the activity of denizens in mid-eighteenth-century London. In America, the city of Philadelphia, by 1770 one of the larger urban concentrations in the British empire, saw similar housing challenges. Labouring families most often lived in sparingly furnished wooden structures, often no more than twenty feet square, on one or two floors (Smith 1990: 158–65).

Labourers and domestic servants alike frequently shared beds with others for practical and economic reasons. Lodging could also be used for a range of purposes, such as prostitution, with landlords often taking a cut of the proceeds. Even for the better off, temporary housing was typical. In London, middling families often rented rooms to lodgers, as way for them to defray costs and for lodgers to secure affordable accommodation (White 2012: 108–12, 354). Student Thomas Adams reported in 1760 that he had, 'taken a small neat Set of Chambers for a small Sum they are very clever and just large enough for me' (LWL, MSS 2/Box 25/Folder 1).

What might the 'small sum' have been that Thomas Adams put out for his chambers? The relationship of income and expenditures is critical to understanding housing arrangements. In London, skilled artisans might earn one shilling a week, resulting in an annual income of between £25 and £50. For many people, though, incomes were £20 a year or less. What could this translate into in terms of housing? Henry Fielding noted in 1751 that lodgers in London could secure space for two-pence a night, and some beds could be had for a penny. A small house of three or four rooms might cost £10 per annum, although in some areas of London many such dwellings were available for £5 or less. Only the wealthiest quarter of the population could afford larger houses. Even the 'middling sort' – merchants, professionals, civil officials – might expect to lay out £20 to £30 a year for a suitable dwelling (Guillery 2004: 15, 27, 35).

Cities combined old architecture with new building to provide housing at a range of price points. In European towns it was not uncommon for earlier houses to have their gable end to the street, and towns and villages in European settlements in North America displayed this feature as well. As classical forms became more prevalent, the façade turned ninety degrees to face the street. George Read I, a prominent resident of New Castle, Delaware, undertook renovations to his house in the 1760s that achieved just this effect (Glassie 1986: 404).

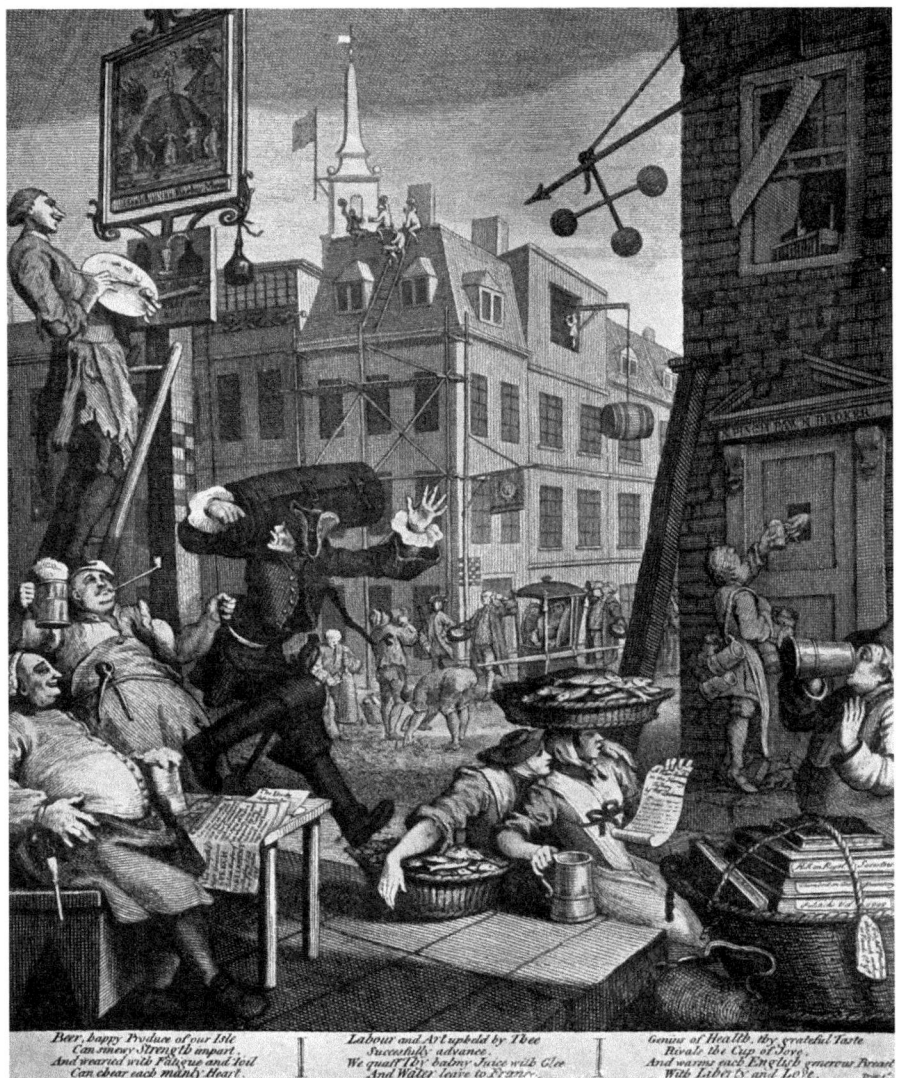

FIGURE 3.3: William Hogarth, 'Beer Street', 1751. From *London in the Eighteenth Century*, by Sir Walter Besant (London: A. & C. Black, 1925). © Print Collector / Getty Images.

Sometimes natural catastrophe brought about urban change. Perhaps the best examples of this during the Age of Enlightenment are the Great Fire of London in 1666 and the Lisbon earthquake of 1755. The Great Fire prompted extensive rebuilding of the City of London. Although accounts of the rebuilding often focus on Christopher Wren's churches and St. Paul's Cathedral, London's fire had a significant effect on housing as well, with 13,000 houses destroyed.

Building codes changed, for example, introducing a series of guidelines for building (Ayres 1998: 230–31). The London Building Acts influenced houses beyond London, although houses did not always reflect these new standards. Cote house near Bristol, built around 1720, is two storeys with an attic with a deep modillioned cornice and flush sash boxes, two distinctive features prohibited by the 1707 and 1709 Building Acts in London but slower to catch on elsewhere. In Lisbon, the massive destruction resulted in changes in architectural practice and the emergence of quickly rebuilt, uniform townhouses known as the *estilo Pombalino*, or Pombaline style, after the Marquês de Pombal who oversaw the rebuilding. These buildings incorporated anti-seismic features and pre-fabricated elements.

To allay some of these problems, urban and social improvement were 'understood as the implementation of the rational and utilitarian ideas' of the Enlightenment (Guillery 2004: 279). As the home to the Enlightenment *philosophes*, France set architectural fashion for the eighteenth century. Parisian architecture in the style of Louis XV was especially exuberant in the period from 1690 until the end of the Seven Years War in 1763. After this, a more rational classicism and a return to Greco-Roman traditions replaced the exuberance and naturalistic inspiration of the rococo (Gallet 1972). At the same time, the development of an urban renaissance in English towns during the late Stuart and Hanoverian periods saw towns become centres of more leisurely activity and consumption, not to mention architectural facelifts. London and other British cities expanded as part of this English Urban Renaissance. A rapid expansion of London's West End, with row upon row of classically inspired townhouses, took place. In London, British aristocrats were not as eager to build magnificent houses in the manner of the French *hôtel*, although a number of palatial aristocratic houses dominated London's streetscape. Rather, British elites preferred London townhouses arrayed around squares, which formed the centrepieces of much eighteenth-century expansion in London. As the eighteenth century moved on, the in-between space of suburbia, where urban houses transitioned into rural space, became a pronounced feature of the London environs. Improvement saw the London built environment transformed, including its housing, by the 1780s (Borsay 1989; Stewart 2009).

Urban development took place elsewhere as well. Bath, a spa town in southwest England, exhibited the most striking town planning, with townhouses arrayed around Queen's Square, the Circus and the Royal Crescent. The townhouses there, exemplified by No. 1 Royal Crescent, today a historic house museum, often combined temporary housing for the genteel visiting Bath for sociable routine with permanent residents. Other cities around the Atlantic World reflected this process, although exhibiting a more varied housing stock. Scottish cities, too, became a locus for improvement (Herman 2005; Harris and McKean 2015).

This was not a process restricted to the British Isles. Late-seventeenth-century Prague experienced a spurt of building in a local Baroque style that 'exerted a strong influence at all strata of society' (Pavlik and Uher 1998: 12). For half a century this movement re-modelled the town, creating new streetscapes and housing, before Prague's building boom ebbed. In Paris between 1775 and the French Revolution, private domestic building significantly shaped the cityscape. Neoclassical and Palladian houses appeared not only as individual façades but entire streets. Although urban housing remained widely variable, it was largely the taste of the upper classes that redressed large sections of eighteenth-century cities in classical garb. Their houses, which have drawn so much attention from scholars, were the capital atop the housing column.

HOUSES OF THE GREAT ELITE

Despite the chasm in housing between most people and elites, many Enlightenment ideals revealed themselves in the aristocratic architecture of Western Europe. Concentrations of wealth and power were evident across Europe. Stylistically, the influence of the Italian baroque and rococo shaped architecture, especially churches, throughout the continent. At the highest level of society, houses expressed state power and control. In seventeenth-century France, Louis XIV's

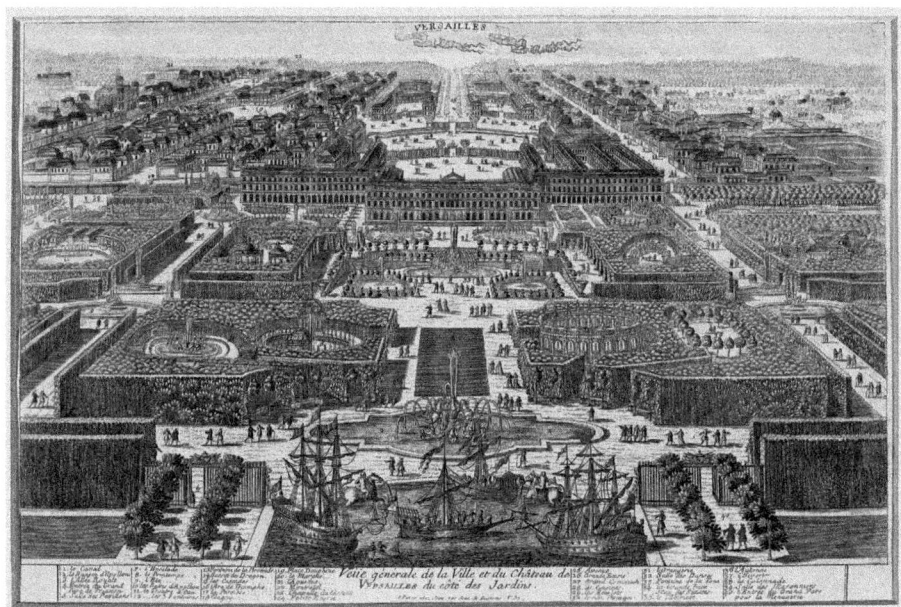

FIGURE 3.4: General view of the town and the chateau of Versailles with gardens on the side, by Pierre Aveline the Elder (1654–1722). © De Agostini / Getty Images.

Palace of Versailles gave physical embodiment to his claim that 'L'etat, c'est moi' (I am the state). Such monumental buildings attempted to present the ideal monarchical state in microcosm: hierarchical, vast and structured.

The Enlightenment challenged the authority of church and king, with wide-ranging repercussions in domestic architecture and the structure of households. Building activity around 1700 profoundly influenced the eighteenth century's domestic buildings and spaces, planting the seeds of a 'revolutionary new architecture' (Millon 2006: 14). The eighteenth century was a period of aristocratic pre-eminence where property was concentrated in larger estates held in fewer hands. In France, large houses in the town and countryside distinguished aristocrats in the seventeenth century, although increasingly life in these dwellings moved from 'an old-style rural, open hospitality' towards more private, urban-focused life (Thomas 2009: 115). In the early-eighteenth century, Parisian *hôtels*, or grand houses for the aristocracy, had a Grand Appartement on the ground floor 'where high society and the nobility customarily forgather', with further apartments on the floor above (von Kalnein 1995: 19). Such large houses for the aristocracy and gentry cost hundreds of times more than cottages for the poor.

Aristocratic mansions served to make a social, cultural or even political statement. The town mansion, or *hôtel particulier*, built by new groups involved in finance, the military and the law, signalled a move away from the court society of Versailles. The most popular arrangement for these houses had a forecourt flanked by service buildings, with a back garden, a standard plan laid out by architectural theorist Jacques-Francois Blondel in the *Encyclopédie*. These are amongst the most significant domestic buildings from eighteenth-century Paris (von Kalnein 1995: 35).

The aristocracy exercised considerable power as a counterbalance to the monarch, with overwhelming representation at the highest levels of the political world, in landed society and in the economy. In 1690, the landed estates of the British aristocracy and the gentry accounted for at least 60 percent of land in England, rising to over 70 percent by 1790; the titled peerage alone, a relatively small number of families, accounted for somewhere between 15 and 25 percent of land ownership over the course of the century (Mingay 1976: 59, table 3.1). Britain's social system, however, also readily accommodated the emergence of active builders further down the social scale who made fortunes from commerce and trade.

Such accumulated wealth amongst the upper and upper middling classes enabled elites to build great houses. Eighteenth-century elites who constructed a country house engaged in a tremendous act of cultural consumption. Indeed, as architectural historian Mark Girouard has argued, 'when a new man bought an estate and built on it, the kind of house which he built showed exactly what level of power he was aiming at' (1978: 3). Stately country houses such as

FIGURE 3.5: Blenheim Palace, Oxfordshire, England, built between 1705 and 1722. © Universal History Archive / Universal Images Group / Getty Images.

Houghton Hall and Holkham in Norfolk, or the Duke of Marlborough's Blenheim Palace, were awe-inspiring works of art and places of power. As a result, these monumental edifices have largely shaped our ideas about domestic space in the eighteenth century. Country houses fulfilled four main functions: they provided income, power, prestige and a pleasant way of life. For those seeking to rise in eighteenth-century society – lawyers, merchants, judges, manufacturers, soldiers or sailors, royal servants, and 'nabobs' who had made fortunes in the East India Company – acquiring a country house could provide a ready path (Girouard 1985: 22–23).

Country house building necessitated a substantial expenditure of money, labour and time. One study of country house builders and their buildings mapped how many houses were built when and at what cost. Between 1664 and 1691, for example, the Dukes of Beaufort spent £29,760 on building and remodelling efforts at Badminton, whilst a century later a smaller country house like Honing Hall in Norfolk cost only about £500 for the exterior 'case', with perhaps the same amount again for the interior. Important country houses sprang up in other areas, such as Scotland, juxtaposed with the rural dwellings discussed earlier. No matter at what level house-building was going on – £1000 for Honing Hall or the £200,000 that Sir Robert Walpole supposedly spent on Houghton – it was time-consuming, costly and complex (Wilson and Mackley 2000: 33, 39–40). As one early-nineteenth-century housekeeper commented to her employer, 'Pray sir, don't think of building, you can't tell the misery of it' (ibid., 145).

Although building and maintaining houses could drain the coffers of an estate, as symbols of power and sociability they exuded cultural importance. The most grandiose domestic architecture of this period, baroque palaces such as Versailles or Blenheim, simply exceeded the money and skill available to be replicated or built elsewhere. To be sure, people below the level of the elite were sometimes influenced by the great houses, but most aimed to secure housing within their means. In 1750, for example, Virginia planter William Beverly 'viewed Chatsworth a noble house', but it is difficult to say what influence this encounter exercised on his own house in Virginia (Carson and Lounsbury 2013: 80).

The domestic building practices of elites nevertheless helped to set architectural standards. By the late-eighteenth century, French domestic architecture, like public building, sought to return to the classical good taste of the seventeenth century by rejecting the rococo. The frivolous style of the rococo, dominant in the second quarter of the century, gave way to a more reasoned and restrained Neoclassicism. Emerging from late-seventeenth-century France and the French notion of *gout*, 'taste', or proper aesthetic judgement, dominated social relations in the eighteenth century. In Paris after the Seven Years' War, tasteful elite housing reflected a more restrained building style, as characterized by the Pavilion de Brancas (1769–71), described as expansive form giving way to cubic compactness (von Kalnein 1995: 131–33, 188, 190).

The French upper classes also placed an increasing emphasis on comfort, which remade physical space and bodily comportment. Elite houses reflected *commodité*, or practical convenience, as illustrated in the more informal design of space in elite houses. In England, country houses evolved from formal, linear arrangements of rooms in the seventeenth century towards the social house of the eighteenth characterized by enhanced freedom of movement and circulation (Girouard, 1978). Throughout the Western world, comfort in building design and furnishing to provide light and warmth became a hallmark of the period (Crowley 2001).

By the mid-eighteenth century, people began to build fashionable houses more from abstract concepts than pragmatic conditions. Taste and comfort shaped eighteenth-century houses in significant ways for other levels of society. Smaller but still genteel houses of the middling classes increasingly dotted the landscape, especially around urban areas. It is in these houses that we can observe domestic space evolve in the Age of Enlightenment. They served as crossroads of social change, as their owners sought to display taste in increasingly comfortable surroundings.

MIDDLING HOUSES AS ENLIGHTENED ENVIRONMENTS

'Inevitably, there comes a time when the yeoman's working farmhouse and the gentleman's exclusive residence will part company', noted Colin Platt (1994: 152). Platt associated a Second Great Rebuilding after the Restoration in 1660 with the shift towards smaller, compact boxes that came to serve as the quintessential English house form in the eighteenth century. Many of the houses constructed during the late-seventeenth and eighteenth centuries originated in moves towards classical forms of architecture that were a key feature of the Enlightenment.

The 'consumer revolution' of the eighteenth century, which emphasized demand for goods, fuelled much of this building. Within a few generations, products that had hitherto been restricted to the wealthy became available to a wider segment of society. Men and women in England by the late-eighteenth century were buying as never before. Between 1750 and 1775, that consumer boom had become so widespread and accessible that it had reached 'revolutionary proportions'. The rich led the way, indulging in an 'orgy of spending' that included 'magnificent houses' in 'a crescendo of building' peaking in the 1770s (McKendrick, Brewer and Plumb 1982: 9–11).

The middling and upper middling classes followed suit, building and remodelling their houses and acquiring new material goods. But calling this emulation is somewhat misleading. Most genteel families, not to mention those even further down the social scale, could not hope to construct large houses like the aristocracy. Instead, houses represented the standing of their inhabitants and were part of 'overlapping spheres of influence between the national and the provincial, the classical and the non-classical, the elite and the everyday' (Arciszewska and McKellar 2004: xxiii). Domestic space also conveyed political identity at multiple levels. In England from the late-seventeenth century, Parliament had largely won the political battle for supremacy. Power rested with the aristocracy and the gentry in the eighteenth century, and it is their houses that attracted attention. In America after the Revolution (1775–83), houses served as the well spring of national identity' (Faherty 2007: 5). Houses structured familial authority and the emergence of a uniform classicism marked a step towards national character as well.

The enhanced transportation networks seen in the eighteenth century – better roads, canals, seagoing trade, commerce and migration – meant that architectural ideas and expertise about appropriate housing could spread as well. In newly settled European colonies, a fresh start made possible buildings that reflected contemporary forms and mentalities, without having to alter previous structures. Builders and architects alike shared architectural design across cultural boundaries, whether between nations or between colonies and metropoles (Bremner 2016).

For much of the period considerable cross-over existed between architect and craftsmen-builders, with the distinction only becoming clear as the eighteenth century went along. In the Chesapeake region of North America, the design process was an exceptionally fluid one involving clients, contractors and craftsmen. Practical experience on the building site governed a great deal when it came to domestic construction.

By the late-eighteenth century, design and pattern books for house design and construction played an increasingly important role in house-building. Several different kinds of books existed. Volumes like Colen Campbell's *Vitruvius Britannicus* (3 vols., 1715–25) set out some of the largest and most significant architectural commissions in the late-seventeenth and early-eighteenth centuries, while works like the enormously popular *A Book of Architecture* (1728) by James Gibbs, was noteworthy for its smaller houses and illustrations of ornamentation. Even here, however, these books were most useful to elite owners and their builders. Other publications, like the extensive works of William Halfpenny and William Salmon, offered designs and costs for a wider range of houses, as did Isaac Ware in his *A Complete Body of Architecture* (1756). By the middle of the eighteenth century, writers like Abraham Swan offered pattern books with details that builders could easily crib. Finally, builders' guides from architectural writers like Batty Langley, William Pain and Richard Neve provided practical, how-to instruction for builders and workmen.

These works especially influenced the construction of houses for middling members of society who profited from the activities of the consumer revolution. Georgian houses in Britain and America shared many similarities. Elite colonial houses increasingly resembled forms found in Britain, and as the North American colonies became more unified under British rule, their regional differences became less marked. In this regard, colonial domestic architecture offers a unique perspective about houses in the Age of Enlightenment.

Tracing the interrelationship of house-building and these important trends in the eighteenth century is critical to the cultural history of the home. As one architectural historian notes, 'The study of eighteenth-century debates on architecture have had little or no part to play in accounts of "the rise of polite society"' (Craske 2004: 97). Middling builders increasingly opted for compact, symmetrical houses above the 'polite threshold', which were distinctly different in plan from larger and more visible country houses. In 1729, Daniel Defoe praised the superiority of English building by comparison with continental domestic spaces, lauding 'our manner of building in England, where neat compact boxes are the usage of the country, not vast pallaces' (Bulbring 1890: 123). Small classical houses built by those on the cusp of elite status – 'the gentleman's house' – became an important fulcrum for social change (Hague 2015). Classicized façades frequently encased older buildings with traditional plans and some vernacular features. Returning to Platt's comment at the beginning of this section, a number of architectural indicators differentiated between a gentleman's residence and a yeoman's farmhouse, although considerable overlap existed between the houses inhabited by these two social groups. Overall size and double-pile floor plan indicated status, as did interior ceiling heights, and 'superior' features such as lateral chimney stacks in the halls and possibly parlours, the presence of a parlour, heated second-floor chambers, moulded stone for mullioned windows, doorways and fireplaces, panelling and grand staircases (Hall 1991). Although many houses demonstrate localized building characteristics, architectural sophistication increasingly communicated their owners' efforts to stake out their position in society.

After mid-century, the middle-class villa set the standard for the ideal house. The distinction between country house and suburban villa is highly complex. As architect Roger North noted in 1698, 'The country model, and that of a suburb villa, are different' (North 1981: 62). Early in the eighteenth century, drawing on Palladian ideals from Italy, a villa was a place of 'retreat or retirement', or 'a house that mediated between town and country and excluded all that was unpleasing of either' (Cooper 2007: 15, 24). Villas were sometimes seasonal residences, the 'little House of Pleasure and Retreat, where Gentlemen and Citizens betake themselves in Summer', as suggested in 1700 (Nourse 1700: 297). From the early-eighteenth to the early-nineteenth century, the villa in Britain suggested a process of democratization, transforming the villa from an aristocratic refuge to a family home. In this conception, the Georgian villa gave rise to a 'state of mind in the Georgian period' (Arnold 1998b: ix–x).

Although Classicism dominated after 1750, Western architecture also displayed a plurality of authority, giving rise to multiple veins of revivalist architecture. Houses could exhibit this stylistic variety, sometimes a source of mockery for those climbing the social ladder. The modern-built villa depicted in the print 'A common Council-man of Candlestick Ward and his wife, on a visit to Mr. Deputy – at his modern built villas near Clapham' (1771) displays the architectural melange caricatured as typical of the middle classes of Georgian England. (Brewer 1997: 70). One notable feature of the print is the Chinoiserie tower surmounted by a dragon, a visible indicator of the increasing influence of goods and styles from Asia in the eighteenth century. Dwellings themselves reflected the importation of tea, ceramics, textiles and other goods increasingly found in domestic spaces.

Such stylistic eclecticism faltered in the face of the triumph of Neoclassical forms, in public building and in domestic architecture at all levels of society. Regional variations gave way to more national or even international architectural style and form, as Classicism became predominant in design at all levels. Widespread adoption of polite classical houses occurred further down the social scale, as improvement took hold and more standardized forms of building occurred. As Matthew Johnson noted, 'for many, the arrival of Georgian houses represents the culmination of the vernacular tradition' (2010: 160). These processes – the end of vernacular building and the rise of Georgian classicism – were closely intertwined. But this transformation marked a significant shift in houses throughout the Western world. This shift had important implications for how people lived in their houses.

FIGURE 3.6: 'A common Council-man of Candlestick Ward and his wife, on a visit to Mr Deputy – at his modern built villas near Clapham', London, c. 1750. © Guildhall Library & Art / Heritage Images / Getty Images.

ORGANIZING THE HOUSE: ROOMS AND HOW PEOPLE USED THEM

As the chapters in this book explore, the spaces people inhabit construct their realities. The interaction of spaces, objects and activities governed their lives, which were dependent on daily routine and ritual. Different spaces focused activity at different times of day. Different categories of people used rooms for different reasons, in different ways. As will be discussed in later chapters, women wielded substantial control over domestic space, especially in constructing the idea of a home as distinct from a house, although scholars have recently highlighted the role of men in homemaking as well. A servant might place a piece of fine ceramic on a table, awaiting the service of the newly fashionable hot drink, tea. A genteel mistress might serve the tea to her husband and guests in a sociable ritual, after which another servant might clear the vessels, transport them through space to be cleaned and then stored. The range of spaces available to a person and how they functioned dictated domestic life.

Increasing segregation of space characterized the eighteenth century, but most houses featured a small number of rooms that inhabitants put to multiple uses. Before 1700, comparatively few spaces formed the core of most houses, and a limited range of terms described them: halls, parlours, chambers, kitchens. In England and France, typical rooms were the hall and parlour, whereas middle and southern parts of Germany and German-influenced regions of North America often displayed the three-chamber division of *Kuche*, *Kammer* and *Stube* (kitchen, bedchamber, stove room), inspired by different European antecedents (Johnson 2010: 145; Weaver 1986).

Whatever their origin, this handful of room names highlighted the limits and possibilities of spatial diversification. Whereas older medieval buildings of various social ranks centred domestic life on the hall, after about 1500 floor plans became more elaborate and sharply defined. By the late-seventeenth century, most yeomen had moved from a common hall at the centre of the house to a centre-hall passage arrangement that served to enable greater segregation. By the mid-eighteenth century, centre halls or passages and dining rooms as segregated spaces became increasingly common, both an outgrowth of changes in urban areas (Johnson, 2010: 120–21; Platt 1994: 157; Carson and Lounsbury 2013: 125–28). The increased idea of privacy went along with room specialization, in such places as the closet. This development indicated a greater separation between owners and servants, although this distinction can be overstated.

The greatest room specialization occurred in larger houses with more spaces. In his classic work on the English country house, architectural historian Mark Girouard traced floor plans from a linear arrangement of rooms to a circular layout that facilitated circulation and sociability. This transition in elite house organization suggested some of the key features of the eighteenth-century home: accessibility, comfort, ease and informality. Smaller but still genteel houses built from the late-seventeenth century usually conformed to a more regular plan. Such buildings typically had four rooms per floor, including several parlours, a hall and occasionally a dining room or study, with bedchambers above. This provided differentiated but inherently flexible space. There were, however, exceptions to the four-room layout, such as the three-cell plan seen in the Delaware Valley region of British North America (Reinberger 1991: 146–54).

Parlours and stairs were especially critical to change in the eighteenth century. Parlours provided spaces for the sociable activities that were an important part of eighteenth-century life. Staircases formed focal points of larger households, allowed both vertical and horizontal movement, and also enabled segregation. At Lower Slaughter Manor in England, William Whitmore constructed a new, centrally positioned staircase in the 1760s, one feature of a series of improvements he undertook to update the *c.* 1660 classical manor house (Gloucestershire Archives, D45/E14). Back stairs signalled a changed approach to privacy, as evidenced by Louis XV's effort to transform parts of the 'model of domestic discomfort, Versailles' into a more private, intimate place through the use of smaller stairs leading to private quarters (DeJean 2009: 5).

In the early part of the period, beds typically stood in the parlour as the most private of spaces. With the extension of houses upward, bedchambers moved to the upper floors. In England this shift largely took place by 1700, although it continued in several of Britain's North American colonies and even parts of Britain. A bedchamber stood on the ground floor in 1688 at Lower Slaughter Manor, for example, and this arrangement remained in 1725. By 1735, however, a desk and bookcase had supplanted the ground-floor bed, suggesting a space altered from an accessible bedchamber to a private space for writing and reflection (Gloucestershire Archives, D45/F4). This change illustrated that specialized rooms developed as well. Libraries as collections of accumulated knowledge, for instance, also typified domestic space in the larger eighteenth-century houses. Although books were an expensive and comparatively rare possession until well into the century, they materially represented Enlightenment ideals of categorization and rationalization of learning.

The kitchen served as a hub of activity providing sustenance to the household, as well as social space. All houses contained cooking arrangements and were heated through fireplaces, although in some regions and at some social levels owners moved kitchens and other functions to outbuildings on account of fire, smell or other factors. Many people continued to inhabit older structures, which functioned largely as they had in the past. In England it was not uncommon for farmhouses to be used for the storage of grains, and for spaces to be devoted to cheese, baking, brewing, even byres for animals. Some of these buildings were altered to accommodate new forms of living and being, but genteel behaviour for inhabitants of even polite houses had its limits. William Palling of Brownshill Court in Gloucestershire, for example, provided generous entertainment in his kitchen rather than a parlour (Hague 2015: 126–29).

Perhaps foremost among changes in the Age of Enlightenment was the emergence of the idea of comfort, which is inextricably tied up with the transition from 'house' to 'home' traced in this volume. This process largely resulted from design and technological changes that provided enhanced privacy, cleanliness, warmth and light. An 'Age of Comfort' emerged in France between 1670 and 1765, marking a significant change in the expectations of inhabitants about the level of comfort desirable in their houses. In architectural terms, the increased access to private rooms, the bathroom, the flush toilet and improved heating, all made for more comfortable domestic surroundings. The concept of the *vie privée*, or private life, first appeared in France in 1690 (DeJean 2009: 49). Bedrooms became more private spaces. Call bells were introduced in France, followed by England, enabling servants to be summoned more easily, although such devices were rarely seen in Germany. While flushing toilets were typical in upper-class French houses, this utilitarian device was slow to spread elsewhere. Such developments began to usher in the modern home.

The senses – sight, smell and hearing – shaped domestic life. The exterior arrangements of doors and windows suggested the social ordering of spaces within. By the late seventeenth century, window glass had become relatively common, and the transition to sash windows had begun. Windows were naturally related to light. Houses in London and some of the American colonies had 25–40 percent of their front façades dedicated to windows and doors, although this percentage was somewhat lower in Virginia. During the period, although houses increasingly reflected classical symmetry, the needs of internal room planning often continued to dictate window arrangements (Carson and Lounsbury 2013: 72, 75–77). The omnipresence of close stools, necessaries, chamber pots, animals, and unwashed bodies shaped inhabitants' olfactory experiences.

Noise was ever-present in houses where exterior walls might be thick but internal partitions thin and uninsulated save in more polite houses. When Thomas Adams, a young law student from Northumberland, arrived in London, he particularly described the city's clamour, especially the traffic: 'There is such a terrible Noise ... that last Wednesday and Thursday my Head was quite discorded' (LWL, MSS 2/Box 25/Folder 1). By the spring of 1761, Adams was 'very seriously thinking of turning my face northward', when he could bid 'adieu to this great and Noisy place.' (ibid.)

As with house exteriors, interiors featured ornamentation and decoration that signalled inhabitants' social standing, beliefs and worldview. Architectural finishes ran the gamut from highly elaborate works of art in the finest houses to remarkably plain for common people. The hierarchy of finish signalled room status and use in even the most modest dwellings. The fireplace and fireplace wall were focal points. Best rooms in middling and upper-class houses exhibited fine wood panelling (later replaced by plastered and painted walls), more elaborate cornices and decorative plasterwork. Later in the eighteenth century, wallpaper began to appear as a fashionable element of interior décor. Although plainly decorated, lower-status interiors frequently displayed some ornamentation or symbolism. Religious texts, symbols and even iconography could be found in various places, especially thresholds of houses such as doorways or chimneys. In societies that maintained beliefs in creatures such as witches, preventing their entry to living space was critically important.

The focus on middle-class housing during the Age of Enlightenment points towards a significant shift in domestic space: namely, the move from an integrated work-life centred in houses to the separation between work *and* life. Previously, 'household and business were part of the same economics' (Hamling and Richardson 2017: 8). In pre-industrial Europe, houses made little distinction between labour and domestic life. London's economy especially depended on the 'putting out' or domestic sub-contracting system, meaning that work in the home continued even during the late-eighteenth-century period of industrial development in Britain (Guillery 2004: 8–9). Through the middle of the eighteenth century, it was not unusual for industry and domestic space to be combined, or at least closely related. Early Bristol industrialist William Champion situated his elegant classical house adjacent to one of the most famous industrial sites in England. One commentator observed, 'The spelter works was built right in front of Mr Champion's windows' (Woolrich 1986: 32). Other examples exist in proto-industrial areas throughout Britain, although the middle classes increasingly separated house from workspace, both in removing work from the domestic setting, but also by spatially distancing houses from industry. As Britain in particular began to move from a pre-industrial to an industrialized society, house and workspace became more sharply defined, a harbinger of things to come in the nineteenth century.

CONCLUSION

Do houses associated with the Age of Enlightenment display a distinctive character? Although by 1800 many in Western Europe retained a way of living little different from their forebears of several generations earlier, significant developments had changed the design and function of houses. As it did with so much else in the Western world, the French Revolution affected architectural practice and attitudes towards domestic space. With Europe embroiled in a twenty-five-year struggle to realize or roll back the ideals of the Enlightenment, 'Architecture became the agent of social levelling' (Platt 1994: 153). Across Europe, neoclassical architecture had won the day, including in the design of houses, a position it would hold until the mid-nineteenth century. At the same time, designers and consumers increasingly emphasized physical comfort, and shaped domestic space to accommodate this desire. New goods pouring into the West from other parts of the world and the domestic products resulting from early industrialization helped to drive this process and facilitate comfort and ease, especially for the upper half of society able to acquire such wares.

The architecture and spatial arrangement of houses, especially for moderately prosperous members of society, altered substantially between 1650 and 1800, reflecting social and cultural change. The move from a one-room deep, linear plan with an asymmetrical exterior to a compact, classical box two-rooms deep mirrored the increased eighteenth-century emphasis on balance, order and symmetry, while simultaneously introducing greater segregation but less hierarchy and freer circulation. Privacy became more valued, but so did sociable routines amongst intimates. Taste – however one defined it – became an important feature of house design and presentation.

In the Atlantic World after about 1750, a common set of architectural principles that can be called 'Georgian' came to hold sway for all social classes. According to Matthew Johnson, the Georgian house marked 'a critical horizon in building' (Johnson 2010: 185, 196). In London, improvement in the first great modern city saw the cessation of urban vernacular house-building by the end of the eighteenth century. The rise of the middling sort as a group, and their efforts to play an enhanced role in society, especially influenced these changes. The aristocracy still predominated, but the 'polite and commercial people' described by historian Paul Langford played an increasingly central role in the literal and cultural construction of the house (Langford 2002: 311–31).

The process of improvement resulted in a single system of architecture drawing on classical design principles, which both the upper classes and the lower orders employed in their house-building activities. This house form increasingly characterized the housing of the Western world. It established national and international norms in houses, with less regional inflection. How such houses became homes during the eighteenth century is the focus of the chapters that follow.

CHAPTER FOUR

Furniture and Furnishings

CLIVE EDWARDS

The twentieth-century sociologist Norbert Elias (1897–1990) posited the idea that civilization, and patterns of behaviours that supported that ideal, gradually developed through *habitus* (the non-discursive aspects of culture that bind people into groups) and *figuration* (a dynamic, shifting set of connections that provides people with established and stable characteristics). Although specifically based in sociology, we can apply the concept to historic analysis as a loose framework to investigate how furniture helped people to make sense of themselves and the world in which they lived.

During the Enlightenment, the growth in literacy, developments in communications, greater social interaction, technical and scientific advances, and changes in women's positions in society reflected characteristics of habitus. Furniture and furnishings were clearly implicated in the figuration of culture. In 1778, Sir Joshua Reynolds expressed this idea of progress in terms of the ownership of goods: 'The regular progress of cultivated life is from Necessaries to Accommodations, from Accommodations to Ornaments'. In other words, the development of enlightened consumption was part of the networked expansion of civilization throughout Europe and its colonies. In addition, concepts of performance and gentility have also shaped the development of civilizations and informed the use and elaboration of 'props' or furniture for domestic spaces. Hence, the history of things, in this case furniture, helps to inform a history of practices.

From this point, a number of sub-themes emerge that explore the furniture and furnishings of the home in the Enlightenment period in terms of habitus, figuration, performance and gentility. These include furniture as a cultural signifier; furniture and its relation to gender; furniture and concepts of function and comfort; notions of fashion and taste; and ideas around self-consciousness, identity, difference and social performance. In addition to these notions, furniture itself was profoundly affected by the enormous developments in global trade and empire building, as exotic materials and techniques were imported into Europe in vast quantities and types, and finished goods were exported around the globe.

HABITUS, FIGURATION, PERFORMANCE AND GENTILITY

Furniture as cultural signifier

In Henry Fielding's *Tom Jones*, the description of Ralph Allen's virtues and good taste are expressed in '. . . his House, his Furniture, his Gardens, his Tables . . . [which] all denoted the Mind from which they flowed, and were intrinsically rich and noble, without Tinsel, or external Decoration' (Fielding 1749). Concerns around issues of class, social status, respectability and taste were associated with the use of furniture and furnishings as signifiers. Any particular total interior effect reflected the differences between the styles and tastes of the urban and the rural, as well as between the various status groups. *The Book of Trades* (1804) commented on the distinctions: 'What a difference is there between the necessary articles of furniture to be found in a cottage and the elegantly furnished house of a merchant or peer. In the former, there is nothing but what is plain, useful, and almost essential to the convenience of life: in the latter, immense sums are sacrificed to magnificence and show'. Thus their consideration of the practices, customs and symbolic meanings of furniture all contribute to an understanding of their context within a larger cultural system.

Gender issues

Recent gender studies have challenged historians' marginalization of women's lives and have opened up the eighteenth-century furnishing practices that operated in a gendered world. As Amanda Vickery has pointed out, the gendering (of any space or object) was not a natural occurrence; it required 'models, training, practice and compliance to handle props as fashion expected' (2009: 288). In practice, this meant being able to follow and interpret other people's use of rooms and furnishings, to be able to follow the journals and publications that expounded upon the topics, and indeed have a willingness to follow the *figuration* characteristics that were current at the time.

Related to both the establishment of social gatherings and the actual planning of interiors, furnishing a home was often a joint exercise, so the opportunities for women to influence the nature and style of homes developed rapidly during the century. In addition to the increased role of women in homemaking during the century, the production of specifically gendered furniture products grew as markets continued to be differentiated. A glance at contemporary pattern books and advertising confirm this elaboration of object types that perhaps suggest an increase in sophisticated marketing rather than actual references to real usage. Nevertheless, the public recognized gendered products as reinforced gender norms such as furniture items that apparently reflected the notion of feminine 'daintiness' and masculine 'bulk'. In fact, any characteristics of furniture that appeared to reflect these ideas show more about contemporary attitudes to gender rather than any aesthetic links with the masculine or feminine form.

Comfort and convenience

The development of the specialization of living spaces (to provide privacy), the increasing importance of the hearth and fireplace (to avoid smoky fires), and the impact of glazing (to combat draughts) were all part of the emerging comfort infrastructure that was well established during the seventeenth century. Apart from these improvements in the physical facilities, the idea of control over one's surroundings and a concern over politeness, respectability and cleanliness reflected concerns with comfort, and could be seen as part of the psychological motivations in considering comfort as being highly desirable.

During the eighteenth century, growing proportions of society were moving from being 'users of things' to being 'consumers of commodities'. If commodities were associated with comfort in a broad sense, this was one of the key issues of the eighteenth century, in the same way as the issue of luxury. Initially, prestige goods and the associated idea of gentility expressed social status, rather than comfort in the purely physical sense. However, part of the agenda of political economy in the eighteenth century was to legitimize material consumption, whether of products related to gentility, or those associated with the comforts of life. Therefore, comfortable furniture becomes the norm. For example, the French *fauteuil*, especially in the 'Louis Quinze' form, was a model of style and comfort which offered not only comfy upholstery through cushioned backs, seats and arms, but also had an elegant and stylish frame. The concept was adopted right across Europe.

Fashion and taste

Furniture like all other consumer products was subject to the vagaries of taste. The period embraced a number of stylistic traits including the Baroque (*c.* 1670s–1725), the Palladian (*c.* 1715–60), the Rococo (*c.* 1730–70), the Neoclassical (*c.* 1750s onward), Chinoiserie (*c.* 1750–65) and the Medieval revivals. These styles were generalized manifestations of taste and often incorporated exotic materials and developing production techniques. In terms of the home, the example of the chintz craze showed how the 'novel' goods were purchased as much for the 'sign-value' as for the 'use-value'; a fact that retailers were very well aware of. Daniel Defoe had noticed this particular demand early in the century. In 1708 he wrote:

> [Chintz] crept into our houses, our closets, and bedchambers, curtains, cushions, chairs, and at last beds themselves, were nothing but calicoes and Indian stuffs, and in short everything that used to be made of wool or silk relating to the dress of the women or the furniture of our house, was supplied by the Indian trade.
>
> —*Weekly Review*, 31 January

The need to change, to be seen to be fashionable and to reject the taste of the previous generation was to become noticeable even in rural districts. James Spershott (1710–89), a joiner of Chichester, Sussex, commented upon these transitions in his memoirs. They included this passage, which referred to his youth in the early eighteenth century:

> I observ'd in those days the household furniture . . . was almost all of English oak . . . but with younger people it was now in fashion to have deal dressers with shelves over for pewter, etc. Their tables and chests of drawers of Norway oak called wainscot. With the higher sort, walnuttree veneering was most in vogue and esteem'd for its beauty above anything else . . . The best chairs were turn'd ash, dyed or stuffed, with Turkey or other rich covers.
>
> —Spershott 1962

The example of 'black' furniture is instructive in the issue of taste. For antiquarians and those with a feeling for the medieval, black furniture represented ancient days and the patina of age was appreciated, whereas in a completely different mode, black ebony Boulle furniture with its brass inlay and gilded mounts represented tradition and authority. Whatever the case, taste was implicit in the presentation of the self.

Finally, some mention must be made of the growth of pattern books that were so important in disseminating the changing tastes. Although design pattern books had been published in the early eighteenth century, Thomas Chippendale's *The Gentleman and Cabinet-Maker's Director* of 1754 was the first to be devoted to furniture and published by a maker. Others followed as tastes changed, with George Hepplewhite's *The Cabinet-Maker and Upholsterer's Guide* published in 1788 and a few years later, between 1791 and 1794, Thomas Sheraton's *The Cabinet-Maker and Upholsterer's Drawing Book* appeared.

FIGURE 4.1: Engraving of a Design for a China Case, 1753 by Thomas Chippendale (1718–79). © Historica Graphica Collection / Heritage Images / Getty Images.

Self-consciousness, difference and social performance

Furniture played an important part in defining self, place and position during the eighteenth century. This role included issues related to intimacy, leisure and materiality, especially in relation to the haptic and visual senses as well as perception and intellectual stimulation. Furniture also met social and psychological needs that related to privacy and secrecy, as well as the intellectual and artistic demands.

The accepted symbolic meanings of objects as 'codes' were intended to establish both differentiation from others and integration within a particular stratum of society. The former was aimed at separating the owner and emphasizing his or her individuality and thus creating distinction, whilst in the latter, the object symbolically expressed the integration of the owner into a context that was both narrow (the building) and broad (the habitus). Therefore, one of the most valuable symbolic functions of goods, and especially of furnishings, was 'making visible and stable the categories of culture' (Douglas and Isherwood 1996: 38).

One such change were the developments in polite social habits, such as tea drinking, social entertaining, reading and writing, which meant that practical, functional furniture forms were required, and this will be discussed further below. Another demand came from people who desired objects for their own intrinsic worth. The polished surfaces with dramatically coloured and grained veneers, rare timbers from the Indies, and contrasting inlays of wood and metals, all excited the visual appetite, as well as satisfying other egotistical demands. When customers desired goods that were financially out of reach, it was often possible to purchase substitutes or simulations.

The development of polite society therefore had ramifications for furniture as much as for other decorative arts.

CHANGES IN EIGHTEENTH-CENTURY FURNITURE, INTERIORS AND USAGE

John Evelyn writing in 1706 expressed his pleasure in the recent improvements in the furniture-making crafts:

> [W]e may see in that late reformation and improvement of our lock-smiths-work, joyners, cabinet-makers, and the like, who from very vulgar and pitiful artists, are now come to produce works as curious for the filing, and admirable for their dexterity in contriving, as any we meet with abroad; and in particular to our smiths and joyners, they excell all other nations whatsoever.
>
> —Upcott 1825: 361

The scope, speed and variety of changes in culture and society during the period that encourage these developments, were such that they can only be touched upon here. Amongst the changes that were to affect furniture, the revisions to the social order that resulted in an interest in differentiation were important. The middle ranks enjoyed growing prosperity but so did the labouring poor to a lesser degree, resulting in a consumer revolution that fuelled diversity and changes in tastes.

The development and exploitation of colonies aided these changes, which also gave an impetus to consumption in both the cities and the provinces and particularly to sites of growth such as ports and industrial areas. Contemporary commentators were quick to see these developments manifest in furniture. In 1727, John Wood wrote of typical Bath premises:

> With cane or rush bottomed chairs the principal rooms were furnished, and each chair seldom exceeded three half crowns in value; nor were the tables, or chests of drawers, better in their kind, the chief having been made of oak; The looking glasses were small, mean and few in number . . .

By the 1760s, Wood noted great improvements in house furnishings that included:

> Walnut tree chairs, some with leather, and some with damask or worked bottoms supplied the place of such as were seated with cane or rushes; the oak tables and chests of drawers were exchanged, the former for such as were made of mahoggony [sic] the latter for such as were made either with the same wood, or with walnut tree, handsome glasses were added to the dressing tables . . .
>
> —Wood 1765: Preface

The differences between 'old' and 'new' wealth illustrate the distinctions between social levels. In old wealth (gentry and nobility), McCracken has considered that 'patina' was an exemplification of prestige before and after the eighteenth century. He further suggests that during the eighteenth century, the fashion system took over and status, at least for 'new money', was found in novel things rather than old (McCracken 1990). However, Pennell indicates that as well as the purchase of new products, older goods or heirlooms suggested some fixed points to people in their image of self, and thus helped to strengthen the familial ties (1999: 559).

The acquisition of goods was not based on a one-off purchase of all requirements, rather the opposite, as the acquiring of home furnishings in particular was based on accretion and accumulation from a variety of sources, as well as disposal of a wide range of goods feeding the second-hand market.

Lastly, there were the major changes introduced in the selection of materials and the developing techniques that were to deal with the increase in demand. The change from walnut to mahogany as the most fashionable timber, the change from woollen to cotton and silk hangings, the move away from wainscot to wallpaper for walls, and the use of rugs and carpets for floors are some of the more obvious examples.

Furniture in the home

It is impossible to discuss the multitude of furniture and furnishings that were used in the eighteenth century. The vast array of types, finishes and styles that reflected the particular status and position of individuals and families through the period can be seen in a good illustrated history of eighteenth-century furniture. This section will thus look at aspects of the furnishings of homes to give a flavour of how domestic space was fashioned and structured and how domesticity was performed so that people could make sense of themselves and their world.

The theatre is a metaphor for the home. The home puts on a show of personality and the accumulation of possessions. Therefore, the home acts as a stage, with its props, its front stage, back stage and private 'wings'. Each area of the home, then, had a particular part to play in the presentation of self. The stage metaphor also reflects the distinctions made by Erving Goffman (1971) in terms of the representation of the self, based on a 'front' and a 'back'. This did not necessarily imply that the public face was more luxurious or refined; indeed, it was often the case that the more private the space, the more conspicuously luxurious were the furnishings. This adds to Goffman's position by suggesting that individuals acted in particular ways to show themselves that they had the appropriate tastes and abilities. In addition, rooms had various functions at different times, so Goffman's simplistic binary division needs qualification and is only partially useful here. It is in all these spaces that furniture and fittings played a starring role.

The materials that covered the walls and floors were the backdrops or scenery to the various rooms in a home. Although oak wood panelling was still used in the early part of the period, more luxurious alternatives such as textile wall hangings and tapestries also remained appropriate for particular spaces during the eighteenth century. However, there was always a constant issue of up-to-date taste. Anne, Countess of Strafford wrote to her husband in 1712 saying, 'I don't much admire your fancy in hanging the Drawing Room with Tapestry . . . you might have plain damask which I believe will cost less than Tapestry' (BL, Add MS 22226). Rather than chastise him for poor taste, she appealed to his pocket. Textiles such as silk damask, and linen/cotton mixes as well as woollen camlet were used to line walls, while printed cottons were beginning to be popular by the 1720s. However, carved wall panelling remained popular in France and was often painted and gilded as part of an ensemble.

Wallpaper was initially very limited but by the 1760s was relatively commonplace. Flocked wallpaper was a popular style used in American, British and French houses. Interestingly, the designs reflected eighteenth-century textile styles, including those derived from damask-woven patterns, and patterns formed of branching stems. The papers exported from China to the West from the seventeenth century onward were sought after and expensive, which led European paper-makers to develop designs with Chinoiserie motifs during much of the period, particularly for the middle market.

FIGURE 4.2: Panelled Room from a Gloucestershire House, *c.* 1740, with Recessed Windows and Chinese Wallpaper. From *Old Furniture*, vol. II, edited by Lieut.-Col. E.F. Strange, C.B.E. (London: Old Furniture Ltd., 1927). © The Print Collector / Getty Images.

Flooring styles also changed over the century. In the late seventeenth century, wooden parquet floors became fashionable, with French models being gradually adopted all over Europe during the first half of the eighteenth century. Although initially carpets were displayed on tables, by the early 1700s they were being used on floors. Carpets could be imported from Persia or Turkey, or made in French workshops such as the Savonnerie or their English equivalents in Moorfields and Axminster. Throughout the century, the choice of floor coverings that reflected status, cost and taste thus reflected the hierarchy of interiors. By the 1750s, fitted carpets such as woven Wilton were used for grander homes, whilst lesser ones used non-pile products such as Scotch carpet and list carpet. Further down the scale, developments in floor cloth and matting meant that people of a wide range of backgrounds could cover the floors attractively.

Drapes and upholstery

The use of window curtains blossomed from the 1670s when the upholsterers supplied them in pairs with pelmets to hide the mechanism. Also popular were pull-up styles and festoons, but by 1770 the divided curtain returned to fashion often with continuous drapery over a number of windows. To produce the notion of unity of style, upholsterers made curtains from the same material as bed-hangings and wall coverings. The range of materials, styles and accessories meant that the soft furnishings of any room were individualized. In the early period between 1680 and the 1730s, the rich covers of upholstered chairs were often removable, allowing them to be stored when not in use. The use of protective loose covers over the fixed better quality materials superseded this practice.

The early part of the eighteenth century is marked by the use of needlework for upholstery, and the rise of the wing chair, which remained popular throughout the century. Introduced from France from around 1725, bergère chairs, characterized by a long seat and a raked back, became popular. By the middle of the century, upholstery had become less visually important, but was used in conjunction with carved wooden frames for chairs and a wide variety of special types of seating furniture and hangings.

The stages in the adoption of seating explored in William Cowper's poem *The Task* (1784) reflected upon the development of seats:

> Thus first Necessity invented stools
> Convenience next suggested elbow chairs
> And Luxury the accomplished sofa last.
>
> —[1784] 1852: 251

The words used closely reflect Joshua Reynolds' comments above regarding necessaries through accommodations to ornaments. Once the backdrop was established, the 'stage' or interior space itself was developed. Thomas Sheraton, in his *Cabinet Dictionary*, emphasized the importance of carefully structuring domestic space in all rooms, to make the right impression:

> The kitchen, the hall, the dining parlour, the anti-room, the drawing room, the library, the breakfast room, the music room, the gallery of paintings, the bed room and dressing apartments, ought to have their proper suits of furniture, and to be finished in a style, that will at once shew, to a competent judge, the place they are destined for.
>
> —Sheraton [1803] 1970

The next sections consider these spaces in turn.

Halls and vestibules

The role of the hall as an introductory statement of what might be found in the rest of the house often meant that the decoration and furnishings would want either to act as a foil to the main interior, or sometimes to be a dramatic statement in their own right. In 1768, Isaac Ware pointed out his distinction between the perceived front and back in the example of halls in town and country dwellings. He suggested that in town houses, the hall did not need to be as elegant, as the area was a place for servants, whereas in the country, it ought to be large and noble, as it could serve for a variety of functions. These functions included 'serving as a summer room for dining; as an anti chamber in which people of business or of second rank wait and amuse themselves; and it is a good apartment for the reception of large companies at public feasts' (Ware 1756: 335).

For much of the century, the main items to be found in the hall were chairs or benches specifically designed for that space. Furniture suppliers were aware that these represented another self-positioning possibility: '[the chairs] are such as are placed in halls, for the use of servants or strangers waiting on business-they are generally made of all mahogany with turned seats and the crest or arms of the family painted on the centre of the back' (Sheraton [1803] 1970). The basic form of these chairs was somewhat standardized but there were variations dependent upon the materials and workmanship. Both Chippendale, and Ince and Mayhew illustrate hall chairs in their pattern books, and both suggest a painted finish if mahogany should prove too expensive. Whatever finish was used, the hall 'ought always to be expressive of the dignity of its possessor' (Ware 1756: 335). The issue of performance was never far away.

Bedrooms

The feature of beds built into the fabric of the house remained for many country homes and in panelled bedrooms in town houses in the Netherlands, for example. 'Four poster' beds remained in general use across Europe and were found in very simple interiors with basic drapes, right up to the complex upholsterers' work of large-scale state beds. These important state or reception beds designed by architects were often replete with luxurious hangings, valances and complicated testers. These beds were much more for show than for sleeping. The French developed a talent for elegance and style in bed design, which was to spread across Europe. Indeed, French names were given to many great confections of textiles, mirrors and carved features in beds, including domed versions such as the *lit à la polonaise* and *lit à la turque*, both of which could be set in alcoves. Other types include the *lit à la duchesse* and *lit d'ange* – even the *lit à l'anglaise*.

The work of Daniel Marot, a French émigré working in Holland, exemplifies this sort of design work. Marot was important in that his wider ideas on the necessity of unity and attention to detail needed for a successful interior were widely published in contemporary pattern books. These books, distributed throughout the period, give a flavour of the fashionable styles as they changed over the century. British upholsterers Ince and Mayhew had suggestions for

FIGURE 4.3: State Bed, English, *c.* 1708. From *Old Furniture*, vol. III, edited by Lieut.-Col. E.F. Strange, C.B.E. (London: Old Furniture Ltd., 1928). © The Print Collector / Getty Images.

rococo beds while Chippendale illustrated not only rococo but neoclassical and chinoiserie design for bedsteads. Towards the end of the century, Hepplewhite offered more elegant neoclassical bed designs with restrained drapery and polished woodwork. At the other end of the social scale, rooms in multi-occupation town houses, or country cottages required products such as folding or press beds to save space in cramped quarters (see further below). Beds remained important pieces of furniture, but gradually became lighter in construction with draperies reduced to a minimum; the woodwork again became important, the posts being reeded and slender, and the canopy often pierced and carved.

A brief snapshot of a moment in a domestic life shows how even prosperous people cleaned and re-used furnishings, matched fabrics and colours, and made up material for curtains themselves. In October 1711, Anne, Countess of Strafford wrote to her absent husband, Thomas, about the furnishings of their home. She reported on the progress of the bedroom furnishings: 'I am extremely Pleas'd wth the work'd Bed for now tis Clean'd tis as good as new & looks very Genteell. I have hung the room with green camlet the same colour of the lace of the bed and made Window Curtains of the same' (BL, Add MS 22226, f. 135).

During the seventeenth century, the clothes press or wardrobe was developed. Initially a cupboard with pegs for hanging, by the eighteenth century drawers were fitted to the base. By the 1750s, the main section was often fitted with sliding trays to accommodate folded clothes, frequently in combination with a hanging section, referencing the growth in clothing collections that individuals accumulated.

Dressing rooms

In 1756, Isaac Ware indicated the changing roles of particular spaces as they changed in response to fashion, use and the performance of domesticity (Ware 1756: 328). In important houses, the progression from the saloon, via antechamber, drawing room, bed chamber and finally to the dressing room, represented a method of social control. Ware points out that

> A dressing room in the house of a person of fashion is a room of consequence, not only for its natural use in being the place of dressing, but for the several persons who are seen there. The morning is a time many choose for dispatching business; and as persons of this rank are not to be supposed to wait for people of that kind they naturally give them orders to come about a certain time, and admit them while they are dressing . . .
>
> —1756: 432

The symbolic importance of the dressing room meant that owners often furnished it with fine quality and high-style furniture and fittings. The space type was also used as a private retreat away from the formality of the saloons. It was here that the owners could indulge their fantasies and, being private, could include a wide range of personal items in the decoration. For women's dressing rooms, a range of special tables, boxes and stools, mirrors and chests of drawers were developed.

Dressing tables were known and used in the seventeenth century, but during the eighteenth, they became much more elaborate. They incorporated a wide variety of toilet requisites and could be very complex and costly objects. An interesting example of an extreme design is the Rudd or reflecting dressing table. This was a four-legged table with pull-out drawers, some fitted with mirrors that lifted up at various angles. First illustrated in Hepplewhite's *Guide* (1788), it was also shown in a simplified form in the *Cabinet Maker's London Book of Prices*. In 1797 it was again published, but by 1803 Sheraton could claim that it was 'not much in present use'. This would seem to indicate the relatively short span of popularity of a novel item.

Dressing tables were not exclusively for women. Sheraton designed one to 'accommodate a gentleman or lady with conveniences for dressing' (Sheraton [1803] 1970: 202). There were differences between these items, the chest usually being a chest of drawers with the top drawer fitted out for convenience. The dressing commode seems hardly different except that the chest might be fitted with a hinged top having a mirror on the underside, whereas the commode would frequently have had a freestanding toilet mirror stood upon it. The dressing chest fits into the taste for multi-purpose furniture in that it was compact and was fitted with a variety of drawers; one for a night stool, one for a square bidet, one for a basin and two cups, and one for a water bottle. In addition, a glass frame was usually hinged under the top.

Apart from these objects, other special-use items included shaving tables and stands, the distinction generally being that the stands did not have basins. Ince and Mayhew's *Universal System of Household Furniture* (1762) showed night tables, introduced mid-century, with one example conveniently offering a rising top for reading. The literal performance associated with furniture such as night tables, bidets and the like meant that they were often disguised to look like another furniture type or were hidden within another form for the sake of politeness.

Dining rooms

The dining room, although established in the seventeenth century, was an ambiguous space. In the preface to their *Works* (1773), Robert and James Adam noted that,

> Dining rooms were considered as the apartments of conversation, in which we have to pass a great deal of our time. This renders it desirable to have them fitted up with elegance and splendour, but in a style different from that of the apartments. Instead of being hung with damasks, tapestry etc. they are always finished with stucco and adorned with statues and paintings that they may not retain the smell of victuals.

The performance of dining and its associated rituals needed specialized furniture. For example, the sideboard table was used 'for a dining equipage, on which the silver plate is placed', whilst the sideboard itself was introduced in the last quarter of the eighteenth century designed to hold all the necessaries for serving and dining. Thomas Sheraton pointed out that 'the dining parlour must be furnished with nothing trifling, or which may seem unnecessary, it being appropriated for the chief repast, and should not be encumbered with any article that would seem to intrude on the accommodation of the guests'.

FIGURE 4.4: Furniture Designs for Kenwood House, Hampstead, London, late eighteenth century. © English Heritage / Heritage Images / Getty Images.

Like other spaces, at any one time there was a particular choice of furniture deemed appropriate for dining rooms. Sheraton also suggested,

> The large sideboard ... the handsome and extensive dining table, the respectable and substantial looking chairs; the large face-glass; the family portraits; the marble fire-places; and the Wilton carpet; are the furniture that should supply the dining room.
>
> —[1803] 1970: 304

The large-scale buffet or cup-board of the seventeenth century declined in popularity and was gradually replaced with sideboards in fashionable houses.

However, versions of the buffet board continued to be used in country homes for a lot longer for both storage and display.

In fact, the habits of dining varied widely during the period. Dining was initially undertaken using medium-sized tables and moveable folding tables that could be casually set up to suit the company. This tradition lasted until the later part of the eighteenth century when sets of tables which could be joined to make one long fixed table were introduced. These changes in fashion altered the nature of the dining room.

Stana Nenadic has remarked upon the rise of the dining 'set' between 1760 and 1810 in middle-rank Scottish households. She suggests that, as the bed had once been the major piece of furniture in late seventeenth-century households, so it was that the dining set became most important in the later eighteenth century. Nenadic also cites a passage recalling early nineteenth-century life in Edinburgh New Town which considers the care and attention lavished on the dining table: 'The furniture was nearly all rosewood or old Spanish mahogany, especially the many leaved dining table . . . which were always in a condition of the highest polish' (Nenadic 1994: 142).

The persistent use of mahogany together with other woods that moved in and out of acceptance is informative. It is an instance of the use of specific timbers accepted as being suitable to a particular item, room or use across the spectrum of incomes. In 1784, the commentator La Rochefoucauld mentioned Suffolk farmers who 'are always careful to keep one small sitting room spotlessly clean and sometimes quite elegant. In this room, they receive their guests, the tables and chairs contained in it are of well-polished mahogany . . .' (La Rochefoucauld 1933: 203). In addition, it was evident to contemporary cabinet-makers that the fashionable rococo designs were well suited to mahogany. The timber's strength allowed delicate ribbon back chairs, cabriole legs, Chinese style frets, and lattice pierced galleries to be successfully produced.

Indeed, the development of the dining chair is instructive in explaining the developing links between material, technique and style. At the beginning of the century, the French Protestant, architect and furniture designer Daniel Marot, presented a chair type with a novel slim framed back that was fitted with perpendicular splats of various shapes. The development of the cabriole leg also transformed chair manufacture by removing the stretcher bars. The effect of the use of the cabriole leg was to create a wider knee at the seat/leg joint, often decorated with carved work such as acanthus foliage. The legs were also finished with a ball and claw foot rather than the old-fashioned hoof and pad style. Shoe-pieces for backs were now pinned and glued to back rails, and rebated seat rails accepted the new drop in seats. Chair seats themselves became broader and there was more concern for an ergonomically shaped back. Legs became even more elaborate with high relief carving and decorated seat rails, with solid splats replacing pierced ones. The use of mahogany from the second quarter of the century allowed for carvers to create chair backs with audacious scrolls and delicate ribbons features. The use of this timber, prized for its colour, strength and exotic connotations, replaced the more ostentatious carved and gilded taste of the first quarter of the century. Other stylistic innovations included the ladder back dining chair initially derived from vernacular models; fretted and latticed work in the Chinese style; various Gothic motifs; Adam style chairs with neoclassical motifs often painted; and Sheraton-influenced square backs and sabre-shaped legs.

Living rooms

The use of domestic spaces varied enormously, often being dependent upon the number of rooms and occupants in a dwelling. Indeed, the naming of the space varied as well. Parlour, salon, closet and drawing room all described these rooms for living. At its best, a house was divided so that rooms could be designated as private, family or guest, and public spaces. During the late seventeenth and early eighteenth centuries in large houses, there was often a great parlour, which gradually developed into the *salon* or saloon, which meant that an everyday parlour was required in these houses. On the other hand, less prestigious homes more often considered comfort and convenience rather than show. In 1756, Isaac Ware wrote:

> The parlour, in a small private house, is a very convenient room; but as it is not the apartment of most shew, there is no necessity it should reduce the passage to an alley; and in larger houses, inhabited by persons of distinction, there must be anti-chambers, and rooms where people of business may attend the owner's leisure . . .
>
> —1756: 293

During much of the century, the drawing room or saloon, as distinct from the parlour, was probably the most important room in the house. In larger houses, the saloon would have been the main reception room, whilst the drawing room was a more relaxed family room. It was the main reception room, and like other rooms, the owner furnished it in accordance with the demands of social politeness, manner and appropriate taste. It was a prime site for the performance of domesticity. Sheraton is very clear as to the purpose of a drawing room; it is 'to concentrate the elegance of the whole house, and is the highest display of richness of furniture' ([1803] 1970: 218). He goes on to say: 'The grandeur then introduced into the drawing room is not to be considered, as the ostentatious parade of its proprietor, but the respect he pays to the rank of his visitants'. Although Sheraton aimed this comment at the wealthy, the idea of decorum and appropriateness filtered down through all classes.

Clearly, the range of spaces designated as living rooms varied enormously. A craftsman potter was relatively comfortable in the 1740s:

> In the Hall, a clock and case, a looking glass, a writing desk and table and stand, a dozen Sedge [matted] chairs. In the parlour a corner cupboard and china and a tea table, an oval table, a tea table, a card table, a dressing table and hand board, twelve cane chairs.
>
> —Weatherill 1988: 33–34

This instance of one comfortable home does not epitomize the full variety of domestic situations. Those who were renting dwelling spaces often had less in the way of home comforts living in one room. The following description of the lodgings of an unmarried clerk, of a 'middling station', living in London in a furnished room rented at half a crown a week in 1767, illustrates the point: 'A half-tester bedstead with brown linsey-woolsey furniture, a bed and a bolster ... a small wainscot table, two old chairs with cane bottoms, a small looking glass six inches by four in a deal frame painted red and black, a red linsey-woolsey curtain ...' (Joy 1968: 834).

Changes in use and configuration continued, and by 1816 Humphrey Repton could write:

> The most recent modern custom is to use the library as the general living room; and that sort of state room formally called the best parlour, and of late years the drawing room, is now generally found a melancholy apartment, when entirely shut up and only opened to give the visitors a formal cold reception.
>
> —1816: 54

Repton illustrated this change in room use, and thus furniture, by comparing images of an old-fashioned panelled room with chairs arranged in a circle for conversation, with a modern library room where people were scattered in groups performing different tasks requiring differing sorts of furniture.

The notion of performance has already been mentioned as a metaphor, but Mimi Hellmann has shown that performance in interiors can also operate in a very real sense. The skill to manoeuvre complex pieces of furniture reflected or denied an appearance of grace and ease with such objects. In a way, the effective operation of these items was a performance by the individual for the onlookers in the assembled company. Furniture had taken on a 'performative role' (Hellmann 1999: 425). If the greater accessibility to furniture and equipment diluted attempts by elites at social exclusion, then as Hellmann indicates, even if the material symbols were easy to acquire, it was important that they were not easy to perform. Participants had to learn how to use furniture and understand its particular role.

Furniture that combined complex functions within one object was often versatile as well. These so-called *meubles à surprises* were celebrated in France and later in England in the later part of the eighteenth century. Many designers turned their attention to this growing market. Sheraton's designs included ladies' writing tables with spring-loaded pen and ink drawers, and a spring-weighted fire screen operated by lead weights and pulleys; a lady's dressing table with a rising back mirror and side mirrors; and the Harlequin table, so called because it used complicated mechanisms that were similarly employed in the *commedia dell'arte*.

Another specialist was John Joseph Merlin, who established a shop selling metamorphic or combined-function furniture. The sorts of objects that Merlin sold included:

> neat little writing-reading-or working-tables, combined with charming soft toned pianos . . . Others with pianos concealed, and clever desks with lights attached for quartettes set up in less than three minutes, which if not required for music might be converted into a nice piece of furniture for playing chess.
> —La Roche [1786] 1933: 140

These adjustable pieces of furniture were more than just amusing artefacts. The more sophisticated and personal ones such as secretaries and jewel caskets demonstrate links to the concept of secrecy and privacy in a culture where property (such as personal letters, jewels and money) was susceptible to prying eyes. In all these cases, cultural practices inform the design of things.

The French influence on style has already been noted in the bedroom. The living rooms also reflected this with the introduction of *bonheur de jours*, *commodes*, *garnitures*, *jardinières*, *girandoles* and *fauteuils*. Sheraton gives an interesting comment about the French *sièges meublants* and *sièges courant*: 'where their drawing rooms are fitted up in the most splendid manner, they use a sett of small plainer chairs, reserving the others merely for ornament' (Sheraton 1802: 444). The distinction between comfort and display is obvious.

Libraries/studies

Libraries were to become important living spaces during the eighteenth century. There was a wide range of furniture products designed and made to meet the particular needs of the users. These included chairs specially designed for reading and writing, tables and stands for books and writing materials and, of course, bookcases and display cabinets. More complex were the combined writing and reading tables with rising tops, drawer space and various accessories. There are variously known as artists, architects or Cobb tables. Cobb tables refer to a design invented by John Cobb whereby the inner desk rises to a convenient height for reading and writing whilst standing.

The freestanding press or library case, often based on architectural forms (and indeed sometimes built-in to the rooms), was not, surprisingly, the foundation of library rooms. In smaller or more secluded rooms, book storage was often incorporated into a combined piece called a bureau bookcase. In addition to these items, furniture needed to access the library was essential, as books were often shelved to the cornice. These were produced in a wide range of types, including telescopic poles, miniature staircases, as well as convertible tables or chairs that had built-in steps. These 'metamorphic' tables, where the function was hidden within the item, were often based upon the 1774 patent of Robert Campbell. In a parallel manner were the metamorphic library chairs that could be adeptly turned from an elbow chair into a set of steps.

Although the library initially had connotations of a masculine retreat, the library gradually metamorphosed during the century towards a family space. The effect of the influence of women meant that a wider range of activities were included in the library that increasingly called for more dedicated furniture. Instances of these include writing tables and bureaux for both men and women; screen tables designed to shield one from the heat of a fire; and specially designed chairs for convenient and comfortable sitting at these table types. By 1820, the changes seemed complete. Maria Edgeworth wrote of her visit to Easton Grey: 'the library drawing room with low sofa, plenty of movable tables, open bookcases, and all that speaks the habits and affords the means of agreeable occupation' (Edgeworth 1894: vol. 2, Letter 11)

SPECIAL FURNITURE FOR SPECIAL NEEDS

In addition to the physical need for space-saving furniture, there was also a demand for dual-purpose items and this was often, though by no means always, related to the size of the family. The press beds are a useful example how domestic space was used and how domesticity was achieved.

The idea of beds in cupboards had, for a long time, been in use in vernacular homes, but in polite society, sensibility and social pressure suggested that a bed in a dining or living room was not acceptable. The nature of these beds also raised concerns about health. As early as 1691, Thomas Tryon was suggesting that press bedsteads did not allow appropriate air flow (1691: 440), and well over one hundred years later Loudon cautioned that press bedsteads were 'objectionable, as harbouring vermin and being apt to soon get out of order when in daily use' (1839: 331–32). However any perceived problems did not deter usage.

Press beds were available in a range of styles, which varied according to customer requirements and pockets. The best qualities were library press beds, which incorporated shelving for books on either side of a middle section that offered the drop-down bed concealed covered by double doors. According to

Richard Gillow, these were intended 'to stand in a Dining Room as a handsome piece of furniture to make an additional bedroom occasionally' (Gillow's Letter Books, 1778–81, 344/169). This pragmatic use of space demonstrates how the practicalities of living had to be dealt with even in higher status homes. A little less imposing was the wardrobe press bed. This was a wardrobe-shaped cabinet that combined a pull-out bed hidden behind the wood or mirror doors. At the bottom of the selection were bureaus and table beds, where the beds unfolded from behind or from underneath. From these examples it is evident that furniture helped people to link the practical performance of day-to-day life with the self-image that furniture could reinforce.

VERNACULAR AND COTTAGE FURNITURE

The discussion so far has dealt mainly with members of middle and high society who had made the distinction between rooms for privacy and rooms for display a part of their house planning for a long time. In the country and outlying districts where one- or two-room cottages were normal, rooms had to act as parlours, bedrooms and eating spaces. Because of this, it was common to find beds in the main room of a cottage, for space-saving furniture items to be present, and functional furniture to be evident over items that were more extravagant. Like urban users, the human needs for furniture to meet the demands of storage, eating, seating, sleeping as well as display were evident in regional domestic spaces. Although these customers did not seek high-style designs as much, this sort of furniture did take its cue from its more elite models.

Whilst simple oak chests were still widely used, cabinet-makers introduced chests of drawers with fashionable brass hardware and bracket or cabriole leg feet. A low dresser continued to be appropriate for large rural homes in dining rooms, but also filtered to humbler dwellings where it was used for both kitchen and dining needs in the same space. The addition of a shelf structure added to its usefulness for displays of ceramics, for example. The use of free-standing or wall-mounted corner cupboards was another example of space saving that was so important in cramped homes. Space-saving initiatives continued with hinged tables with drop-down flaps, small-scale side tables that could serve a number of various purposes, and tripod pedestal tables that were popular as occasional tables or for serving tea or supporting candle stands.

A rare 1768 inventory of a cottage in New Brentford, Middlesex, illustrates the range of household effects that an artisan-labourer possessed. It shows a remarkable mix of the old and new, mingled with some considerations of comfort. The bedroom furniture comprised a four-poster bedstead and a half tester turn-up bedstead, both fitted with textile furnishings. The home also enjoyed five tables, two of which the inventory described as wainscot dining

FIGURE 4.5: 'Cottage Life', *c.* 1750, An idyllic portrayal of Eighteenth Century cottage life. © Edward Gooch Collection / Getty Images.

tables. There were four cane and five rush-bottomed chairs as well as a leather-covered elbow chair. For storage purposes, there was a deal clothes chest, a wainscot chest with drawers veneered in front, and a mahogany tea chest. Other items included eight prints and two small looking glasses (Joy 1968: 592).

An enormous variety of chairs were produced that either reflected local traditions and materials, or attempted to copy high-style models suited to local needs. Whether 'thrown chairs', ladder back chairs, Windsor chairs or 'country Chippendale', the sheer range of styles and types that was available is astonishing. Windsor chairs, probably first developed for outdoor use and painted green, soon became an important furnishing item and were made in an enormous range of shapes and styles that reflected local tastes and craft.

SECOND-HAND FURNITURE

As with clothes, there was a flourishing trade in second-hand and used furniture in the eighteenth century. The easy disposal of second-hand and unwanted goods had a twofold influence on the market. First, it made space for new and fashionable goods in the homes of those who could afford them. Secondly, for those who could not afford new, it gave them access to furniture which when it was new they could only aspire to. This eventually gave them an opportunity to participate on the fringes of style and quality. Second-hand furnishing goods were usually sold by auction, through furniture stores or through specialist brokers. These sales were not just for those who could not afford to buy new. There is some evidence of the collecting of old things for their own sake. John Hervey's *Book of expenses* showed that in 1690 he bought 'a parcel of old china for my dear wife, and a pair of china rowlwaggons' (tall cylinder vases). In 1692, he paid £1.17.6d for a chest of drawers bought at Stow Green Fair. This was the same John Hervey who, in 1696, paid fashionable London cabinet-maker, Gerrit Jensen, £70.0.0 for a set of pier glasses, table and stands (Wills 1971: 104).

Stana Nenadic has pointed out that in the eighteenth century, in Scotland at least, there was an extensive market in second-hand goods, which by definition were unfashionable. The twin attractions of second-hand goods appear to be that they often represented quality and usefulness and retained some resale value as well as the more pragmatic issue of simply being available and affordable. This apparent willingness to include second-hand goods in an interior may appear to negate the argument about goods 'going together' but it is likely that owners used second-hand goods in non-public rooms or in homes that were not aspirational. Indeed, as Nenadic points out, people made second-hand purchases because of their functional value rather than their status value (1994: 129). However, this was not always the case. Parson Woodforde noted in his diary for August 1783 how 'Mr and Mrs Townsend behaved very genteel to us. The drawing room in which we drank tea &c. was hung with silk. The chairs of the same kind of silk and all the woodwork of them gilded, as were the settees. The looking glass, which was the finest and largest I ever saw, cost at second hand £150.0.0 . . .'. The reference to the second-hand nature of the mirror would have no hint of any pejorative suggestion.

CONCLUSION

In the eighteenth century, domestic space can be seen to have been fashioned, inhabited, structured and performed through the concepts of *habitus* and *figuration*. The furniture and furnishings that were bought and used expressed habitus or the unarticulated but experienced symbols of life. The figuration or the networks of interdependent humans that created and sold the styles, types and materials that helped people to make sense of themselves and the world in which they lived, informed these. Supplementing these two considerations was discussion of furniture as a cultural signifier whereby people were defined by their furnishings. In addition, furniture and its relation to gender has suggested that although there was differentiation in products, home furnishings was often a joint venture for married couples. It was during the eighteenth century that furniture and the concepts of function and comfort were fully developed, whilst the notions of fashion and taste and ideas around self-consciousness, identity, difference and social performance all played a role in the furnishing choices made for the home.

CHAPTER FIVE

Home and Work

LEONIE HANNAN

CONNECTING THE DOMESTIC WITH THE INVESTIGATIVE IN EARLY-MODERN ENGLAND

The early-modern home was a complex space, through which people, things, materials and knowledge circulated. Masters and servants alike, exercised a wide range of technical competencies and material literacies in the activities they conducted at home – using minds and hands to achieve work of both a necessary and of a more exploratory nature. A raft of historical and anthropological literature has revealed the dynamism of domestic space and its constitutive role in the realms of gender relations, family life and servants' work.[1] Meanwhile, architectural and art historical scholarship has explored the material and aesthetic dimensions of the home, especially of larger households, making connections between design and the social.[2] In each of these realms, the work of the home is visible, whether that is the work of design in building and decorating homes, the gendered division of labour between the master and mistress of a household or the conditions of domestic service.

Recent scholarship across a range of disciplines has also generated diverse definitions of domestic experience, referring variously to the intellectual, behavioural and experiential facets of human lives lived at home. Historical studies have focused in particular on the operation of 'private' and 'public' spheres, responding in varied ways to Jürgen Habermas's proposal that the eighteenth century witnessed a transformation of the latter.[3] The increasing separation of these spheres has been traced as an important feature of emergent 'modernity', but many historians and especially those focused on the study of gender have argued convincingly for the blurring of these boundaries.[4] As Amanda Vickery has stated: 'the issue of privacy still haunts the history of space'.[5] Michael McKeon's weighty contribution to the intellectual history of domesticity reveals that whilst many more aspects of society were drawn into the public-private division in our period, domesticity itself increasingly came to embody both of these characteristics.[6] McKeon's work reinforces the notion of the domestic as a porous space capable of promoting both privacy and public activity at the same time. This exploration of how domesticity has been represented and understood, in intellectual terms, is complemented by a recent surge in scholarship that addresses the emotional or experiential dimensions of domestic space. Encouraged by a revived interest in material culture as an historical source, embodied and tactile engagements with home have brought new interpretations to the fore – Carolyn Steedman's analysis of domestic service being a prime example.[7] As literary scholar James Krasner has argued:

> While the home is both a cultural formulation and a building, it is, more than either of these, a cluster of tactile sensations and bodily positions that form the somatic groundwork through which we experience its emotional sustenance.[8]

Krasner speaks of the 'home's resonantly familiar materiality' as opposed to its material form and function – a space 'contiguous with the body's sensorium'.[9]

In studying the home, sociologist Elizabeth Shove has suggested that we need to 'focus attention on the formation of regimes and concepts of service, on how meanings, practices and technologies hold together'.[10] By focusing attention on the circulation of materials that provisioned the home, domestic space can be seen as both porous and connected with other domestic, commercial and artisanal spaces. Through the countless people (servants, visitors, traders) and materials (fuel, foodstuffs, linen, ash) that moved through this space, the home was integrated in networks that connected urban and rural environments. By considering the household in this way, this chapter engages with the status of the home as a site of production and circulation of both consumable goods and knowledge. Thinking of the home as a networked and dynamic space casts a different light on the work of home, allowing connections between domestic labour and intellectual endeavour to become visible.

DOMESTIC WORK

To date, some of the most significant scholarship on the home as a place of work has focused on the role of servants, the substance and meaning of their labour, and the relationships that existed between them and their employers.[11] For many historians of the twentieth century, trends within domestic service offered valuable insight into the larger socio-economic shifts associated with industrialization and 'modernity'. Tim Meldrum's London-focused study substantially shifted the emphasis from the (easier-to-research) employers' perspectives to the servants' experience of service.[12] Furthermore, Meldrum placed gender at the heart of his research, revealing the agency some servants exercised in their lives, the sheer diversity of their experiences of service, and the inadequacy of the 'separate spheres' and 'growth of privacy' narratives to explain these experiences. More recently, Carolyn Steedman's intervention in this field has further emphasized the importance of female servants (75 percent of all servants) in this period and her analysis casts new light on the qualities of servants' labour and the feelings it provoked. Even more pertinently for this chapter, Steedman examines the material dimension of domestic service, arguing that 'material things – jokes, jests and the well-set jam a maidservant had just produced – were objects and entities, part of the social world' and as such critical to our understandings of the 'social order' of that time and place.[13] Of course, some early modern thinkers did not even acknowledge domestic service as labour in the strictest sense because it did not produce saleable goods.[14] Nevertheless, the work of servants in early modern households was constitutive of social relations and hierarchies and, as such, was fundamental to understandings of identity and authority in this period.

Over the last fifty years, gender historians have debated women's experiences of domestic life and labour at length, also addressing male contributions to domestic work.[15] In particular, Leonore Davidoff and Catherine Hall's seminal work, *Family Fortunes: Men and Women of the English Middle Class, 1780–1850*, not only revealed the configuration of class as a gendered phenomenon but also brought women's roles in family businesses firmly into the foreground.[16] Davidoff and Hall expertly illuminated the 'private' or hidden dynamics of family life and since this publication, much historical work has been committed to developing our understanding of female action in the 'public' arena.[17] As mentioned above, substantial critiques have been made of the separation of public and private spheres as described in *Family Fortunes*, most notably by Amanda Vickery,[18] but for our purposes here, Davidoff and Hall developed understanding of domestic ideologies as they operated in the middle-class home and provided the foundations for many subsequent and nuanced studies of home.[19] Moving into the present day, the unwaged – and therefore unrecognized and unrewarded – labour of women in the home remains an important issue globally, underlining the ongoing significance of this topic in our studies of society past and present.[20]

One of the unhelpful features of the public/private dichotomy has been its tendency to reinforce the notion that work largely took place outside of the home. As we have seen, this was not the case for many kinds of labour, but the separation of spheres also overlooks the prevalence of intellectual endeavour that took place 'behind closed doors'. The home as a site of intellectual labour has been considered most concertedly in relation to elite households, especially those owned by significant patrons of the arts.²¹ Research has shown that from at least the seventeenth century onwards, grand houses were built with intellectual endeavour explicitly in mind.²² Once these buildings no longer served a defensive purpose, as they had in earlier centuries, they took up the task of displaying an aesthetic ideal in their outward manifestation and also providing space for the practice and display of the arts in their internal dimensions. Their visual appearance 'always bore witness to decisions that had been made to engage the mind and delight the eye'.²³ Art and literature occupied an important place within the life of elite households, both in terms of the performance of gentlemanly masculinity and in the cultivation of feminine accomplishments. However, large houses could facilitate a wide range of intellectual interests, from the horticultural to the alchemical, and provided opportunities not only to collect knowledge (books, artefacts and specimens) but also to share that knowledge with wider networks via the calendar of social visits and events that shaped elite life in this period. Political activity was also underpinned by the sociability promoted by these homes.²⁴ In this sense, elite homes were important spaces for both the production and dissemination of ideas.

As Dimmock, Hadfield and Healy have commented: 'increasingly significant areas of private, internal space led to the provision of rooms such as closets, studies and libraries where objects were gathered for their curiosity and intellectual value, and scholars encouraged to discourse and write about them'.²⁵ Libraries were swelled by the rapid expansion of print culture in this period but closets – often characterized as spaces for devotional activities – came to play a key role in reading and writing practices in the eighteenth century. As Tita Chico has emphasized, the closet or dressing room's associations with female writing was amplified in the literature of the day and this phenomenon had its roots in everyday practice – as men and women used such small, private household spaces to read, write letters and keep accounts.²⁶ Writing in the summer of 1741, Jemima, Marchioness Grey described using another woman's closet and the clutter of materials she found there:

> I have taken Possession of the Lady's Closet, (which I may now again call Mine) & all her Papers & Books which strew the Floor, cover the Tea-Table & fill every other Table & Chair in the Room. So that after having committed great Devestations, displacing Drawers & laying out of the way many Curious Miscellanies, I have with some Difficulty found the Corner of a Table (which is at present cover'd with no less a Book than Dʳ Middleton) to write upon.²⁷

Likewise, Sarah Hutton has highlighted the importance of the closet to the seventeenth-century theologian and writer, Damaris Cudworth, Lady Masham, a room in which 'the works of Descartes, More and others rubbed shoulders with recipe books, cures and that symbol of female obedience, the spinning wheel':

I can but think how you would smile to see Cowley and my Surfeit Waters Jumbled together; with Dr More and my Gally Potts of Mithridate and Dioscordium; My Receits and Account Books with Antoninus's his Meditations, and Des Cartes Principles; with my Gloes, and my Spinning Wheel; for just in this order They at present ly[e].[28]

In this scene, we glimpse the 'jumbled' nature of domestic life and work, where the labour of provisioning a household had a subtle but significant relationship with the labour of scholarship.

The intellectual currents of the eighteenth century were intimately connected with the form and function of elite households. Antiquarian activities lent themselves to the lifestyle and interests of the gentry and aristocracy, rooted in their locality and motivated to trace their own ancestry and heraldry back to ancient times. The very broad network of antiquaries that grew over the course of the century, anchored by the Society of Antiquaries, provided a basis upon which detailed histories of local buildings and sites could be produced. Such networks were facilitated by the sociability of elite households, but not confined to them, and the antiquarian project promoted the possibilities of the regions (distant from the institutions of intellectual note) to offer intellectual reward.[29] As Rosemary Sweet has shown, even in the early 1700s, there was an attempt to realize the commercial potential of antiquarian writings – mainly produced by members of the landed classes.[30]

Studies of the intellectual culture of this period have brought to life the vibrancy and wide-reaching influence of the Bluestocking circle's domestically situated intellectual activity of the later part of the century. Certainly, Bluestocking hostess – Elizabeth Montagu – played a significant role in shaping the literary culture of her time, maintaining networks and using her influence amongst aristocratic peers as well as with London's book printers and sellers to promote her preferred authors. As Elizabeth Eger has emphasized, Montagu's London assemblies offered a 'particular kind of virtuous yet opulent sociability'.[31] Montagu's household was a preferred space for cultural discourse and diversity of company, removed from the 'factional politics of court'.[32] Amy Prendergast has also highlighted the 'flourishing literary associational life' of Ireland in these same decades, with a focus on Elizabeth Rawdon, Lady Moira's Dublin-based salon.[33] In each case, cultural debate was framed by opulent interior décor and whilst 'diversity' of participation was often remarked upon, the domestic settings emanated aristocratic ostentation.

Historians of science have also identified the genteel household as an important site for scientific experiment, but they have tended to do so via the particular biographies of important men of science. Steven Shapin's brilliant study, 'The House of Experiment in Seventeenth-Century England', published as long ago as 1988, makes the case for the importance of domestic space for experimental science and lists some of the most notable examples as follows:

FIGURE 5.1: Valentine Green (1739–1813), engraving 'An Experiment on a Bird in the Air Pump' (after Joseph Wright of Derby), 1769. Found in the collection of the State Hermitage, St. Petersburg. © Fine Art Images / Heritage Images / Getty Images.

the laboratory equipped for Francis Mercury van Helmont [1614–98, Flemish alchemist and writer, Kabbalist] at Anne Conway's Ragley House in Warwickshire; the role of Towneley House in Lancashire in the history of English pneumatics; Clodius's [the physician and chemist Frederick Clod] laboratory in the kitchen of his father-in-law Samuel Hartlib's house in Charing Cross; [natural philosopher] Kenelm Digby's house and laboratory in Covent Garden after the Restoration; the Hartlibian laboratory worked by [scientific writer and Fellow of the Royal Society] Thomas Henshaw and [alchemist – writer on natural magic] Thomas Vaughan in their rooms at Kensington; [natural philosopher] William Petty's lodgings at Buckley Hall in Oxford, where the Experimental Philosophy Club originated in 1649; Thomas Willis's house, Beam Hall [worked on the anatomy of the brain], where the Club met during the early 1660s.[34]

Shapin's article makes clear the importance of homes and households to the study of science in the seventeenth century. Likewise, Deborah Harkness has shown how different members of natural philosopher John Dee's household worked to ensure that the 'business' of science was conducted effectively and profitably within their home in Mortlake – his wife Jane Dee playing a key role.[35] Moving outside the walls of the house itself, Clare Hickman has illuminated the eighteenth-century garden as a dynamic space of scientific experiment and medical practice.[36]

Whilst the home was a site where science was conducted, its importance has been overlooked and an emphasis has tended to be placed on the new manufacturing in a period of increasingly rapid industrialization. While economic historians might see the household as a manufacturing site in decline in this period, it was still the key space for scientific enquiry until well into the nineteenth century, when homes were gradually displaced by specially built laboratories as sites for scientific research. As historian of science Simon Werrett has shown, most natural philosophers conducted chemical experiments in kitchens, cellars or rooms adapted for this purpose. These domestic investigators employed common household utensils, furniture and spaces to serve experimental ends, and employed materials ready-to-hand in the home to learn about nature – everything from candles and cups to mice and clay pipes.[37] The motives for such practices were varied, ranging from practical and economic constraints of poverty and scarcity to religious and social values of thrift and stewardship.

The ways in which these different activities, or types of work, interacted is less well understood. Our histories reflect the differentials in status attributed to the process of making jam versus the process of conducting a scientific experiment, despite the fact that these activities might both involve an in-depth knowledge of material properties, the use of specialized equipment, the heating and cooling of materials to change their quality, the tacit knowledge of having performed these actions repeatedly and with particular aims in mind.[38] Moreover, our scholarship can sometimes compound this distinction by failing to recognize the high status of some domestic labour – especially the kinds of knowledge and skill that were required to operate a stillroom effectively. There is a network of connection (material, embodied, technique, equipment, space) between domestic labour and domestic enquiry.

HOUSEHOLD MATERIALS, EQUIPMENT AND TECHNIQUES

Evidence of the myriad of materials and things that circulated through an eighteenth-century household can be found in a variety of domestic record-keeping. As Karen Harvey has argued, the particularities of domestic authority can be seen within the documents of home 'oeconomy' and these shed light on the different tasks that were done and by whom.[39] Account books, lists of household expenses, recipe books, diaries and letters all provide an insight into both the mundane and the rare and sought after. This extract from the Household Book of Dunham Massey in Cheshire gives a feel for consumption during one week in late February/early March 1743:[40]

From Saturday the 26 of February to Saturday the 5 of March 1743
Mrs Kinaston
Pounds of Butter, Eggs
25 Partridges 7 fowls
Veal, Cod, Whitings, Turbats
Flounders, Shrimps, sand
Grocer's Bill
From the Dairy
Milk, Cheeses Turkey
Fowles
Used this Week
Fowls, Partridges, Turkey
Pounds of Soap
Butter, kitchen. Stillhouse
Thomas Hardey
Malt 25 Measures
Wheat 6 Measures
Barley 4 M.
Groom, Oats, Beans
Coachman, Oats, Beans
Draughts, Oats, Colts
Cows, Oats 6 Measures
Partridges, Corn, Pecks
Poultry, Barley
Pigeons, Corn
Two Sheep
Brooms
Mrs Walton
Quarts of red Port
Quarts of white Port
Pint of sack
Quarts of Birch Wine
Quarts of March Beer
Barrel of Ale tap't the 3
Hogshead of Small Beer
Pounds of Hops
Candles from the Garden

This record shows that Dunham Massey operated a mixed economy of buying in some items from local suppliers and generating other products on site from raw ingredients. As Beverley Lemire has highlighted, practices of household accounting were bolstered by the 'quantitative culture' that was growing in this period alongside rising rates of numeracy. She argues that the older concerns of reciprocity and hospitality were gradually overtaken by numerate reckoning and precepts of debit and credit in the domestic sphere. Likewise, Margaret Hunt has described the increasing accessibility of book-keeping skills as a phenomenon that gave certainty to the managers of households:

> A democratic mystery in the best Baconian tradition, it [accounting] promised its initiates an unprecedented control over the intimidating universe of credit, debt, and cash flows.[41]

In this way, household accounting can be seen as a powerful 'mode of writing' and 'representing hours of careful labour over years and years or over a lifetime' a way in which individuals expressed themselves and represented their domestic environment.[42]

Take the eighteenth-century kitchen, this was a room in which many different materials and processes took place and a space that was connected closely with other productive parts of the household, such as the dairy, brewery or stillroom, and also with the scullery, larder and cold stores. Of anywhere in the home, the kitchen exemplified the incredible diversity in the materials and processes that domestic servants administered on a daily basis and its contents were carefully accounted for.[43] The kitchens of large households would typically be fitted with

FIGURE 5.2: Vicar of Wakefield by Oliver Goldsmith. 'Mr. Burchell's First Visit' by Thomas Rowlandson, English artist (1757–1827). © Culture Club / Getty Images.

a wide range of equipment, including a fireplace (invariably with a roasting range), a roasting screen (a tin-lined open-fronted cupboard to keep dishes warm), an oven (most likely as part of a range in the later part of the century), boilers or coppers (for boiling meat, vegetables or puddings), and a range of smaller articles like mills, mortars, chopping blocks or marble slabs.[44] The Gells of Hopton Hall in Derbyshire had a well-equipped kitchen including apparatus to make the most of the roasting potential of the fireplace ('Three coal rakes', 'two racks with hooks', 'six large spitts & one bird spit'), pans that indicated the existence of a stove or hot plate ('nine Sauce pans; four stew pans; five brass pans; four fish pans; two leaden fish pans') and a wide range of other equipment from wooden scales to an egg slice.[45] Likewise, an 1825 inventory of Styche Hall in Shropshire revealed the kitchen packed full of specialized equipment that would facilitate the production of diverse consumables, including '11 Copper Stew pans & preserving pan', 'Two tin fish strainers', a 'Lanthern & two reflectors', a 'Cradle Spitt 20 Meat hooks in ceiling' and 'Two loafs of Sugar'.[46] This household also benefitted from a larder, scullery, brewhouse, malt room and salting room, each offering further apparatus and supplies for provisioning the household.

The everyday apparatus of domestic production is often overlooked in an era that is synonymous with an explosion of new, consumer goods and the exotic products of global trade.[47] Whilst the allure of the new was more than evident in eighteenth-century homes, especially those of the elites, it was the mundane but essential articles of daily use that made life possible in these spaces. Moreover, in our rush to understand the 'consumer revolution', features of domestic life that were focused on repair and re-use have tended to be overlooked.[48] As Karen Harvey has noted, in her study of male domestic authority, the evidence of household accounting does not 'uncover individual consumers excited by advertising or searching for the fulfilment of fantasies of pleasure driven by "modern autonomous imaginative hedonism"' but rather 'exposes men striving to manage their property well'.[49] In these documents, 'the unit of the household is palpable'.[50] By the same token, those householders that wished to learn more about the natural world might invest large sums in cutting-edge instruments such as a microscope or even an air-pump, but they could equally be aided by the existing material conditions of their domestic environment.[51]

Managing or conducting the many and varied tasks of home economy demanded a wide range of skills and tacit knowledge. All too often, the recipes that appear in domestic collections gloss over the intricacies of process, assuming a range of competencies that are alien to the twenty-first-century reader. However, the kitchen was not the only space that demanded specialized equipment and dexterous skill. The stillroom (or still house) was of particular importance in the production of a range of household remedies and luxuries and, as the name suggests, principally included a still or alembic for distilling liquids – heated by a furnace. In the seventeenth and early eighteenth centuries, this room and mode of production was the domain of the mistress of the household, which designated the higher status of these activities as compared with cooking, curing or cheese-making. Mary Evelyn (c. 1635–1709), wife of the famous diarist John Evelyn and a regular at Court, remarked that she had 'the care of piggs, stilling, cakes, salves, sweet-meats, and such usfull things' in 1674.[52] The salves (medicinal remedies) and sweet-meats (luxury confectionary) were two products strongly associated with the stillroom. This interesting facet of early modern domestic space has not been given the scholarly attention it deserves, most likely because stillrooms fell out of use at the end of our period and have not survived the household improvements of subsequent centuries. In fact, there appears to be only one extant stillroom in the British Isles, at Ham House in Surrey.[53]

There is good evidence, from an earlier period, that Thomas Smith of Hill Hall in Essex took great pride in his still house, carefully recording its contents in a separate, dedicated inventory and keeping a close eye on the work of this space even when he was abroad.[54] Smith's still house activities were part of a broader engagement with intellectual and antiquarian pursuits – interests that he fostered by equipping his home not only with books, but also with an incredible number of stills: five pewter, one of copper and a further enclosed 'pelican' still.[55] By the eighteenth century, most stills were kept in a room in the main house, although earlier household plans had tended to position them in an outbuilding (hence the term 'still house'). Likewise, the use of this space shifted over the early-modern period. Having principally been used for extracting the potent aspects of plants to produce health-giving medicinal ingredients, by the seventeenth century stillrooms were routinely also used for making and storing confectionary. The reason these functions were combined was partly because there was overlap in the techniques of production of health-giving herbal waters and celebratory spiced cordials.[56] Moreover, both activities were considered the responsibility of the mistress of the house rather than that of a servant. As Mary Evelyn argued in a letter to a friend: 'wee [women] are willing to acknowledge all time borrowed from family duties is misspent', the priorities of a wealthy mistress was 'the care of Childrens education, observing a Husbands com˜ands, assisting the sick releeving the poore, and being serviceable to our friends'.[57] Assisting the sick by providing homemade medicines and entertaining visiting friends with lavish banquets both required time spent in the stillroom.

Another field of home production that required a dedicated space and the administration of a skilled practitioner was the brewery or brewhouse. The 1825 household inventory for Styche Hall reveals the following as contents of the 'Brewhouse':

FIGURE 5.3: 'A Brewhouse', 1747. Designed and engraved for the Universal Magazine, (January 1747). Hand-coloured later. © The Print Collector / Print Collector / Getty Images.

> Brewing furnace
> nearly new stack lead Curve & Grate
> Iron furnace & appendages
> Five Mashing Tubs
> Three Large oval coolers
> Six small Round Coolers
> Rince Tub and Gasser
> Tun[ing] dish Gaun & pail
> Cleansing scieve & Mash
> Rules
> Old Barrel & Small Cask
> Oven Peel Scraper & fork
> Water Trough & Spout
> Four large stillages
> One Bench
> New Round Tub & old ditto
> Iron Water dish[58]

Traditionally, brewing was women's work and public ale houses had often been run by women too. However, by the eighteenth century, the brewer in large households was much more likely to be a man. As Christina Hardyment has commented: a brewhouse – whether large or small – 'was an important domestic office from the days of the Saxons until the nineteenth century'.[59] Such a space contained a large copper vessel, sometimes two, which would heat water (fuelled by a furnace) and 'had a high ceiling, to allow the clouds of steam from the boiling copper to be dispelled'.[60] Sometimes bakehouses and brewhouses would be built adjacent to one another so that one furnace could facilitate both activities. For example, at Foremark in Derbyshire (built 1759–61), the two are situated next to each other. At a very grand house like Castle Howard in Yorkshire (built 1699–1712), the brewhouse and bakehouse occupied the same outer wing, although there were very many other formations besides.[61] Once boiled, the water runs off into a large barrel called a 'mash tun' and malt, known as 'grist', is added and stirred with a mash paddle. The process of mashing takes several hours and turns the grain starch into sugar, producing 'wort'. Once this is complete, the contents are returned to the copper so that it can be boiled again, this time with hops and sugar. The 'hopped wort' can then be emptied into cooling trays. Once cooled, the liquid is drained into a fermenting tun – where yeast is added. The yeast used might also have been used in baking, another connection between these two domestic offices. After a few days of fermenting, beer is produced and can be poured into casks and moved to the cellars.[62] A wealthy household would have produced beer of three different kinds on a regular basis and this required adjustments to the process described above to achieve the variations in flavour and alcoholic strength desired.[63]

In the process of researching and restoring a brewhouse at Shugborough Hall in Staffordshire, National Trust staff had to consider where the differences might lie between the (better documented) commercial breweries and the prevalent and often large-scale domestic versions. It appears that the largest eighteenth-century households might support brewhouses that could compete with the commercial breweries for the sophistication of equipment and quantities produced. Pamela Sambrook has estimated, based on accounts dating from 1819, that the inhabitants of Shugborough Hall consumed 24 gallons of beer a day.[64] However, by the nineteenth century the commercial operations outstripped domestic ones in their adoption of new technology. That said, towards the end of the eighteenth century, even domestic brewing adopted refrigerators as part of their set-up.[65]

Whilst essential to the household, brewing was arduous work, but more importantly it was work that demanded expertise in the process of fermentation and the combinations of ingredients, heatings and coolings that would achieve the desired end. Brewing skills were consequently highly valued amongst domestic servants throughout this period and it was a selling point for both male and female servants (whether coachmen or housemaids) to be able to conduct brewing alongside their other household work.[66] Moreover, a beer allowance often substituted for part of a servant's wages and so the domestic production of beer remained fundamental to the economy of a large household in this period.[67]

The flow of goods and people through the house was reflected in floorplans. For example, the scullery was used for washing and cleaning dishes and cooking equipment, preparing vegetables, fish or game and, therefore, it was desirable for there to be direct communication between this room and the kitchen, the yard, coal cellar, wood house and ash bin. However, owing to the heat and odour that emanated from the scullery, it was usually ensured that it did not connect directly with spaces that contained fresh produce, such as the larder, dairy, pantry or other food stores.[68] Eighteenth-century householders and servants had to be attuned to the relative heat and cold of adjoining, working spaces in order to ensure that produce didn't spoil. Julie Day's study of the elite Yorkshire homes of Temple Newsam, Nostell Priory, Harewood House and Hovingham Hall confirms that:

> Eighteenth-century country house design evolved entire new wings and blocks to accommodate the arrangement of kitchen space and its associated departments to lessen the effect of fire risk. This also proved acceptable on the grounds that cooking smells could no longer permeate through new or expensive remodelled interiors, including the dining room itself where it might have been the height of neo-classical fashion.[69]

Likewise, in the later eighteenth century, Susanna Whatman remarked in her housekeeping book that 'Butter, radishes, or anything that spoils in a hot kitchin should be placed near the parlor door, as should the cheese, to be ready to come in'.[70] Peter Brears has analysed a range of formations used in the layout of domestic offices in substantial country houses. This survey reveals Palladian architectural design as a driver of 'spinal corridor basement plans' keeping domestic offices 'below stairs' but arranged in such an order as to facilitate the production, storage and delivery – to principal apartments – of food and drink.[71] This model was further developed in the mid-eighteenth century by designs that added wings beyond the main house – sometimes offering a whole pavilion for the kitchen and its attendant offices. This development allowed for greater separation – as Whatman desired – between the dirtier and bad smelling activities and those involving fresh food.

Here we have discussed a couple of the more specialized kinds of domestic space in order to reveal the tailored skills and understanding demanded of both masters and servants in the early-modern home. These practices shaped inhabitants' days and how they saw themselves. In these tasks, status could be derived, gendered roles could be performed, care for others could be undertaken. When gentlewoman Anne Dormer of Rousham House in Oxfordshire complained of her husband being 'much taken with all sorts of cookery and spends all his ingenuity in finding out the most comodious way of frying broileing resting stewing and preserving his whole studdy'[72] or 'loiter[ing] aboute, somtimes stues prunes, somtimes makes Chocolate, and this somer he is much taken with preserving',[73] her point was clear – these tasks and who did them mattered, not only for home economy but also for the moral order of her household. However, it was just this kind of domestic experimenting – forays outside of the norm – that is the subject of the next part of this chapter. Whilst conduct manuals of the period were clear in their prescriptions for how domestic work should be undertaken, for what purpose and by whom, there were householders who sought to use their tightly honed domestic skills to explore a wider field of enquiry.

WHERE HOME ECONOMY MET 'INNOVATION'

The archives of the Royal Society of Arts, formerly the Society for the Encouragement of Arts, Manufactures and Commerce, hold important insights into the investigative practices of a wide range of eighteenth-century men and women. The Society was founded in 1754 by the drawing teacher and inventor William Shipley who wished to encourage creative thinking that could be put to public uses with a view to fostering beneficial social progress. To this end, the Society offered prizes for submissions by the general public that contributed to contemporary problems in a variety of fields. There were two types of prize: 'premiums' for entries that responded to a call issued by the Society and 'bounties', which were awarded to unsolicited submissions. The categories were:

> *Agriculture* (which might concern the growing of vegetables, turnips, madder, tree planting, sowing techniques or new farming technologies)
> *Manufactures* (e.g. improvements in techniques for dying leather; ways of manufacturing milled hats in imitation of the French; loom-woven fishing nets)
> *Chemistry* (a wide-ranging category, including things such as perfume production or food innovation)
> *Mechanics* (focused on innovation in technology – although these innovations were often put to agricultural use)
> *Polite Arts* (drawing, decorative arts, paints and pigments, but experiments with natural dyes were sometimes reported here)
> *Colonies and Trade* (this covered initiatives such as vines being transported from the Old World to the New and the collecting of botanical samples).

Amongst the letters submitted to the Society describing efforts to innovate for the 'public good' of the nation, there is evidence that the home was a key site for such informal investigative activity. Sometimes the ingenious new observation, adaptation or product was even prompted by a domestic problem. Other contributions clearly displayed the knowledge and skills honed by work in the home, garden or field – knowledge and skills that could be put to a different and, perhaps more noble, purpose.

In June 1756, an A. Curteen of Haverhill in Suffolk wrote one such letter to the Society. Keen to establish his knowledgeability on the subject, Curteen stressed that he had made 'manifold and repeated experiments' over the course of 'fourteen or fifteen years together' but understood that there were some obstructions to 'this great discovery . . . becomeing an universall good'.[74] The topic was preserving the flesh of animals, with a view to the product provisioning sailors during long voyages at sea. Following a critique of the common practice of salting the 'flesh of sheep', Curteen proposed an alternative method: drying meats 'under a covered roof but laid open on every side to the wind', which he felt both reduced the likelihood of flies getting to the meat and also reduced the 'smell and taste of putrefaction' present in some salted products.[75] In a similar vein, 'A.B.' wrote in 1761 about his 'Observations on the process of manufacturing oils' with a procedure that would improve the quality of 'any kind of fish or seal oil, that pitrifid & stinking' and 'the drain oil called vitious oil'.[76] In the case of the former:

> When the oil is taken off from the dregs & brine: the dregs which swim on the brine should be taken off it also & put into another vessel of a deep form: & on standing, particularly if fresh water be added & stirred with them, nearly the whole remaining part of the oil will separate from the foulness: or to save this trouble the dregs when taken off may be put to any future quantity of oil that is to be edulcorated by this method. Which will answer the same end.

But for vitious oil that was even 'more putrid & foul', this process would remove the bad smell 'however stinking it may be' and adjust 'the brown colour . . . to a very light amber'.[77] The innovator referred to domestic practices when he commented that these oils might be used in lamps and referenced a kind of oil commonly known as 'Kitchen stuff'. However, the potential to use these methods in a manufacturing context was the object, thereby not only attending to the needs of the frugal housekeeper, but also contributing to the prosperity of the nation. Sadly, it seems that 'A.B.' did not receive the response he required from the Society – he would write a further three times about oil (a letter on 10 May 1761 running to thirteen large sides). He also sent specimens, which he worried about:

As I have heard nothing from you in relation to the proposal I made concerning the edulcoration of train oil, I presume nothing is hitherto decided with respect to it: & as I am apprehensive that the specimen sent is not purified equally to what my process can effect, & that as it may probably if kept in a warm room be less perfected than when it was sent, as all animal oils when kept warm in a small quantity will change, I have sent another sample of crude & purified oil, which I fancy will be found more different from each other than the first.[78]

Some submissions included detailed descriptions, diagrams and even models of a particular innovation. When Richard A. Clare wrote from Clarendon in Jamaica on 21 April 1799, addressing himself to the secretary of the Society, Samuel More, he enclosed a diagram to which he referred to in the text of his letter. His communication was concerned with a new design of 'Still and Refrigeratory, calculated to save expence in the distillation and refrigeration of ardent spirits, at the same time that it renders these more pure than can be done by stills of the usual construction'.[79] He felt sure that distillation on the principles that he described 'may turn an advantage' and noted that he would 'esteem himself honoured' should the Society approve his design.[80] The cross-referencing between image and text worked as follows: 'It consists of a copper Body A, from the top of which proceeds a hollow Trunk. a. b, forming the Refrigeratory, which terminates in a large Receiver. b, made globular'.[81] Clare cautioned More that 'Every part of the apparatus must be made air tight'.[82] Unfortunately, a year and three months later, Clare was forced to write to confess that the still of his invention had 'By some accident ... got leaky, admitting the air when the vacuum was made'. For the time-being, he was waylaid: 'as I have little leisure from my business as a Surgeon &c, I have not as yet set myself to repair it; for you must know there are no workmen in this country to execute a thing of this kind'.[83] However, he fully intended, 'when I have time' to 'resume the inquiry, respecting the advantages that may arise from distilling in vacuo, and the result of my experiments shall be laid before the Society'.[84] Such correspondences with the Society could, in some cases, span years with willing experimenters sending updates on their observations and new adaptations that might be of interest to the arbiters of commercial and artistic merit.

In 1756, a Reverend Dr Stephen Hales contacted the Society about some experiments he had been conducting to find a method for 'checking in some Degree the Progress of Fires'.[85] He had been prompted to do this on hearing about the 'late destructive fire in Cornhill London' but his method was designed for use in ordinary houses.[86] Hales explained:

> I made the following Experiment, in order to form some Judgement of the Matter. Viz: I placed on two Garden Potts a dry Fir Board, which was half

an Inch thick, & nine Inches Broad: and covered nine Inches length & breadth of it, with an Inch depth of common damp Garden Earth;[87]

Hales used 'two Course of Bricks' to make a fireplace to enclose the fuel of wood and coal and encouraged the fire with the use of the bellows 'in order to keep the Fire to a vigorous Heat'.[88] After two hours,

> before the Fir Board was burnt thro', when there was only a weak lament Flame at the under Part of the Board; for it could not flame out for want of proper Fewel, because the Substance of the Board was reduced to a brittle Charcoal, by the Heat of the Inch depth of Earth which lay on it; & which hindred the burning board from flaming.[89]

Hales 'reasonably inferr'd' that the use of earth in this way might considerably 'retard the Progress of the Fire'. He suggested that, in such an emergency, householders 'cover with Earth the Floors of several of the adjoining & more distant Houses; which stand in the Course of the Progress of the Flames. The thicker the Earth is laid, so much the better'.[90] He calculated that 'a Cubick Yard of Earth will cover 36 square Yards of Floor, an Inch thick'.[91]

In 1796, Elizabeth Wyndham was awarded a silver medal by the Society under the category of 'Mechanicks'. Her innovation was a Cross-Bar Lever, which she had designed to help resolve her workmen's difficulties in moving large and heavy rocks, or as the Society put it: 'her ingenious contrivance of a method of using to the best advantage, the power applied to the Cross-Bar Lever, for raising large weights'.[92] On 28 October 1795, Wyndham had sent a drawing of the lever and a model (which was then stored in the 'Society's Repository for the inspection of the Public') alongside her explanatory correspondence. She wrote:

> I assure you, it has proved of great use, and the workmen all approve of it very much ... I observed that the men made use of the Lever in a very ineffectual manner, by standing three or four at a time on the bar of the Lever; by which means some of them were placed so near the fulcrum, that their power was in great degree lost; besides they were obliged to steady themselves upon sticks, for fear of falling, which took off from their weight upon the Lever.[93]

Wyndham explained how her invention worked, cross-referencing the drawing and model, showing how her design 'inclines backwards, which increases the power' and included 'a cross-bar for the workmen to hold by' and another for them to stand on – both 'additions are made to take on and off, and are only to be used when the strength of the rocks require an increase in power'.[94] Elizabeth

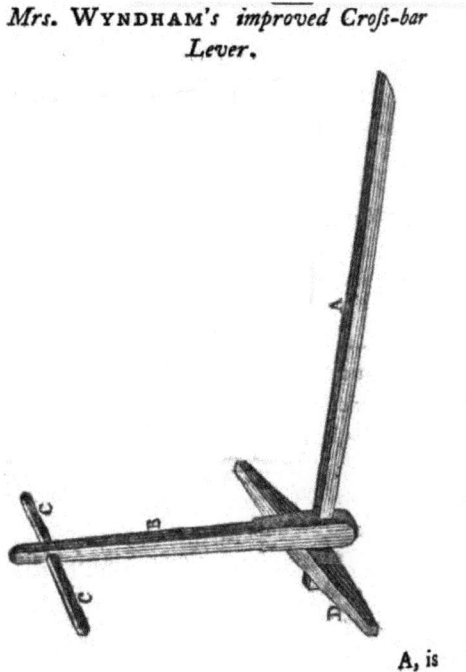

FIGURE 5.4: Mrs Wyndham's Improved cross bar Lever. She received the Society of Arts silver medal in 1796 for her 'ingenious contrivance'. This was an improved method for using the manpower applied to a cross bar lever to raise large weights, such as stones. © Royal Society of Arts.

'Wyndham' was actually Elizabeth Ilive, the mistress of George Wyndham, third Earl of Egremont of Petworth House in West Sussex. She had broader scientific interests, having established a well-equipped laboratory at Petworth in the later eighteenth century.[95]

Whilst many of the submissions to the Society came from the aristocratic, well-to-do or professional classes, this was certainly not the whole story. On 26 May 1791, a joiner – Alexander Thomson – living on the Nutts River Estate in Jamaica wrote to the Society about a mathematical instrument he had designed and made:

> I beg leave to Acquaint you that I have found out to Perfection A Mathematical Instrument (of my own making intirely of wood and made By myself being A joiner By Trade) which solves By Inspection all Quest[i]ons in Right Angled Obliq[u]e and Accute angles and likewise at pleasure solves Obliq[u]e and Accute Angled Quest[i]ons When Required to be reduced into two Right angles.[96]

Thomson assured the Society that he had 'Already Proved the Instrument and in all Cases and Quest[i]ons above mentioned finds it Accurate Both By Geometrical and Trigonometrical proof'.[97] Submissions such as this give a snapshot of the domestic ingenuity of eighteenth-century householders. Some of their letters addressed the challenges of the domestic environment itself, the vast majority reported on experiments undertaken in that environment using materials and equipment close at hand.

Whereas the Society for the Encouragement of Arts, Manufactures and Commerce's records provide qualitative material on the activities of eighteenth-century innovators, other records corroborate this picture of a diverse range of individuals working to improve techniques and apparatus for a broad spectrum of uses. A snapshot of all patents issued in Shropshire during this century reveals products designed by a 'Gentleman', 'Yeoman', 'Clerk', 'Forgeman', 'Mathematician', 'Engraver', 'Ironmaster', 'Flax Dresser', 'Engineer', 'Clockmaker' and 'Coal Master'.[98] Some of their innovations were focused on improving their trade, others used the specialized skills of a given trade to create something of use in an entirely different realm. For example, the yeoman Thomas Jackson of Wellington registered a 'Tincture for curing wounds, burns &c' in 1747.[99] Meanwhile, a team of mathematician and engraver (John Duncombe and Joseph Pokle of Ludlow) collaborated to design a new method of measuring timber and a mechanical turning spit to replace a jack.[100] In these cases, the patents suggested a financial motivation alongside the more public-minded considerations often invoked in the Society's transactions.

CONCLUSION

This chapter has sought to provide an overview of domestic spaces, busy with consumables, equipment and people – performing diverse and often complex tasks. Whilst many of these operations were ordinary in the sense that they were necessary, daily activities, when taken together, the actions of the brewhouse, stillroom or kitchen; the dairy, the laundry or the garden created a fertile context for investigation. Whilst beyond the scope of this chapter, other kinds of domestic record – such as letters, diaries, journals and commonplace books – speak to cultures of observation and documentation that leant themselves to intellectual enquiry. Many of the wealthier households of this period augmented the run-of-the-mill domestic equipment with well-stocked libraries and drawing rooms that featured orreries, telescopes and other scientific instruments. The individuals who chose to write about their experiments to the Society for the Encouragement of Arts, Manufactures and Commerce reflect this culture of enquiry. Often they conducted their investigations with no more equipment than the average domestic space could offer them. Nonetheless, they were driven to enquire, to make some record of their observations and to offer them up in service to the nation. These fragments of evidence begin to build a picture of eighteenth-century society that saw a broad population concern itself with matters of the mind and to do so by employing their hands from the comfort of their own home.

CHAPTER SIX

Gender and Home

RUTH LARSEN

In Madrid in 1786, Francisco Cabarrús reacted negatively to the idea that women should have full membership of the Real Sociedad Económica Matritense de Amigos del País.¹ He argued: 'How do we expect those to be friends of the country who are not friends of their homes? And good citizens those who scorn the obligations of wife and mother?' (cited in Smith 2006: 97). Cabarrús, who has been described as the 'Rousseau Español', believed firmly that women had a place in society, and that place was within the home (Smith 2006: 96–98). Although Cabarrús may have been out of step with many of his fellow society members, as a significant number supported female membership, his ideas were shared by many other writers in Europe and North America in the late eighteenth century. They believed that women had an important function within society, and this was familial and domestic.

Mary Douglas describes the home as 'the realization of ideas' (1991: 290). During the eighteenth century, this was especially the case for gender ideas. The shifts in the different forms of hegemonic masculinity in this period (Harvey 2005) and the resultant impact on feminine ideals did have an impact on the home. This is no surprise, as the home can act as a 'setting through which basic forms of social relations and social institutions are constituted and reproduced' (Saunders and Williams 1988: 82). Central to these ideas was the growing focus on domesticity. Carole Shammas defines domesticity as 'making home the center for most non-market social interaction' (1980: 3), and it was during the eighteenth century that the home attained an increasingly important status within many societies. It was in this period that the shifts began to take place, so that by the 1830s and 1840s the ideal of home had become a cultural norm (Tosh 1999: 30).

It is important to remember, however, that there was a distinction between ideals and practice, and this is where there is another key connection between the home and gender. Academic scholarship on home has often made a distinction between the ideal and the real home, with some writers suggesting that they are binary terms. However, increasingly there is an awareness of the need to see how the ideal and real are interconnected ideas and 'not pure and distinct concepts or domains. They are mutually defining concepts and experiences' (Mallett 2004: 70). Similarly, while most people did not fully conform to hegemonic gender ideals, because if they did they would not be hegemonic (Connell and Messerschmidt 2005), the real and ideal of gender roles were often connected. Taking as a starting point the idea that 'the term home functions as a repository for complex, inter-related and at times contradictory socio-cultural ideas' (Mallett 2004: 84), this chapter focuses on the interconnections between prescribed ideals and lived experiences. It examines the eighteenth-century discourses of home and domesticity and how they connected to gender, exploring themes within didactic literature, novels, art and the writings of enlightenment philosophers and historians. As well as exploring the examples of specific individuals in order to understand the lived experience, there is also a focus on the interconnections between the house and home. This is because buildings are not only shaped by the society that created them, they also impose restraints on subsequent social actions, and space both reflects and shapes the ways in which gender is constructed and experienced (Massey 1994: 186; Locock 1994: 9). This chapter considers in turn the ideas of 'public' and 'private', the idealization of domesticity during the eighteenth century, the impact of sentimentality and politeness on the home, and the different forms of 'homemaking'. The ways in which the home created or reflected notions of masculinity and femininity in the period are discussed, and throughout it is argued that the home was of central importance in shaping gender relations in the Age of Enlightenment.

THE 'PUBLIC' AND THE 'PRIVATE' IN THE HOME

The idea of separate spheres has dominated gender history in recent decades, especially works focusing on nineteenth-century Britain and North America (see Vickery 1993a; Davidoff and Hall 2002: xii–l). The close connection between the private and the domestic has also meant that it has been of distinct importance to historians of the home. However, although the notion of the public sphere is especially associated with the eighteenth century because of the work of Jurgen Habermas (1989), the idea of separate spheres where the private sphere was distinctly female is generally more associated with the nineteenth century, and with the Christian bourgeoisie in particular (Hall 1979). The extent to which there were gendered 'separate' spheres in the eighteenth century has therefore been the subject of significant debate (e.g. Barker and Chalus 1997; Kerber 1988; Rendall 1999; Vickery 1993a; Wahrman 1993). As Ben Griffin, Lucy Delap and Abigail Wills note, 'regrettably "separate spheres" has become a straw man, a reductive caricature of an argument that presents an easy target for historiographical potshots' (2009: 5). However, Matthew McCormack argues that although the notion of separate spheres can be unhelpful, 'home and "public life" were gendered in importantly contrasting ways' (2005: 20). Therefore, for historians of gender and the home, it is important to recognize some of the different ways that modern historians and eighteenth-century commentators have understood the concepts of 'public' and 'private'.

One of the main causes of the 'potshots' is that although Jurgen Habermas (1989) used a very precise definition of the public sphere in his writing to mean neither state nor institutions but rather the sphere of private people who come together in public, this does not reflect the ways that the terms were used at the time. Instead, during the eighteenth century the 'public' had multiple meanings, including to mean the state or nation (Vickery 1998: 288 ff.; Dwyer 1987: 95). Similarly, the extent to which the public sphere was exclusively male has been challenged; even if we use the Habermasian understanding of the public sphere, there is evidence of women being involved in gatherings to discuss the affairs of state. Many aristocratic women were active in politics, for example, both local and national, canvassing votes for their family members, hosting influential parties, and using philanthropy as a way of encouraging the electorate (Chalus 2005; Lewis 2003; Richardson 1996). Also, this form of the public sphere was sometimes located within domestic buildings; by transforming a house from a place to a space, it was possible for a home to be also part of the public sphere through being the location of a salon or a politicized dinner party (Beggs 2014: 127; Chalus 2000). The salons of Paris and London allowed political debate and literary discussions to take place, and in England they often had the additional feature of the gaming table, which was used by both sexes (Beggs 2014; Deutsch 1996: 647–48). If we broaden the definition of the public to include commerce, which some writers during the eighteenth century did (Harvey 2012a: 60), again this was not exclusively male nor separate from domestic buildings. Women of all classes could be also influential in trade, and their family links, friends and social networks as well as their sociability were all important elements of running effective businesses (Hunt 1996: 168). This support was not necessarily just for male kin; Boston businesswoman Elizabeth Smith supported her nieces in their business ventures, including utilizing her London-based networks to help give them access to goods (Norton 1979: 54). Although these forms of the public sphere were dominated by men, it was an arena that involved both genders and was not necessarily distinct from the home.

Likewise, the extent to which the private sphere was either distinctly feminine or wholly domestic during the eighteenth century has also been questioned (e.g. Harvey 2009). It is important to remember that not only is the association of home with women a cultural construct, but also that it is one that was questioned by some enlightenment writers. James Fordyce, for example, argued that the ancient Greek practice of the seclusion of women in the home was problematic for men and women alike, while David Hume wrote that it was better for a marriage if women left their firesides (Taylor 2004: 131–32). Some texts directly connected the domestic to the public sphere; in her *A Vindication of the Rights of Men* (1790), Mary Wollstonecraft introduced discussions about the family, female education and children, for example (Tomaselli 2001: 241). Wollstonecraft also saw the family as the cradle of patriotism, and Linda Kerber's (1976) model of 'republican motherhood' shows how politics and domesticity were interconnected in post-revolutionary America. However, privacy, along with seclusion and familial intimacy are central themes in many modern definitions of the home (Lewis 2009: 340) and there is evidence that because of the changing nature of work, the home was becoming increasingly private during the eighteenth century. Industrialization played a significant role in changing the meaning of home. The establishment of gendered divisions within capitalist production had an impact on gender relations, both within the domestic sphere and more generally (Hall 1992: 59). As Hareven (1991b) argues, the idea of the home as a 'haven' developed within French and British bourgeois households in the mid-eighteenth century because of the changing relationships of family and work. As work moved away from the household and the number of boarding apprentices declined, the home became more private and more of a retreat and less sociable (1991b: 257). Also, as home became much more than the space for the household or their location in this period, and it had increasingly powerful emotional connections too, so the sense of privacy in the home became more valued. Although the notion of privacy did not emerge during the eighteenth century, and privacy had been an important part of English culture since the Reformation, it was a period of increasing interest in the topic (Spacks 2003: 6; Vickery 2008: 145). This included a growing sense of the public sphere as a location of moral danger combined with the associated 'gender panic' regarding the permeability of gender boundaries, both of which shaped evangelical ideas about the home (Wahrman 1998; Griffin, Delap and Wills 2009: 6–9). There were also emerging discourses that led to the feminization of the world of goods, both those bought and made, which further encouraged a sense of the home as feminine and was part of the growing language of separate spheres (Fennetaux 2009: 91).

However, this does not mean that the home became either work-free or wholly private; as Sylvanna Tomaselli argues, conflating the domestic sphere with the private sphere is problematic (2001: 239). State and economic forces continued to have a bearing on the family (Tague 2007: 189; Staves 1990: 223) and work continued within the home, as the 'business household' was the main model of living in most small towns in Europe and North America (Tosh 1999, 14). In many ways, the degree to which the home was a private space was more closely connected to status than to gender. Large country houses in Britain and Ireland did see an increase in the number of private and domestic spaces during the eighteenth century, and in the Ottoman empire within elite homes there was a clear distinction between the public space, the *selamık,* and the private family space, the *hermlik* or harem (Dadabhoy 2014: 54–55). However, for the middling sort, while there was a shift within eighteenth-century German houses for the bedroom to be increasingly considered a private space where the domestic altar was often located, other spaces, such as the privy, were not considered to be intimate spaces (Schubert 1996: 358). For those who lived in poorer houses, not only was much of their space shared with lodgers and other non-family members, for those in urban areas the close proximity of their neighbours meant that quarrels and other disputes may have been public rather than private (Bryden and Floyd 1999: 12; Cockayne 2007: 118–21). However, it would be far too simplistic to suggest that the wealthier an individual the greater their privacy. While it was the case many of those living within poorer housing, especially within the urban areas, had little space that could be described as private on a modern understanding of the phrase, this does not mean to say that they did not enjoy any sense of privacy (Hewitt 1999). Likewise, it was important to remember that in this time period the private lives of members of the royal family was subject to immense scrutiny and that country houses and townhouses were often locations of public parties and gatherings (Morris 1996).

It is thus possible to see some of the ideals and experiences of notions of public and private within the architecture of the home, the house. Some literary and critical analysis has used the interconnections between architecture and the public and private as a way of understanding female vulnerabilities, for example in the work of Charlotte Smith, or female resistance, as seen in the work of Anne Finch (Ladd 2014; Jeong-Oh 2014). Also, many scholars have argued that there was a growth in privacy as an ideal within domestic architecture during the seventeenth and eighteenth centuries. The development of corridors within large houses meant that, for the first time, private rooms offered privacy (Stone 1977: 253–54; Girouard 1978: 123; Spacks 2003: 6–7). Interior spaces were increasingly subdivided and, following the seventeenth-century Dutch model, there was a growing separation of work spaces, social spaces and private spaces in urban houses (Rybczynski 1986: 51–76). In Philadelphia, Pennsylvania, for example, the changing form of middling houses reflected the growing desire to segregate public and private spaces and there was a clear distinction in levels of decoration between the 'best' and 'lesser' spaces (Herman 2006). There appears to have been a growing impulse towards personal privacy that was not exclusive to the aristocracy. As Michael McKeon notes, 'what had begun as an elite withdrawal from collective presence had become the architectural expression of an emerging individualist norm' (2005: 252). Although writers such as Olwen Hufton have suggested that across much of Europe, 'the mud cabins and rat-infested hovels of the rural poor remained unchanged' (1995: 14), there was a growing awareness of the need for better housing. In England, local landowners or parishes were increasingly building new houses for their villagers, and many of these plans were driven by the desire to provide greater privacy, which was increasingly associated with decency, or to promote domesticity (McKeon 2005: 259–67; Lloyd 2004). It is important to note, however, that although there was an emerging focus by architects and social reformers in providing private spaces, this was tempered by a growing demand for sociability within the home too (Girouard 1978: 181–212). This reflects the ways in which a binary understanding of the public and private space within the home is unsatisfactory and that, similarly, a binary separation of spaces along gendered lines may also be problematic. Although domestic manuals may have suggested that there was a gendered segregation to the house, those ideals were not always experienced in practice; we need to identify the difference between the 'world-as-lived' and the 'world-as thought' (West 1999). As Amanda Flather has argued: 'space could be theoretically defined but male and female experience of it could not be so ordered. People lived in space as social beings, and the way they did so could not be organised in so orderly a pattern' (2007: 1).

Despite this, specific parts of the house have been gendered by some architectural scholars. Writers such as Lynne Walker argue that gendered binaries are part of architectural language, especially the separation of public and private and that this distinction and 'the use of genders as an organising principle in architecture have been the tools of architects since antiquity' (2002: 826). As houses were pre-eminently symbols of status and public worth, so the exterior has been associated with value and, in turn, with masculinity. Colin Cunningham, for example, assumes that the 'public' spaces of a house were implicitly 'masculine', as they served the needs of the male household head (1994: 67). Likewise, the categorization of the drawing room as a feminine space is a common feature of many interpretations of the Georgian elite houses, and this is suggested in Jane Austen's *Northanger Abbey* ([1817] 2006: 219–20). The architect Robert Adam noted its role as a space for women to escape the noise of the dining room and to drink tea and coffee after dinner while the men would talk about politics elsewhere (Cunningham 1994: 69). However, as we have seen, women would not have needed to flee the discussion of politics, but that they often drove these discussions themselves (Chalus 2000). During the eighteenth century, many patrons and architects alike noted the need for the drawing room to be a separate space from the dining room. When the plan for Hagley, Worcester, was being discussed in 1752, Lyttleton told the architect that his wife wanted there to be a room separating the dining room and the withdrawing room 'to hinder the ladies from the noise and talk of the men when left to their bottle, which must sometimes happen, even at Hagley' (cited in Girouard 1978: 204). The latter part of this comment is of note; it indicates that the need to flee drunkenness would be only an occasional occurrence rather than part of the everyday. Therefore, while the withdrawing room might have been understood architecturally as a feminine space by some builders and patrons, in practice, it was not a space of retreat for women. Instead, it was a space where men and women spent time together; as Girouard (1978: 205) has noted, by the eighteenth century country house families were spending less time in private apartments and more in the common rooms in the houses. The spaces were increasingly sociable, and while in the largest of houses there were more individual rooms than in previous centuries, they were often multi-functional. While they may have been ascribed an ideal function within the architectural plans, in practice spaces could be formal and informal, public and private, at different times of the day (Vickery and Styles 2006: 10). Even Robert Adam acknowledged this; in his design for Syon House, Middlesex, he intended the Long Gallery, a space that was also used as a library, to act as the withdrawing room too (Cunningham 1994). This reflects the way that libraries became the main informal living room in many country houses in the later eighteenth century (Williams 2017: 50).

FIGURE 6.1: Thomas Rowlandson, 'Dr Syntax with a Blue Stocking Beauty', reproduced in William Combe, *Doctor Syntax's Three Tours: In Search of the Picturesque, Consolation, and a Wife* (London: John Camden Hotten, 1868), p. 448. British Library Board, Public Domain.

In many houses, neither the library nor the withdrawing room appear to have been the part of 'territory' of one gender, only to be used by the other with permission (Walker 2002: 826). Instead, this combining of rooms traditionally understood to be distinctly male (library) or female (drawing room) shows how the notion of gendered spaces in theory soon unravelled in practice. As Benjamin Heller (2010) notes in his discussions of London houses, men and women both played important roles within the houses and their roles often overlapped, and this was true of houses across the social spectrum. Rooms were spaces in which gender ideals could be expressed, asserted and challenged, but these ideals were much more focused on the way in which the space was used rather than the ideals of those who built it; as Amanda Flather notes, 'space had a range of gendered meanings that were fluid rather than fixed' (2007: 16).

For the vast majority of Georgian people, the public and private were closely entwined in the eighteenth century, and the home was one of the places where the two spheres came together. As many gender and cultural historians have argued, the domestic was not private and the boundaries between the public and the private were 'blurred and porous' (Harvey 2012a: 11; McKeon 2005). The extent to which there were gendered separate spheres, in the modern understanding of these terms, has rightly been questioned, and their emergence was 'an incremental rather than a rapid historical process' (McKeon 2005: 268). As Amanda Vickery has commented, 'Georgian men and women were not cardboard illustrations of sociological theories, but flesh and blood individuals capable of mixed feelings and contradictory reactions' (2009: 9–10). Likewise, homes were not static architectural plans, but rather homes for living in. However, this does not mean that ideas of private and privacy were unimportant to eighteenth-century understandings of the home, nor does it exclude the possibility that, in some discourses, the domestic sphere was a gendered one. If we use the idea of gendered spaces that were associated with idealized masculine and feminine qualities rather than gender exclusive places, than we can gain a more nuanced understanding of the domestic sphere in the eighteenth century.

IDEALIZATION OF THE DOMESTIC SPHERE

Although the public and private may not have been distinct, there was a changing recognition of the importance of the domestic sphere during the eighteenth century, so much so that many scholars believe that modern domesticity was invented in England in this period (Harvey 2012a: 9). As Abigail Williams has noted, 'the idea of home and the wholesome domesticity within it acquired an increasingly privileged status in the ethical vocabulary of the later eighteenth century' (2017: 11). Much of this was driven by didactic literature, which became increasingly popular and read by wider audiences during the course of the period. While at the beginning of the century many of the texts were a mixture of devotional and manners books that were aimed at members of the aristocracy, by the mid-eighteenth century this genre incorporated more humble texts that featured recipes and hints for managing the domestic economy and essays about self-improvement in periodicals such as *the Gentleman's Magazine* and *The Spectator* (Armstrong 1987: 62–69; Davidoff and Hall 2002: 156). While many of these texts were addressed to both sexes, much of the conduct literature did promote the interconnections between women and the domestic sphere. Periodicals in particular presented women as separate but equal within the home and utilized the language of binary opposites in order to identify the feminine role with the household (Shevelow 1989: 3–11). This led to the emergence of the 'domestic woman', which scholars have closely connected to the rise of the middle classes from the 1780s and the evangelical revival (Davidoff and Hall 2012). This movement wanted to develop a new morality that was based in the home, as this was seen as the best location to fight the constant struggle against sin (Hall 1992: 75–84). However, despite Edward Shorter's depiction of domesticity as the family's awareness of itself as a 'precious emotional unit that must be protected with privacy and isolation from outside intrusion' (1976: 227), evangelical domesticity directly linked the public with the private, as it argued that the sincerity of the home needed to be carried out into the wider world (Hall 1992: 86). For the middling sort, domesticity was a moral endeavour and meant hard work, for both men and women (Hunt 1996).

This idealization of domesticity was not confined to literature addressed to the English middling sort. Writers such as François Fénelon celebrated domestic qualities and promoted educational practices for French elite women that moved them away from luxury and display to virtuous household work. In his *Treatise on the Education of Girls* (1687), Fénelon warned of the dangers posed by the culture of polite society, writing that 'all is lost if your daughter becomes infatuated with *bel esprit* and disgusted with domestic cares' (cited in Lougee 1974: 88). This idealization of domesticity also featured in the work of other enlightenment scholars, some of whom, such as Voltaire, closely connected the domestic with the feminine (Rendall 1985: 15). By the end of the eighteenth century there was a growing use of 'scientific' reasoning to 'prove' that women were only suitable for domestic roles (Hunt 1992: 158). Not all writers saw this role for women in wholly negative terms; some, such as John Millar, argued that women needed to be educated so that they could fulfil their important role within the domestic sphere and not be swayed by the outside world (Rendall 1985: 27). However, it is important to remember that the basic premise underpinning these ideas was not new; Amanda Vickery notes that 'the notion that women were uniquely fashioned for the private realm is at least as old as

FIGURE 6.2: Frontispiece from Hannah Glasse's *The Art of Cookery Made Easy* (edition from *c.* 1775, printed in London for a company of booksellers, and sold by L. Wangford). © Wellcome Collection, Attribution 4.0 International (CC BY 4.0).

Aristotle' (1998: 6). There were significant continuities in the representations of women, and the 'new' eighteenth-century woman was in many ways created by the need to control women outside of the traditional religious paradigms (LeGates 1976: 33). However, while the association of women within the domestic sphere was not new, the ways in which domestic space – that is, the home – was feminized, had changed; as Kathryn Shevelow (1989: 192) argues, this period was a time when gender roles were reshaped, with women equal in name although subordinate in custom and law.

Beyond didactic and philosophical literature, in practice there was a presumption that women should be good at housewifery, and it was considered important for a wife to possess domestic qualities (Crane 2000). Within the diaries of middling and lower-class men in eighteenth-century Manchester, the desire for a wife who could provide a comfortable and domestic home was notable (Barker 2008). Those men who did not marry also recognized the importance of having a woman that they trusted to head the household, and would use female relatives to fulfil the domestic duties of the wife, as Winifred Constable did for her brother, William, in their childhood home of Burton Constable, near Hull (Connell 1998: 38). The Reverend Enoch Warriner wrote in 1806 that while his wife was not wealthy enough to help his finances, 'she is one who will more than compensate for this by faithful attention to her duty and my interest' (cited in French and Rothery 2012: 193). Across the social classes, this idea of duty, along with virtue was seen as the crucial quality of a good housewife, and so was sought in potential wives, as they needed to be able to provide moral guardianship over the household. Michael McKeon has suggested that the home was part of '"public" agency of moral control (government, management, employment)' and that this was especially associated with the wife and mother who was associated with the business 'of the pedagogy of self control' (2005: 298). This can be seen in the anonymous children's book *Virtue in a Cottage; or, A Mirror for Children in Humble Life* (c. 1790), where the excellent housewifery skills of Betty Bark and the positive impact of these attributes on her daughter Sally were held up as examples of feminine hard work, industry and cleanliness. Personal probity and the ability to manage the household were closely linked throughout this period, and so it was believed that a man needed a virtuous woman he could trust in order to run the home. This was especially important for those who lived in larger households who had to manage staff who were significant social actors in the domestic household (Dwyer 1987: 95). The family needed the servants in order to ensure the smooth running of the household, and reliable upper staff whom the household head could leave in charge of the administration were crucial. However, the servants' actions would have reflected upon the householder's virtues and abilities, rather than those of the housekeeper or steward (Richardson 2010: 148–50). Because domesticity was associated with virtue, a poorly managed staff or a disrupted household were seen as the result of personal impropriety. As John Dwyer notes, if 'the family was meant to be a harmonious symphony, a virtuous woman was its conductor' (1987: 132); discord needed to be avoided in the ideal home.

However, although the role of the domestic woman was idealized, the household should not be considered as a 'separate sphere' that was a specifically female concern, nor was the house 'simply a place of inactivity where women played out an elaborate game of femininity for their husbands' (Higgs 1983: 209). Although roles in the household were often gendered, they were neither 'oppositional' in nature nor mutually exclusive categories; the male head of the family played an important role too, and husbands and wives would manage the household together (Reynolds 1998: 21, 31, 41; Weatherill 1996: 138; Harvey 2014). One example of this can be seen in the ownership of keys; while English Church court cases suggested that house keys were the property of the male head of the household, it was usually the wife who carried them (Vickery 2008: 168–69). This reflects the ways in which domestic life was also important to men as well as to women, and both men and women played a role in creating a culture of home. The discourses of morality amongst the middling sort were expressed in the ideal of private domesticity that acted as the basis for public virtue (Hunt 1996: 193–215). This was especially important for men, as masculine citizenship became increasingly related with enlightenment ideas of domesticity and the associated qualities of being the head of a household (McCormack 2005: 27–28). For poorer men, much of the late eighteenth-century rhetoric around the improvement of the Poor Law in England directly connected to manliness. Independence and morality were linked to domestic happiness and associated with self-sufficiency, the ideal championed by those who were critical of the workhouse system and wished to enable the poor to be, in Richard Elsam's phrase, 'the monarch of his mansion' (Elsam 1816, cited in Lloyd 2004: 98). It was not just about virtue and citizenship, though; men valued their domestic roles and were active household managers, consumers, decorators, fathers and husbands (e.g. Vickery 2009; Harvey 2009, 2012a; French and Rothery 2012; Stobart and Rothery 2016). Home was also, to use Tosh's phrase (1999), 'a man's place'.

This, though, is not to suggest that the ideal form of domesticity in this period was one of equality for men and women. For example, a number of Scottish historians saw the feminization of society during the eighteenth century as a process that benefitted men; the status suggested for women following their freedom from 'slavery' was not one of equality but one of domesticity (Sebastiani 2013: 134). Lynn Hunt argues that domestic ideology only emerged in France because of the need to justify the exclusion of women from political participation in the country in the period 1793–1804 (1992: 158, 203). Within England, the development of a domestic and sentimental family ideal can be seen as providing a fresh rationale for the subordination of women within political theory by the late eighteenth century (Okin 1982: 65). Even enlightenment writers who had praised female qualities, such as Dr John Gregory, saw women's main duties as softening and polishing men; in both public affairs and in the home, power remained in the hands of men (Sebastiani 2013: 149). However, while domestic patriarchy did not collapse during the eighteenth century, and there is evidence of its ongoing importance, its form did change (Harvey 2012a: 6; Tague 2007: 189). In many ways, the changes reflect the shifting ideals of masculinity, reflecting the move from a Godly patriarchy to sociable and polite gentility to sensibility (Harvey 2005). As David Hussey notes, 'the home formed one of the main arenas through which conceptions of polite masculine gentility . . . were encoded' (2008: 51). Masculine identity and the home were closely entwined in this period, although it remains unclear whether the home made men or men made the home; it was probably both.

THE POLITE AND SENTIMENTAL HOME

The idea of politeness has been subject to considerable discussion amongst historians of masculinity, and it has been argued that it was a masculine ideal that was seen across national boundaries in the mid-eighteenth century (Stobart and Rothery 2016: 126; Carter 2001; Langford 1989; Harvey 2005). Although there is not a single definition, politeness was associated with manners, morals and taste, and the importance of the idea that external behaviour reflected upon an individual's inner character (Tague 2002: 162–65). Although traditionally associated with masculinity, women were very much part of the sociable world which politeness encouraged. This polite sociability was a central feature of British society in the eighteenth century (Harvey 2012b: 170), as reflected in the changing nature of the house and the home. Entertaining became increasingly part of domestic life, as can be seen in the high number of goods associated with dining found in probate inventories from North America and England (Shammas 1980; Weatherill 1996)

Spaces for mixed-sex socializing (heterosociability) also developed – for example, the bourgeois living room became increasingly popular in eighteenth-century Germany (Schubert 1996: 359). For all social classes, visiting was important and so 'domestic recreation was closely linked to display' (Williams 2017: 45). Visiting meant that being seen to be conforming to ideals both inside and outside the house was important. For Quakers in eighteenth-century America, socializing children through visiting was a central responsibility for mothers, as it encouraged sociability within the religious community (Maples Dunn 1979: 127). Therefore, being seen within the home to be fulfilling shared gendered, social and moral ideals was important; aspirational display was central to the activities and decoration of the domestic interior, especially when

FIGURE 6.3: 'Farmer Giles & his Wife shewing off their daughter Betty to their Neighbours, on her return from School', by James Gillray, London, 1809. © Victoria and Albert Museum, London.

one had guests (Williams 2017: 46). This meant a growth in heterosociability which was encouraged by some writers; the enlightenment historian William Alexander wrote, 'Man, secluded from the company of women is not only a rough and uncultivated, but a dangerous, animal to society' (1779, cited in Sebastiani 2013: 133). Not all men enjoyed this heterosociability; Dudley Ryder, in his youth in 1715, noted that he found that he was 'mighty apt to look silly and a little uneasy when I am in the company of ladies' (cited in Williams 2017: 47). Likewise, not all women welcomed too many visitors; for example, because she was tired of always being 'open to callers' in her main house at Welbeck Abbey, Nottinghamshire, Lady Oxford moved out into a small cottage in the estate for half of the week (Lewis 2009: 342). Usually, though, the home and sites of polite sociability were habitats where women were perceived to be comfortable, although as Shammas notes, 'the evolution of the house into a home made social interaction more accessible to women and put it more under their control' (1980: 18). The second half of the eighteenth century was a period where there was a growing instability in the boundaries between men and women and as Taylor has argued, this led to 'an unprecedented cultural convergence between the sexes' (2004: 132).

The model of politeness and sociability, however, did not remain for the whole of the eighteenth century and it is important to remember that the polite gentleman was just one form of masculinity in the eighteenth century, and not all men aspired to the hegemonic ideal (Harvey 2012b: 170–71). Some writers were critical of the idea of politeness and sociability; Montesquieu, for example, mocked French men for their excessive sociability ([1721] 1973: 167–68, Letter 87). In particular, there was concern that politeness could just be mastered through learning behaviours, and so this led to the shift towards sentimentality (Tague 2002: 164; Carter 2001, Ch. 3). Sensibility was in many ways as difficult to define as politeness and, as Markman Ellis has shown, was the subject of much discussion during the eighteenth century (2004: 5–8). However, it was marked by an emphasis on informality, sincerity and sentiment. There was a growing element of religiosity to it, whether that be Christian evangelicalism or a secular faith, and it became associated with genteel decorum (Harvey 2005: 304). The cult of sensibility had an impact on male identity in France, where the eschewing of the seductions of luxury was an important ideal (Vila 2007). Despite the fact that in the cult of sensibility it was the man of feeling that was celebrated, there was a close association between sentiment and femininity (McKeon 2005: 673). Writers such as Dr John Gregory saw the main differences between men and women being shaped by feeling, with men associated with bravery, strength and intelligence and women with sentiment, sensibility and taste (Sebastiani 2013: 136–37). Therefore, the man of sentiment was one who was seen to be engaging in feminine ideals. This, though, was not necessarily injurious to his identity, and it is important to remember that male and female was not always the same as masculine and feminine; effeminacy could be part of male identity. There is some suggestion that this connection of both men and women with feminine ideals was empowering; Katharine Rogers (1982) has argued that the growth of sentimental literature gave women an opportunity to express their feelings and to claim emotional fulfilment. In France, it was important to homosocial ideals and when the revolution led to the abandonment of *sensibilité*, by 1789 any feminization of the public realm was reversed (Outram 1989: 86–87). This did not mean that sentimentality had gone; in France and in England it was embodied by the family group who spent more time at home with one another than before, a trend that began to appear in France in the late eighteenth century (Shorter 1976: 228). The sentimental became closely attached to the home (Barker-Benfield 1992; Mullan 1988; Brewer 1997).

Part of the reason why sentimentality was so closely connected to the home was because of the growing belief that domesticity was not simply about virtue; it also had emotional qualities. Being devoted to one's family and home life were also important features of the life of the sentimental domestic man and woman. Writers such as Rousseau discussed the values of sentiment and sensibility in their work, and he argued that the patriarchal model of the family was a sentimental one, as a father's feelings for his family meant that he was the most appropriate person to lead the household (Okin 1982: 76–77). Many works from this date idealized the home as the location of 'felicitous sentimental' domesticity, with the affectionate husband and natural mother at the centre of the stories (Brewer 1997: 114–22). The idealization of family life often led to public displays of familial affection, and acting out the features of a 'domestic' life. While George IV, as the Prince of Wales, faced criticism as 'a despiser [sic] of domestic ties', his father and his family were particularly keen to demonstrate their domestic virtues in the late eighteenth century (Davidoff and Hall 2002: 152–53). Queen Charlotte played a central domestic role, managing the king's household during his illness and educating Princess Charlotte, the only legitimate granddaughter born during her lifetime (Campbell Orr 2002: 22–23). Her 1779 portrait painted by Benjamin West further publicized her domestic role, as she was painted in front of a tableau of her own family, and she was likewise depicted in her role of mother in her *c*. 1765 portrait by Johann Zoffany (Colley 1992: 269, 273)

Beyond that associated with the royal family, wider literature and art during the eighteenth century increasingly celebrated the ideal of home. The family became one of the main themes in novels and, in conversation pieces, such as William Hogarth's *The Wollaston Family* (1730), the home was increasingly

FIGURE 6.4: Johann Joseph Zoffany, *Queen Charlotte (1744–1818) with her Two Eldest Sons*, *c*. 1765. © Hulton Archive / Getty Images.

romanticized as a location of virtue, affection and, by the later eighteenth century, sensibility (Flint 1998: 15, 37; Barker-Benfield 1992: 218; Solkin 1993: 87). In many British elite women's letters, especially from the 1750s onwards, it is possible to identify an increasing romanticization of the 'home'. Their fondness for their home was often expressed through the language of familial affection, describing the place in relation to the love of their family, rather than as an architectural structure, reflecting Bachelard's descriptions of intimate locations as 'felicitous space' (1994: xxxv). For example, in her 1760s letters to her London-based friend, Frances, Lady Ingram wrote with delight about her happy marriage, and her comfortable life, noting that her domestic pleasures gave one 'the sort of happiness one perceives is really what makes life desirable'. In her letters, Frances clearly separated herself and her family, whom she described as 'the homely ones' from the 'fine folks' of fashionable society, and presented her home as a 'retreat', a safe haven (TNA, PRO 30/29/4/2). While among elites the idea of the house as a retreat from the Court had classical origins, eighteenth-century commentators stressed this ideal for all classes, especially emphasizing the idea of the home as the retreat for women, but one where they ruled (Ackerman 1990: 12–13; Saumarez Smith 1993: 233). Women increasingly sought to make the home a place where their husbands would come for their leisure time, as opposed to the alehouses (Barker-Benfield 1992: 99, 157). It was therefore important that the house was made into a home.

MANAGING AND MAKING HOME

The domestic and gender ideals discussed above fed into the ways in which the house was managed and made into a home. As Hareven notes, 'homemaking was idealized as part of the cult of domesticity, and was accorded special social status' (1991b: 262). However, while it was a cultural ideal, it did need to be put into practice. Virtue, sociability and sentiment, along with prudence, could move from idealized texts into lived experience. This can especially be seen in the responses to household management. During the eighteenth century, the literature that discussed oeconomy took two main forms, one that dealt with the practice of running a household and the other that explored the theory of housekeeping (Harvey 2012a: 26–27). Both forms encouraged men in particular to play a proactive role, and by exploring the household accounts, Harvey (2014) has noted that these theories were often put into practice. The careful management of credit, in all its meanings, was an important attribute of masculine identity (Shepard 2015). This is not to say that men engaged with the household economy alone; in the idealized household, in a similar relationship between the master and his steward in elite families, when it came to oeconomy the husband led and the wife supported him (Harvey 2012a: 34). Isabella, fourth Countess of Carlisle, advised young women in her *Maxims Addressed to Young Ladies* (1789) to 'study such occupations as will render you of consequence to him [the husband], such as the management of his fortune, and the conduct of his house; yet without assuming a superiority unbecoming of your sex' (1789: 2). Some women, though, did lead, whether it was due to necessity, capability or interest (McDonagh 2018: 39–69). Isabella Irwin, of Temple Newsam, Leeds, very much managed the family's finances both as the wife of the third Viscount Irwin, and as dowager and adviser to her sons, five of whom held the title during her lifetime. The Irwins could be described as 'poor nobles' (Bush 1988); the estate inherited by Isabella's husband in 1690 was in poor condition financially and they were deeply in debt, with much of the land mortgaged. She therefore encouraged her husband to reduce his personal expenditure, ordered her steward to find the best value for household goods and complained when prices rose. When managing the estate on behalf of her son she wrote in 1709: 'I never remember provisions so dear as this year. You can't buy a good chicken for under 8 groats . . . for my part I grudge everything that is more than plain meat' (WYAS, Pawson MSS, Ac 1038, vol. 8). Isabella was not only fulfilling her duties as a good housekeeper in being aware of the price of commodities, but she was also publicly displaying her efficiency and self-sacrifice in maintaining household standards. There was a close relationship between prudence and personal probity in the didactic writings of the early-modern period, and the ability to manage the family finances was evidence that an individual could manage their own bodies (Crane 2000: 212, 219). Restraint was a central element of middling sort morality and it was an important element of running the home as well as one's business and managing one's self (Hunt 1996: 72).

Although prudence was an important virtue, consumption was also important in homemaking. Amanda Vickery (1993b) highlights that the eighteenth-century growth of domesticity along with the growth of consumer outlets offered greater purchasing opportunities, especially for women. In the Age of Enlightenment, women were the symbol of the commercial society who drove the demand for luxury and domestic items (Sebastiani 2013: 133). They were able to control the purchasing and management of goods, and domestic products gained new social prestige during the Georgian period that was in addition to the increased appreciation of their sentimental worth (Brewer and Porter 1993: 5). Women appear to have used goods to establish their families' status, to control its moral and ideological image, and to negotiate personal qualities of taste, sociability and worth (Glennie 1995: 179; Miller 1995: 35). Smaller items, such as tea sets, card tables and small domestic goods were consumer markers of a woman's interest in polite sociability, and reflected her concerns with home and her role as a domestic woman (Vickery 1998: 168–69). The ordering and display of these items could work as signifiers of their feminine credentials, as well as being objects needed to fulfil household or business activities. For example, the homes of dressmakers Sarah Melton and Mary Smith in eighteenth-century Philadelphia, Pennsylvania, both had the best furniture in the most public rooms of the house, as this is where these women met their clients (Herman 2006: 53). The value attached to dining as social contact can be determined through the increasing use of highly decorative ware at social gatherings for tea drinking or dining that offered women the opportunity to display their domestic credentials (Weatherill 1996: 137). Material culture was increasingly seen as forming the home and women played a central role in identifying and purchasing it.

It is important, however, that we do not turn eighteenth-century consumption into an activity that was exclusively female. In her study of household ledgers, Amanda Vickery has noted that the spending on interior redecoration usually fell to men (2009: 12–13) and, as Margot Finn (2000) and David Hussey (2008) have shown, men were involved in purchasing a wide range of goods for the home. The accounts of excessive spending on the country house amongst elite men is well known, with examples such as Willam Beckford at Fonthill in England and Count Jørgen Scheel of Ulstrop Castle in Denmark being just a couple of examples (Beckford 1957; Stobart and Rothery 2016: 115). However, for most men the expenditure on the home was modest and reflected their good taste and domestic interests (Vickery 2009: 49–82; Stobart and Rothery 2016: 109–39). For example, the Frenches, members of the Irish parliamentary gentry, ensured that they spent enough to impress visitors to their Dublin properties, but not so much for them to be considered either too fashionable or ostentatious (Barnard 2008: 158–59). The way that a home was decorated was thought to reflect upon the personality of its inhabitants; during the eighteenth century, novelists such as Richardson and Austen used depictions of domestic interior as a way of constructing their characters (Grant 2005). Good taste was also directly associated with sensibility, and a failure to demonstrate an appropriate aesthetic response could be seen as the result of a lack of virtue (Campbell 1993: 49). However, identifying what was good taste could be difficult, and sometimes this meant asking a woman. Although in the early eighteenth century women were often associated with poor taste (Vickery 2009: 258), Charles Saumarez Smith notes that from the mid-eighteenth century women were increasingly considered to hold a privileged position in relation to their ability to comment on fashion and the decoration of homes, in order to display 'a special form of visual sensibility' (1993: 233). What often mattered most was appropriate taste. As Bernard Herman notes, for people of the Atlantic World taste was not a monolithic construction but 'a process that enabled the expression of sensibilities linking them to the economic and social contexts in which they lived' (2006: 57); spend too much and one could be seen as vulgar, while too little could be seen as miserly. In England, labouring women who spent the family finances on inappropriate goods, such as tea and gin, were subject to particular criticism. However, despite these risks, engagement with commerce was seen as the route to civilization and so the right type of consumption by the labouring poor was encouraged by some social reformers (White 2006). In eighteenth-century representations of the cottage, the power of 'domestic endearments' to turn a hovel into a cottage, and thus into a home, was a popular trope (Lloyd 2004: 101–2). For men and women, the balance between the 'private vices' and 'publick benefits' of consumption, to borrow Bernard Mandeville's (1714) phrase, was an important balancing act for those making a home.

As well as being consumers, the family were also makers. The process of craft and production in the home was increasingly gendered during the eighteenth century. While there is evidence of 'crafty men' (Ilmakunnas 2016) and, of course, artisans continued to work in the home throughout this period, the idea of a commercial/domestic divide in production that followed gendered lines has some traction. Women were often involved in crafting and making, reflecting gender ideals and their role in making a house a home. While for women of the labouring classes, making continued to be an important part of domestic life, for many middling women, the nature of domestic labour changed during the eighteenth century as they became more involved in the final processes in their house work, such as cooking, sewing and decorating, rather than making the primary materials from scratch (Shammas 1980: 17). They became more concerned with being seen to do the work that made the house a home and they became much more family-focused in their labours. For example, the fact that the wife or the housekeeper, rather than the general servants, was responsible for the food in middling and gentry houses reflects how cooking was part of the woman's duty of providing care in the early-modern household (Weatherill 1996: 149). Even amongst elites, through writing recipe books and sending food gifts women shared their knowledge of food and cooking, demonstrating that they were conversant with the domestic arts (Aspin 2000; Pennell 2009: 182–83). Although they would have employed staff to cook their meals, the idea of cooking for pleasure began to develop, and by the later eighteenth century there was growing interest in the work of the dairy amongst genteel women, made popular by Marie Antoinette (Barker-Benfield 1992: 156; Arnold 1998a; Valenze 1991). Likewise, the creation of decorative items for the home was also important for many women of a range of social classes and reflected gendered ideas (Vickery 2009: 231–55; Fennetaux 2009; Ilmakunnas 2016). Paper cutting was determined to be an acceptable and domestic craft for women, and they often used the parlour for their work. The subject was often domestic too; the silhouettes created by Luise Duttenhofer in Germany often portrayed women at home, whether they were engaging in crafts, reading, taking tea or, for the service class, undertaking domestic work

FIGURE 6.5: Sampler of woollen canvas embroidered with silks, made by Elizabeth Brain, England, 1785. The verse reads: 'In Conversation speak with ease / Shun Barbarous words as Rocks in seas. / Elizabeth Brain: 1785'. © Victoria and Albert Museum, London.

(Sedda 2009). Likewise, embroidery offered women a route to demonstrate publicly their domestic sensibilities.

A task associated with patience and purity, embroidery was not a meaningless pastime to keep idle hands busy, but could allow women to engage with the discourse of homely virtue and, in the view of Rousseau, was natural to women (Parker 1984: 124). However, it was not necessarily a lonely act; in Sweden and Finland women often sewed together and it may have been one of the ways in which women and girls formed and maintained their social and emotional bonds (Ilmakunnas 2016: 310). As Rozsika Parker notes, during this period it was thought that 'women embroidered because they were naturally feminine and were feminine because they naturally embroidered' (1984: 11). Handicrafts offered women a useful way to employ their time that could demonstrate their domestic virtues, decorate the home and, if they were good enough quality, attract visitors to the home, bringing the practicality and performance of the duties of the domestic woman together (Vickery 2009: 254–56).

CONCLUSION

During the eighteenth century, discourses of home began to develop a new focus. While patriarchal concerns remained, there was a growing focus on heterosociability within the domestic sphere. In the same way that ideas about public and private did not fall neatly into inside and outside or state and family, neither did they conform to male and female. Although there may have been writers and thinkers, such as Francisco Cabarrús, who closely associated the home with women, the home was a place for both genders. In many ways, the ideals of domesticity were closely connected to ideals of masculinity; the prudent, sociable and sentimental men who dominated the conduct literature needed the home in order to fulfil the prescriptions of their sex. This is not to claim that the home was masculine; the idealization of feeling and the focus of felicitous domesticity, especially in the later eighteenth century, was closely connected to femininity. However, this did not exclude men. Like women, or, ideally *with* women, men played a central role in domestic life. They were both crucial in making and managing the home and their relationship can be seen as reflecting a combination of the ideals of both patriarchy and Lawrence Stone's (1977) idea of the companionate marriage. The shifting idealization of home life reflected and shaped the gender roles.

The development of domestic identity with womanhood during the eighteenth century had a significant impact on gender relationships during the next century too. Therefore, as Nancy Armstrong notes:

> to consider the rise of the domestic woman as a major event in political history is not, as it may seem, to present a contradiction in terms, but to identify the paradox that shapes modern culture. It is also to trace the history of a specifically modern form of desire that, during the early eighteenth century, changed the criteria for determining what was most important in a female.
>
> —1987: 3

By the nineteenth century, the domestic and the feminine were very closely intertwined. The American writer Sarah Lewis anonymously noted that a woman's education was

> to vivify and enlighten a home. What a paradise even this world might become if one half of the amount of effort expended in vain attempts to excite the admiration of strangers, were reserved to vary the amusements and adorn the sacred precincts of home!
>
> —1839: 120

This does not mean, though, that men became more distant from the home. While the codes of masculinity connected to politeness and sensibility began to wane in the nineteenth century and were replaced by 'character' as the keystone of respectable manliness (Griffin, Delap and Wills 2009: 6), domesticity still played a central role in male identity. Discourses of domestic virtue remained and the ideal of home life became a measure against which men's conduct could be assessed (Tosh 1999: 7–8). However, we should not see the eighteenth century as simply an incubator for Victorian society; it had its own important role in the history of gender relations, and the home is one of the best places to see these emerge. It was not just women who were, in Cabarrús's phrase, 'friends of the home'; men were too.

CHAPTER SEVEN

Hospitality and Home

WOODRUFF SMITH

EARLY MODERN HOSPITALITY

Like 'home', the English word 'hospitality' and its equivalents in other languages had a range of meanings in the European world between late medieval and modern times. And as was the case with 'home', those meanings changed between the sixteenth and the eighteenth centuries, not entirely but substantially, especially in terms of the cultural norms and practices and the social structures with which they were associated.

Felicity Heal has shown that hospitality, as a set of named cultural practices, was situated within the social structure of pre-Reformation England mainly in the Church and the secular elite, particularly at the upper levels of each where intersection between the two estates was most pronounced: among noblemen, prominent gentry, bishops and abbots.[1] Institutionally, it was located primarily in larger elite households and in religious establishments such as monasteries and 'hospitals'. In these contexts, hospitality meant essentially two things: providing support, mainly in the form of food but also sometimes accommodation, to the poor and to others in need of help (such as the sick and travellers), and promoting sociability and thereby helping to maintain a peaceful community. People of high status were expected to practise hospitality in standard ways, and they were criticized if they did not do so to the extent that their resources would seem to permit. In an English 'great household' – that of a nobleman or wealthy gentleman or senior cleric – customary hospitable practices included making food available on set occasions to all comers 'at the gate', dining in the house's hall with recognized guests and with as many of the unknown travellers and the poor as could be accommodated (all properly

FIGURE 7.1: A medieval great hall in later use for more private hospitality. 'The Baron's Hall', print, 1844. Accession Number B1977.14.14821. © Yale Center for British Art, Paul Mellon Collection.

distributed according to rank and expected to show appropriate deference), entertaining distinguished visitors courteously and convivially at the proprietor's table, and inviting locals of all classes and neighbouring gentry to special festive occasions.

Occasions of hospitality performed a welfare function in the guise of charity, a public order function by re-enacting the distribution of wealth and power in a way that emphasized its beneficent character, and a social peace function by promoting sociability among members of an elite whose relations often tended towards violent competitiveness. If nothing else, hospitality afforded the opportunity to compete for status in more or less pacific ways.

The boundaries of the segment of society expected to practise these forms of hospitality were not firmly fixed. Households of poorer gentry, wealthier freeholders, tenant farmers, and urban tradespeople and merchants often followed similar patterns at reduced levels of munificence, although the farther down the conventional social scale one stood, the greater the opportunity one had to opt gracefully out of the full range of hospitality.[2] There were differences between parts of Europe with regard to specific expectations. In general, the more urbanized an area, the more likely it was that the poor relief function would be performed by specialized institutions; before the late sixteenth century, these institutions were more often religious than secular or municipal. In most of Western Europe, the function of promoting sociability within the elite was associated with practices of courtesy and tended to follow fashions increasingly emanating from Italy.[3]

Between about 1500 and the early eighteenth century, the predominant meanings of hospitality altered as their social, ideological, institutional and discursive contexts changed. These alterations were complex and, for the most part, gradual, and they were probably the result of many causes. The main factors leading to change that Heal cites for England were the expansion of the market economy (and an attendant proliferation of commercial establishments for accommodating business travellers), the growth of the central state, and (more limited in effect than the others) the appearance of Protestantism, primarily in its Puritan form.[4] By the early eighteenth century, although vestiges of medieval practices and the pre-1500 ideology of hospitality survived, they did so mainly as received memories of the 'good old days': good, but not so good that it was necessary to revive them. Hospitality at the gate had largely disappeared and been replaced by official poor relief administered by local authorities. The poor were no longer welcome to dine in the great halls of the nobility, who in any case had long since ceased to take their meals under public gaze and had turned their halls to other uses. Travellers, unless personally known or vouched for by friends or relatives of householders, no longer expected to be put up gratis in private houses. They stayed instead in inns or other paid lodgings. Except for the kinds of occasion that became village fetes in the nineteenth century, public festivals paid for by local elites where they hobnobbed with ordinary people became rare. Patterns of sociability grew more complex, but also more uniform and broadly spread among the gentility and the middling sort, and more private. Heal presents these developments as a stage on the way to what she describes as the present practice of hospitality:

> For modern Western man hospitality is preponderantly a private form of behaviour, exercised as a matter of personal preference within a limited circle of friendship and connection. As such, it is also considered a social luxury, to be pursued when circumstances are favourable, but abandoned without serious loss of status when they prove adverse. Few would claim that it possesses any centrality in our value-systems, or that the obligation to entertain could be described as a moral imperative.[5]

Developments in other parts of Europe varied with regard to timing and to cultural specifics, but the general process described by Heal could be seen nearly everywhere.[6]

In summary, if we followed Heal we could say that hospitality transformed itself over time from being a 'public' function, performed predominately by the upper classes and possessing cultural meaning in a context of a hierarchical social order and a charitable moral one, into a largely private, optional practice, with no generic connection to any significant social or moral imaginary. People today still hold social events in their homes to benefit particular charities, but it is no longer obligatory to do so. They invite subordinates to dinner so as to promote a degree of sociability in the work environment. But such exceptions do not really invalidate Heal's general proposition that hospitality in the home has lost the moral and social meanings that it possessed in medieval and early-modern times.

Nevertheless, what occurred in the eighteenth and nineteenth centuries was not a straightforward transition from an older culture of public hospitality to the present, more limited, more personal one. A great deal changed in between, much of it bound up with what happened to the home. It is not necessary to cover the ground of other chapters in this volume, but one development is particularly significant: the imaginative construction of the home as a framework for imparting moral behaviour and maintaining moral order. In medieval and early-modern England, it had been 'hospitality' that bore a moral meaning connected to the virtue of charity; 'home' or 'house' merely designated the location where (upper-class) hospitality was practised, possessing significance in that context mainly in terms of social status. In the eighteenth and nineteenth centuries, 'home' took on a complex set of meanings, many, to be sure, having to do with status and social function but most of them framed by morality and by notions of taste and sociability closely linked to morality. The most important of these meanings were encompassed within a cultural construct that was evident in Western Europe and the Americas by the late eighteenth century. The English word most commonly used to name the construct (wholly or in part) was 'respectability'.[7]

Other developments occurred in the course of the eighteenth century that affected the relationship between the home and hospitality, among them a 'consumer revolution' that included recognition of the family as the principal unit of consumption, a recasting of the home as a bastion of comfort and relief for men working outside their domiciles, a growing emphasis on the family as a site for shaping the characters of children, and a reorganization of household space to reflect these and other changes.[8] But we will concentrate here on respectability as a context for mentally constructing the home and for living within actual homes. Most of the developments just listed intersected with respectability: a large proportion of family consumption in the eighteenth and nineteenth centuries was shaped by the perceived need to be respectable; respectability defined the kind of comfort that the home provided and the kind of moral education children were supposed to receive; housing was increasingly designed to accommodate respectable practices. Among these practices was hospitality, which, at least as conducted in homes, tended to conform closely to respectability.

FIGURE 7.2: An idealized respectable family of the late eighteenth century, illustrating the central role of children. A print from 1793 entitled 'Virtuous Love', after a painting by William Hunter. Accession Number B1978.43.693. © Yale Center for British Art, Paul Mellon Collection.

RESPECTABILITY

What was respectability? In the first place, it was a word, derived obviously from 'respectable'.[9] 'Respectable' was not new, but in the late eighteenth century one range of its meanings became predominant. In the *Oxford English Dictionary*, these are described as 'Worthy of respect, deserving to be respected, by reason of moral excellence', and 'of good or fair social standing, and having the moral qualities regarded as naturally appropriate to this. Hence, in later use, honest and decent in character and conduct, without reference to social position, or in spite of being in humble circumstances'.[10] In or just before the 1780s, the noun 'respectability' was coined to denote the condition of being respectable in the newly-predominant sense. Similar developments occurred in other languages: words such as *honnêteté* in French and *Anständigkeit* in German took on particular meanings that paralleled the English meanings of respectability. Direct borrowings – *respectabilité* and *Respectabilität* – came somewhat later.[11] Respectability was also by the late eighteenth century the central term of a distinctive discourse, one which incorporated some, but by no means all, of the senses of older words such as gentility, civility and politeness.

Along with its discursive dimension, respectability encompassed a cognitive one, an imaginary that offered a kind of map of respectable behaviour and the logic that lay behind it. We will see examples of this map in operation shortly, but we can outline three of its principal features now. Two can be represented as ideal traits of respectable individuals, while the third was a particular view, which could be expressed in words and displayed in behaviour and attitude, of the proper relationship between morality and society.[12]

The first trait was legitimate *self-respect*, based largely on manifest moral qualities and, as a secondary factor, aesthetic taste revealing moderation in general outlook. The second was *moral competence* – that is, the capacity to recognize the right thing to do and the strength of character to do it. (If you want a classic example of someone displaying these two characteristics in a context of respectability, think of any Jane Austen heroine – except on occasion Emma Woodhouse and Catherine Morland.) The third feature was more complicated. The basic idea was that there exists a hierarchy of status in society in which people have standing on the basis of their manifest moral virtue more or less regardless of where they are situated in other hierarchies. The moral hierarchy does not necessarily constitute a challenge to the more conventional structures of power, prestige and wealth, but the presumption is that the other structures need to acknowledge and accommodate the moral one – and also to emulate it as much as possible.

Instead of continuing in this abstract way to discuss the relationship between respectability and hospitality, we can examine specific textual examples from the late eighteenth and early nineteenth centuries. Let us begin by looking at two references in a single text. In 1783, William Pitt the Younger, William Wilberforce and a few other friends, all in their twenties, decided to take advantage of the recent outbreak of peace with France and the fact that Pitt was (as it turned out, temporarily) out of office to make a brief cross-channel tour. In a sketch of Pitt written long after Pitt's death and not published until long after Wilberforce's, Wilberforce included a short narrative of the tour.[13] When they got to Rheims, they discovered that they had no letters of recommendation to distinguished people in the town – which is to say that they lacked the standard means by which high-status persons from elsewhere legitimately imposed upon the hospitality of social equivalents, not usually for lodging but for invitations to dine and to converse with people of the right sort. Not to worry. A well-connected grocer whom they met put them in contact with the local lieutenant of police, a M. Du Chatel, whom Wilberforce describes as 'an intelligent and apparently a respectable family man'.[14] Not much is said about the specifics of the hospitality Du Chatel supplied, but presumably it included an arranged dinner where young English gentlemen could converse with French counterparts. For our purposes, the important point lies in Wilberforce's description of Du Chatel. This otherwise insignificant functionary obviously made a sufficiently strong impression that Wilberforce remembered him many years later. And what Wilberforce remembered was that he was a 'respectable family man', not that he was, say, an elegant conversationalist. That seems to have been what was important to Wilberforce about Du Chatel's hospitality.

The second instance occurred a short while later, when Wilberforce, Pitt and their party were in Paris. They were invited to dine with the Marquis de Lafayette, together with other guests who included Benjamin Franklin.[15] On this occasion, both the conversation and the 'home' presentation of the host made an impression. Wilberforce says that 'it is due to M. le Marquis de la Fayette to declare that the opinion which we all formed of his principles and sentiments, so far as such a slight acquaintance could enable us to form a judgment, was certainly favourable, and his family appeared to be conducted more in the style of an English house than any other French family which we visited'.[16] There is not enough detail to allow us to know precisely what was talked about or what specific patterns of behaviour were observed by the guests. But again, we note the impression that stuck with Wilberforce long afterwards: not only that what Lafayette said made sense, but that he 'conducted' his family in a desirable way, which is specifically described as being consistent with 'the style of an English house'. What might these statements have meant?

As it happens, we know a little about life *chez* Lafayette before the French Revolution. One notable element was the role of Adrienne, Marquise de Lafayette. She and her husband appeared as equal partners at social gatherings in their home, as joint heads of their family, and as a couple devoted to one other.[17] This presentation should be qualified by an admission that the Marquis had a mistress – as he almost always did except when he was in the United States. But at this particular time, Adrienne and the current mistress knew and apparently liked each other, both being 'pious ladies'.[18] Wilberforce does not mention Adrienne, so her prominent role probably was not what impressed him, but a consequence of the fact that she was 'pious' may have been part of it. Adrienne enforced certain rules at gatherings in her home. No gambling was permitted. Appropriate language was encouraged and conversation was supposed to be interesting and moderately informal, but also morally edifying.[19] That would have been attractive to Wilberforce, who, although he had not yet made his celebrated leap into Evangelicalism, was already showing proclivities in that direction.

What about the 'family' to which Wilberforce referred? It is clear from the context that he meant a nuclear family, not 'family' in the sense, say, of a nobleman's lineage or a gentleman's establishment. Because the Lafayette children were far too young in 1783 (six and one) to have been physically present at dinner with distinguished visitors, it is unlikely that Wilberforce would have seen the Lafayette family in operation. It might very well, however, have been a subject of conversation. The rearing of children, the stages of their growth, their moral development, their education, these were significant and popular topics in the late eighteenth century.[20] From the way in which his hosts discussed their children, Wilberforce might have inferred the kind of family they 'conducted'. If this were the case, it would suggest something about the kind of performance of hospitality in which Wilberforce participated: that it involved serious discussions of domestic matters as well as political and literary subjects.

We should also think about what Wilberforce might have meant by describing the Lafayette household as operating (relatively) 'in the style of an English house'. We don't know for certain because he doesn't specify. It might simply have reflected a deliberate political performance on Lafayette's part. In the 1780s, Lafayette was projecting his American experience in his public life, which consisted mainly of ostentatiously avoiding the court at Versailles and gathering people of 'advanced' (although not *too* advanced) views at his house for dinner and a kind of salon.[21] It is possible that what Wilberforce perceived as an 'English' style was in fact North American, modelled on practices in the households of American gentlemen such as Lafayette's patron George Washington – or perhaps on a French notion of what a social occasion at a 'republican' American gentleman's house should be like. But judging from what Wilberforce wrote, he was thinking about something quite different. He seems to be implying that in England, at least among people with whom he usually had contact or in a social imaginary of household life that was so widely accepted that Wilberforce could refer to it as characteristically English, there was a mode of performance centring on the family that was revealed when rendering hospitality and to which parallel performances in other countries could be compared. Wilberforce does not apply an adjective to this mode, but the word he used for Du Chatel, 'respectable', would seem to fit. It appears that in both instances, Wilberforce interpreted performances of hospitality in France as embodying the cultural construct that was just coming to be called 'respectability' and that he tended to think of as particularly, but obviously not exclusively, English.

TEA

Before we examine other textual representations of respectable hospitality, it might be helpful to consider a generic image of a familiar performance displaying some of its principal features: tea (the meal). Although tea (the drink) was consumed in many countries, the mode of conducting tea as an occasion that was adopted in Britain in the late eighteenth century became an international model consciously denoted as 'English'.[22]

HOSPITALITY AND HOME

FIGURE 7.3: Elements of a presentation of respectability: family tea-drinking and musical performance. An anonymous painting entitled *A Family Being Served with Tea*, probably from the 1740s. Accession Number B1981.25.271. © Yale Center for British Art, Paul Mellon Collection.

Tea was a performance constructed around mutual respect. The person directing the performance from behind the teapot (usually the senior woman in the household) received the respect of the others in symbolic exchange for the tea. It was expected that conversations would be polite and that everyone would respect everyone else's self-esteem. Behaviour and conversation were governed by the rules of civility generally applicable to everyday life. It was presumed that the sensibility of the ladies present determined the boundaries between what could and could not be said. Self-restraint was expected, but not to the extent that it seriously constrained sociability among the participants. Tea was supposed to be an enjoyable occasion, and one of the principal sources of enjoyment was conversation. At least among people who thought that they possessed gentility, participants were expected to display that quality, but the kind of gentility appropriate for ordinary tea had little overtly to do with the specifics of one's birth and almost everything to do with manners and behaviour.

We can analyse tea from several perspectives: as a ritual, as an instrumental practice with conscious purposes, as a celebration and as a means of identification.

A notable point about tea as a ritual was its participatory nature: everyone present, with the exception of servants if there were any, took part on essentially the same basis as everyone else. The person pouring had a special status, there were some minor gender differences with regard to the tasks of distributing tea and food, and children, if present, were subject to standard constraints, but apart from that, everyone possessed the same standing (and seating, which was not, apart from the place of the person at the teapot, prescribed). If there were guests, they were essentially temporary members of the family. They did not just share the meal and observe; they *belonged*, and they played active roles in the performance. The ritual format of tea was transparently different from that of the hospitality practised in the great halls of late medieval times, with its heavy emphasis on the proper placement of people and on reinforcing the high status of the host and the most prestigious guests.

Tea incorporated several instrumental elements. For one thing, it was regarded as a device for training in proper language and manners and for their reinforcement. For another, tea was an understood opportunity for creating social linkages. If invitations to tea were reciprocated between members of different families on a regular basis, this implied a common connection within a framework of shared respectability. Invitations to tea were a recognized means of vetting potential marriage partners and their families by allowing them to

FIGURE 7.4: Respectable hospitality. A print from the 1790s entitled 'Ladies at Tea', by Thomas Rowlandson. Accession Number B1975.4.702. © Yale Center for British Art, Paul Mellon Collection.

demonstrate how respectable they actually were. The promotion of sociability can also be seen as an instrumental function, in a particular way: tea was a conscious demonstration that groups of people could enjoy themselves peacefully without consuming alcohol.[23]

Tea also, quite overtly, celebrated respectability – both respectability in general and the particular respectability of the people participating in it. Tea and similar occasions were frequently represented as symbolic of what came to be called towards the end of the former century, 'civilization'.[24] But like many other rituals, tea not only *presented* symbols; it was seen as *constituting*, in a small way on each occasion, that which was symbolized. In late medieval times, occasions such as dining in a nobleman's hall represented the ideal order of society, while the treatment and behaviour of those receiving hospitality actually constituted the order in operation. In a later era, rituals such as tea both represented and constituted a different order, a respectable order in which standing denoted in terms of birth and wealth was paralleled, and under some circumstances trumped, by manifest moral and aesthetic standing. We shall see textual examples of this shortly.

Tea can also be perceived as a performance in which people signified their respectable identities. Hosts might consciously stage tea in order to display respectability and other claims to social standing to guests as a kind of outside audience, but the identification function was clearly more complicated than that. If guests at tea were supposed to be not merely spectators but participants and performers, we can presume that the guests were also identifying themselves. By joining in the performance, everyone was validating everyone else's respectable identity. Moreover, the same kind of performance, more or less, occurred at family tea even when no one from outside the family was present. Thus in a sense a respectable family having tea was identifying itself as respectable *to itself*, according to publicly established standards. This characteristic is consistent with the centrality of self-respect within respectability: by qualifying legitimately on grounds of morals, manners and taste to respect oneself, one was supposedly respectable whether or not anyone else noticed.

Tea was of course only one of several typical occasions involving hospitality in the home on which performances of respectability could take place. These included other meals, calls made by visitors, salons, formal festive occasions such as balls and less formal ones such as picnics and parties after excursions. Across Europe, middle- and upper-class families organized evening activities according to standard patterns; house guests and visitors, if there were any, were integrated into these activities.[25] Patterns of evening entertainment of house guests are frequently described in contemporary novels. Although the full range of occasions for respectable hospitality was available only at the upper end of society, a substantial sub-set (tea, for instance) was evidenced fairly far down the conventional social hierarchy, not only among middle-class families but also those of tradespeople, artisans and workers: people who, by adopting such practices, identified themselves as 'respectable'.[26]

REPRESENTING RESPECTABLE HOSPITALITY

In order to observe in more detail how respectability worked in the context of hospitality and what it meant in the late eighteenth and early nineteenth century, we can turn to novels from the period. Novels are obviously not perfect texts for this purpose. For one thing, their representations are fictional, although it may be assumed that, in the works of good writers, they are based on intelligent observation. For another, novels are sometimes vague about forms of practice because authors usually presume that their readers are contemporaries and do not need to have such things fully explained. The compensation (again, with good writers) is that meanings and intentions are typically explored more thoroughly than they would be in straightforward reporting of actual events. There is also the difficulty that the performances of respectability to which novelists give the most attention are often in some sense transgressive. In such cases, however, it is usually clear by inference what the proper performance would be. Sometimes the author tells us directly.

Let us start with something very familiar: the first ball in Jane Austen's *Pride and Prejudice*, the local assembly at which Mr. Darcy speaks slightingly of the ladies present within earshot of Elizabeth Bennet, and then compounds his offense by referring to her specifically as merely 'tolerable'.[27] Elizabeth thereupon constructs her prejudice against Darcy on account of his pride and sets the novel's main plot in motion. Darcy's misstep and Elizabeth's response are essentially framed by respectability. Although neither Darcy's party nor Elizabeth's family is acting as host, obligations of general civility fall equally upon everyone present. It is not just Elizabeth who thinks that Darcy has offended. Although his handsome appearance and the rumour of his great wealth had caused people to admire him at the start of the ball, after a while 'his manners gave a disgust which turned the tide of his popularity; for he was discovered to be proud, to be above his company, and above being pleased; and not all his large estate in Derbyshire could then save him from having a most forbidding, disagreeable countenance, and being unworthy of being compared with his friend [Bingley]'.[28]

Admittedly, we are not dealing (yet) with serious questions of moral identity, but Austen makes it clear that behaviour with regard to smaller matters contains evidence about individuals' general character – if one can evaluate the evidence correctly. The last is obviously a major theme of *Pride and Prejudice*, as it is of almost all of Austen's novels: Darcy, despite his *hauteur*, is actually a good person, while Darcy's foil Wickham, despite his manners and sympathetic air, is not. Elizabeth initially misjudges both, although later she learns to do better.

FIGURE 7.5: A provincial ball of Jane Austen's era. A print entitled 'A Ball at Scarborough', about 1820, by Thomas Rowlandson. Accession Number B2001.2.1155. © Yale Center for British Art, Paul Mellon Collection.

All three of the major elements of respectability noted previously are engaged in the first ball scene. Self-respect is obviously central: Darcy imagines that his natural diffidence among strangers, together with his sense of his own social and aesthetic status, constitute legitimate self-respect. They do not, as he learns when he falls for Elizabeth and she explains why she dislikes him. Until he corrects his fault, he offends against the self-respect of many more or less worthy people. The principal key to displaying respectability on occasions of hospitality, whether one is a guest or a host, is not to injure other people's self-regard. If one is among strangers at a respectable function, one should treat everyone as respectable unless there is strong evidence that they are not, and even in that case, there is seldom a good reason to be offensive. The second element, competence, is also present, although mainly by suggestion for future development. Again, it is not *moral* competence in the most serious sense of the term that is initially at issue, but rather competence (or the want of it) in civility, politeness and regard for others. Nevertheless, deeper matters are suggested, mainly by Elizabeth's failure to read Darcy's character correctly. Judging overt behaviour in order to evaluate moral character is an important part of respectability, but it is not an easy thing to do well. The third element of respectability, the notion of a moral hierarchy, is also present in the attenuated form of judgements of manners more or less independent of conventional social standing. Because of his behaviour, Darcy is identified as someone not entirely respectable despite his 'large estate in Derbyshire'.

Some of the workings of respectable hospitality as a set of meaningful rituals are also displayed. For example, the dancing at the assembly conforms to established patterns: the dances themselves, as well as conventions about requesting, accepting or refusing partners for particular dances, about introductions to strangers, and about subjects of discussion during and in between dancing. The next ball in *Pride and Prejudice*, the one at Netherfield, Bingley's house, shows these patterns more specifically.[29]

Darcy, by now thoroughly taken with Elizabeth (and, as we learn later, conflicted because of his low opinion of most of her family), makes a special effort to attach himself to her, but she continues to avoid him. She finds herself, however, in a situation in which she cannot escape dancing with him without transgressing. She uses the occasion to twit him for his silence, which she implies is unsocial. She explains sarcastically that dance partners are supposed to converse and suggests standard but inane topics. This indicates, although ironically, that a proper performance of respectability requires conversation and a display of sociability.

Several social occasions in *Pride and Prejudice* feature a prominent ritual: musical performances by guests, especially by young women who are 'accomplished'.[30] Elizabeth, although she is only moderately adept, is frequently asked to play the piano. Her sister Mary, who is not adept at all, insists on playing after her, especially at the Netherfield ball. On most of these occasions, the presence of Darcy, said to have good musical judgement, makes Elizabeth feel self-conscious. She does not seem to be more than a little concerned about his assessment of the quality of her own playing. She knows what her limits are and would be perfectly capable of refusing to play if she thought that her abilities were inadequate for the occasion. Her sister's playing, however, embarrasses her greatly, not only because Mary really is inadequate but also because Mary insists on continuing to play beyond the point at which other guests should be expected to listen. The embarrassment is compounded by the sarcasm with which her father detaches Mary from the piano at the Netherfield ball.[31] Elizabeth knows that Darcy has noticed all this this and that he disapproves – justifiably.

Austen's descriptions of this kind of musical performance suggest comparisons between respectability and other modes of social identification such as *gentility*. The acquisition by girls of 'accomplishments' such as music was an aspect of a fashion for aesthetic distinction that became a significant part of the culture of European gentility in the seventeenth and eighteenth centuries.[32] It informed much of the education of women of elite (or aspirant elite) status and made the possession of musical instruments, especially pianos, practically obligatory. In the context of gentility, young women performing on occasions of hospitality could be seen as demonstrating the success of their educations, validating the social claims of their families, and advancing their own interests as potential marriage partners. From the perspective of respectability, however, the ritual appears in a somewhat different light. Hannah More, a major exponent of respectability, strongly disapproved of constructing women's education around 'accomplishments'. Young women, she wrote, should prepare themselves for their proper roles as educators of their children and contributors to the moral uplift of society.[33] Jane Austen was not so negative about accomplishments such as playing an instrument, but she thought that they should reflect primarily the interests and talents of individuals. For players of moderate ability like Elizabeth (and Austen herself), performing at social gatherings ought to be a voluntary contribution to the pleasure and sociability of the occasion or a service if guests want to dance or sing. Darcy's sister Georgiana is a player of unusual ability. This is treated favourably, but as an individual calling; it has nothing to do with playing at balls or establishing status.[34]

In *Pride and Prejudice*, Austen includes several instances of hospitality specifically in homes. In these, Austen typically portrays people not behaving properly, from which we can infer how they *should* behave. The most notable of these instances come when Elizabeth is in Kent visiting her friend Charlotte, who has married Elizabeth's absurd cousin Collins, a clergyman.[35] Collins' patron is Lady Catherine de Bourgh, on whom he fawns disgracefully. Shortly after Elizabeth's arrival, the Collinses and their guest are invited to dinner at Rosings, Lady Catherine's house. The highlights of that evening and of subsequent visits after the arrival of Lady Catherine's nephew Darcy consist mostly of violations of unspoken rules of courtesy and respectable hospitality by Lady Catherine, with some assistance from Collins. Neither Lady Catherine nor Collins is apparently aware of the rules, but everyone else is. Lady Catherine tries to place herself at the centre of every conversation, establishing its subjects and presuming that her opinions, although uniformly unintelligent and ill-informed, are definitive on all subjects. She asks her guests, especially Elizabeth, highly impertinent personal questions and is surprised when, on one occasion, Elizabeth puts her off with a joke.[36] To Lady Catherine, Elizabeth's response, not her own rudeness, is a sign of questionable breeding.

In terms of the ritual procedures of hospitality, there is little that is overtly wrong when Lady Catherine entertains guests. Invitations are given in proper form, gestures of courtesy follow the standard, individuals go through the appropriate physical motions. On Elizabeth's first visit, everyone is a bit too stiff to afford a desirable degree of collective sociability, especially since the proceedings are dominated by the hostess's monopolizing tendencies and Collins' sycophantic ones. But later, after the arrival of Darcy and his cousin Colonel Fitzwilliam (who enters into conversations 'with the readiness and ease of a well-bred man'),[37] things loosen up a bit. What is really wrong, at least when Lady Catherine is in control, lies in the absence of respectable meaning that is supposed to be manifest in the rituals. This is what permits the reader to identify Lady Catherine as someone who is, despite her rank, decidedly not respectable. We can employ the three characteristics of respectability noted previously to specify her failings, both as a hostess and as a person.

In the first place, Lady Catherine appears not to be conscious of the self-respect of her guests and certainly is unaware of any obligation to acknowledge it. If she actually knew anything about the subjects on which she utters pronouncements, we might say that she at least respects herself (in the sense incorporated in respectability), but she doesn't. Her esteem for herself is based on the belief of a stupid person that because she is who she is, she must know more and have better taste than anyone else. She is abetted by Collins, who gushingly confirms her wisdom in all matters and thereby displays his own lack of real self-respect. A truly respectable hostess, like any respectable guest, acts under the assumption that everyone present is worthy of regard, that it is impolite to slight anyone (although one may certainly disagree with what they say), and that it is everyone's responsibility to make the occasion of hospitality a successful and pleasing one. Respectable hospitality is founded to a large extent on mutual recognition, perhaps even celebration, of self-respect.

From the perspective of social order associated with respectability, it appears that Lady Catherine's failings signify more than mere absurdity and hurt feelings at dinner. Lady Catherine's view of herself as empress of all she surveys is not entirely delusional. It is based on the reality of her social position and wealth and of the power that she believes these things afford her. In the local community, she apparently wields real power.[38] Collins' subservience reflects not just his personality but also a view of the nature of social hierarchy that is, from Austen's point of view, deeply flawed. Moreover, Collins is a dependent: he owes his living to Lady Catherine. Because of this, Charlotte must gesture at imitating her husband's behaviour. One reason (apart from simple politeness and her own respectability) that Elizabeth does not overtly challenge Lady Catherine at Rosings is concern for her friend. But when, towards the end of the novel, Lady Catherine directly insults Elizabeth by denigrating her social and moral standing (and in Elizabeth's own home), Elizabeth gives her what she deserves: a lecture and a request that she leave.[39] Austen is clearly not insinuating that the conventional hierarchies of wealth, social status and power are irrelevant or even that they can or should be dispensed with. She is indicating that morality, taste and other elements of respectability define their own legitimate hierarchy, within which Elizabeth stands high and Lady Catherine, whether she knows it or not, very low. Ideally, the other hierarchies should be congruent with the hierarchy of respectability, but sadly, Lady Catherine demonstrates that this is often not the case.

Here we can see a major difference between hospitality in an upper-class home around 1800 (as portrayed by Austen) and its counterpart of two centuries before. Collins' behaviour towards Lady Catherine, which is so out of place in a context of respectability as to be extremely funny, would have been entirely appropriate and expected in an earlier era. Lady Catherine would probably have been guilty of incivility in 1600, but it would most likely not have registered as a fault of great importance. The rationale of earlier rituals of hospitality, at least in households at a social level comparable to that portrayed by Austen, revolved around the reproduction and reinforcement of the conventional social order, which demanded lavish praise of the host by guests privileged to speak.[40] The performance of hospitality in a respectable home of Austen's time signified something quite different. To pursue this point, we can turn to the third aspect of respectability, the notion of personal competence.

Although fictional presentations of respectability generally do not employ situations of hospitality to display serious moral competence, they often suggest that moral competence is linked to the social and aesthetic competence required for entertaining guests. The most striking examples in *Pride and Prejudice* are constructed in negative terms. Lady Catherine's failings as a respectable hostess lay out the framework of the moral incompetence that she displays later – when, in order to maintain her illusion that Darcy will marry her daughter, she tries to force Elizabeth to swear that she will never accept Darcy's (as yet unrepeated) proposal of marriage.[41] It is not difficult for Elizabeth to resist this demand because of her self-respect and strength of character, but the implications of the attempt are significant. Lady Catherine has no real hold over Elizabeth, but she might take revenge on Collins and Charlotte. Her incompetent performance as respectable host suggests that she is equally incompetent in exercising power over her local community. In other words, respectability properly acted out in contexts of hospitality in the home parallels and resembles the respectability that society's governors are supposed to demonstrate in settings of power. Rituals of respectability enacted in the home provide evidence of fitness for wielding power and perhaps afford training in its proper use.

It should be noted that although there is an obvious class element in all this, in Austen's presentation it does not constitute a critique of specific classes as such. Lady Catherine is an incompetent member of her class, but there are plenty of competent ones in Austen's novels: Darcy, for example, once we get to know him better. Perhaps the most striking is Mr. Knightley in *Emma*. Elizabeth, in standing up to Lady Catherine, is not representing one class in a moral confrontation with another. She insists that, as a 'gentleman's daughter', she belongs basically to the same class as Darcy and Lady Catherine.[42] The critique focuses instead on how members of that class behave, and they are supposed to behave respectably.

The relationship between class and respectability is a complicated subject disguised, in conventional historical understanding, as a simple one. We tend to assume that respectability was a 'bourgeois' phenomenon.[43] The fact that many of the ritual aspects of respectability and much of its terminology ('gentleman' and 'lady', for instance) clearly derived from the aristocracy can be explained, up to a point, by postulating a process of diffusion, imitation and, particularly in language, adaptation. ('Gentleman' and 'lady' had taken on two overlapping sets of meanings by the late eighteenth century, one in what purported to be a more traditional, aristocratic sense and one in a context of respectability which featured moral behaviour and respect for other people as its distinguishing signs.[44]) But this kind of explanation does not wholly account for what was going on. To see more, let us look for a moment at *Evelina* (1778), the first novel of Frances ('Fanny') Burney, Jane Austen's predecessor and one of her models.[45]

Evelina was written just before the time that the word 'respectability' was coined. Whereas Austen uses 'respectability' and 'respectable' (in the sense of 'displaying respectability') very often, in *Evelina* Burney employs 'respectable' in the same sense only occasionally. Nevertheless, the attitudes that the central character, the *ingénue* Evelina, reveals in her letters (it is an epistolary novel) correspond closely to those which we have been discussing. Social events involving hospitality are, even more than in Austen's novels, occasions for the heroine to comment on behaviour. After one such occasion, for example, Evelina remarks, 'But I knew not, till now, how requisite are birth and fortune to the attainment of respect and civility'.[46] She is obviously not pleased with her discovery, which contradicts the respectable notion that respect and civility should be accorded to worthy people regardless (or almost regardless) of where they stand in the hierarchy of birth and fortune. Is this a bourgeois sentiment? Not in *Evelina*.

Burney herself came from a family that could be considered middle class (although her father, one of the earliest British musicologists, represented himself as a gentleman), and the character Evelina is the ward of an impecunious clergyman.[47] Nevertheless, Burney describes a world in which social life is legitimately dominated by aristocrats, and although many of the aristocrats are by no means respectable, many of them are – especially Lord Orville, to whom Evelina is eventually betrothed. Evelina herself turns out to be the daughter of a nobleman. Many of the most egregious violations of proper behaviour – especially on occasions of hospitality – are committed by non-aristocratic people overtly described as such. The woman at whose house Evelina stays outside of London for most of the novel is the wife of a naval captain. She is perfectly respectable, but her husband is not. He is crude and nasty, and speaks like a common seaman. There is no hint of the respectable professionalism and 'gentleman-like' qualities that Jane Austen emphasizes in most of the naval officers she portrays. Even more notable is the description of a dinner to which Evelina is invited at the home of a well-to-do tradesman in London.[48] The description is intended to be funny, but it clearly gives an impression that the manners of people in trade are often mere attempts to ape their betters, that many such people recognize no obligation to respect the feelings of others, that they lack moral, aesthetic and social competence. So while Burney, through Evelina, may subscribe to the notion that the behavioural traits associated with what would shortly be called 'respectability' are not dependent on wealth and birth, she does not even hint that they are peculiar characteristics of the bourgeoisie. Rather, they constitute a model for all classes, or at least for all that provide hospitality in their homes.

It would be possible to examine a great many other novels of the late eighteenth and early nineteenth centuries, both English and continental, to obtain a fuller picture of the ways in which hospitality was practised, or was supposed to be practised, in a respectable home. What we have seen, however, is enough to suggest that the history of hospitality in the home does not proceed *directly* from a premodern cultural pattern of meaningful, obligatory elite performance centring on charity, on enacting the conventional social order, and on performing various political functions to a contemporary setting in which hospitality is optional and has very limited meaning. Rather, it moves in the eighteenth and nineteenth centuries through a period in which hospitality is incorporated into and given meaning by the cognitive map of respectability that defines a large part of what 'home' signifies. Modern practices of hospitality are not as formal in any sector of society (apart from the 'hospitality industry') as they were two hundred years ago. Nevertheless, the basic principles of ideal behaviour in the home have not changed completely, although we usually do not employ words such as 'respectable' to describe them. And if we do not have as pressing an obligation to offer hospitality in our homes, the fact that home life retains a substantial legacy from the past ensures that when we do offer it, we follow patterns that once constituted respectability.

CHAPTER EIGHT

Religion and the Home

MATTHEW NEAL

Eighteenth-century England was not ubiquitously genteel (Gatrell 2007; Dickie 2011), but nor did it experience the kind of violent social breakdown that blighted the seventeenth century (Klein 1994; Thomas 2018). This fact is the more remarkable given how vast were the political, social, economic and cultural changes which English men and women experienced between 1660 and 1832 (Price 1999). The relative success with which an increasingly diverse society managed its diversity in these years must be counted among its defining features. The proximity of the seventeenth century, in part, explains this success, for the horror of bloodshed is often an antidote to more. On the other hand, in a time 'before liberalism' (Skinner 1998), so far was diversity from being thought self-evidently a good thing that the instincts of English men and women may be said to have been positively for conformity. Those instincts had led to civil war in the seventeenth century, when all sides had sought to impose religion at the point of a sword. In the eighteenth century, excepting periodic outbursts of violence, instincts that had once led to war were tamed in favour of peace. Civil peace was a precondition of the artistic and intellectual 'exuberance' characteristic of the eighteenth century (Greene 1970). Contemporaries knew this, figuring theirs as an 'Augustan' and 'enlightened' age (Lund 2012; Porter 2001). That wit, satire and curiosity should have flourished when only several decades earlier leaden faith had wrought a deadly mess is extraordinary. How had English men and women tamed instincts that had once been so destructive?

Since they lacked any liberal instinct for diversity, the best answer would appear to be that they learned to do so, developing tools for the purpose. Such 'moderation' as prevailed in eighteenth-century life did not come naturally. As

Ethan Shagan has argued, it was always 'an act of control' (2011: 3). Sometimes the tools developed to facilitate it were legal, like acts of parliament granting toleration, relief and indemnity (but never a plenitude of rights) to non-anglicans (Grell, Israel and Tyacke 1991). At other times they were institutional, such as improved access to courts of law – particularly King's Bench -- for the purpose of dispute resolution (Halliday 1998). They might also be cultural: modes of thought and patterns of life, like 'politeness' (Klein 1994) or 'reasonableness' (Rivers 1991), which gave to men and women of the period structured ways of navigating the complexities of their society.

These tools were instruments of socialization. Making social diversity manageable, if not universally welcome, their effect was to reconcile men and women to the facts of their lives. They are crucial to any effort to understand such stability as eighteenth-century Britain achieved. The present essay forms an additional contribution to that effort. To the roll-call of tools by means of which men and women of the period learned to manage their diversity this chapter adds another: eighteenth-century home and home-life. It puts the eighteenth-century home centre-stage, arguing that it should be seen as a forcing-house for a variety of attitudes and behaviours underpinning one process of socialization in particular: the growth of religious toleration. In doing so, it proposes to see the eighteenth-century home as more than 'the preeminent machine for living' of Amanda Vickery's memorable description (2009: 292). Home *was* such a machine. But insofar as it helped to beat seventeenth-century swords of religion into eighteenth-century ploughshares, it was also something more: an instrument for cultivating ways in which to live *better together*.

Standard narratives of eighteenth-century domestic life have tended to be narratives of invasion. It is an affecting story which figures the home as an 'affective' and 'companionate' space which had thrust upon it the impersonal economic forces of commerce and industry (Stone 1977, chs. 6, 8, 13). These forces give us one of the quintessential images of the period: Britain as the world's first mass-production, mechanized economy, with a market-oriented mentality to boot. According to the 'invasion' narrative, the new economy dumped on eighteenth-century domestic life a dizzying range of new, production-line goods with all the advertising, sales and marketing paraphernalia that an expanding economy naturally produces (McKendrick, Brewer and Plumb 1982). Nor was it only the consumption of mass-produced goods which invaded the eighteenth-century home. Production processes also crossed the threshold into the domestic space, with cottage industry furnishing another classic image of life and work in the early age of manufactures (Hudson 1981; Houston and Snell 1984; Berg 1985).

Pro-market histories applaud this as the birth of a modern, dynamic economy with the power to enrich; anti-market histories deplore it as life within. 'Public' and 'private' were never entirely separate spheres, however much moralists of the period may have wished them to be (Vickery 1993a). It is clear, for example, that discourses of domestic morality that did so much to shape the ideal of home-life in the period cannot be understood apart from the growth of new social structures in the form of the working and middle classes (Thompson 1963; Davidoff and Hall 1987). Nor can we grasp the power of what Phyllis Mack has called 'heart religion' without recognising the way in which 'Enlightenment ideals and Protestant theology' in public life, not to mention the daily grind of working life in the industrial economy, 'confronted' men and women in their innermost selves with a set of existential questions to which the 'aggressive spiritual agency' of Christian revivalism was the psychological response (2008: 14).

But if in these and other ways the world outside the home impinged upon the life within, so too did life within impinge upon the world outside. Private flowed into public, just as public affected private. Historians of education, for example, tell us that in an era before compulsory state education, schooling was often organized from within domestic or semi-domestic spaces (de Bellaigue 2016; Woodley 2009). In similar vein, Jan de Vries' (2008) recent work on 'industriousness' reminds us that not all economic forces in the eighteenth century were impersonal, or originated outside of the home. Hardworking, desirous allocators of household resources drove eighteenth-century consumption patterns as decidedly as consumption patterns refashioned consumers' homes. Even trends as large and faceless in scale as rising population have their roots in a set of highly personal decisions made in the most intimate of domestic spaces (Wrigley and Schofield 1989). This essay follows the model of historians of education, industriousness and population in figuring the eighteenth-century home as more than just a space invaded. It was a complex space which bore upon the world, no less than it was borne upon by it, in ways that were as many and varied as homes themselves (Vickery 2009).

To build its case for seeing the home as a forcing house for a set of attitudes and behaviours underpinning toleration, this essay draws upon eighteenth-century conduct literature. In particular, it draws upon a number of authors and texts known to have been influential in the period. The aim of the essay is to show that it is possible to trace an irenic sensibility of the kind that governed eighteenth-century religious life to sources concerned with Christian conduct in the domestic sphere. That is not to say that it was *in* such sources that that sensibility originated; my claim is the more modest one only that in some of the more widely read conduct literature of the period do we find a homespun version of it articulated.

Chief among the sources in which we find that sensibility articulated is *The Whole Duty of Man*, a Christian advice manual first published in the late 1650s, most likely by the Royalist churchman Richard Allestree (Elmen 1951). (This

FIGURE 8.1: *The Whole Duty of Man* frontispiece, Wenceslas Hollar (1607–77) from first edition, 1658. © University of Toronto / Wikimedia Commons, Public Domain.

essay follows Elmen in assuming Allestree's authorship.) The text went through scores of editions, and has been described by Charles Stranks as 'the dominant book of religious instruction' in the eighteenth century (1961: 125). Cherished alongside other staples of the Protestant bookshelf – the Bible, *Pilgrim's Progress* and Foxe's *Book of Martyrs* – its appeal likely lay in its 'denominational openness' (Alblas 1991: 94). Stranks observes that, though 'a High-Church book', *The Whole Duty of Man* 'was admired by all parties' and 'intended for the widest possible audience' (1961: 125). Paul Elmen suggests that the text's commitment to the doctrine of passive obedience in particular should be read as an overture to dissenters (1951: 26). It is therefore a useful text in seeking to reconstruct what we might call the domestic context of religious toleration.

The Whole Duty of Woman, published anonymously in 1737, was understood by contemporaries to form a companion volume to *The Whole Duty of Man*. According to W.R. Irwin, it had a 'long history of popularity' (1952: 290), Paul

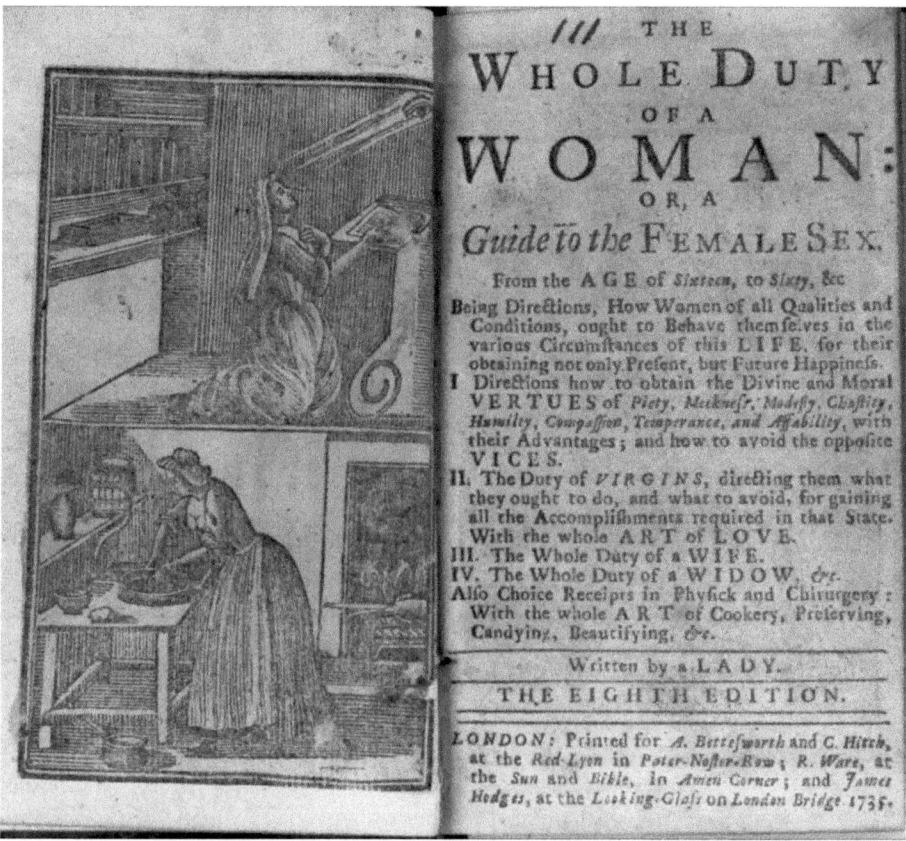

FIGURE 8.2: Engraved frontispiece with two illustrations: 1. A woman kneeling and praying; 2. A woman preparing food; and title page of *The Whole Duty of a Woman; or, a Guide to the Female Sex*, 1735. © Library of Congress, Public Domain.

Fussell, Jr. noting that 'by 1831 it had gone through sixteen editions' (1951: 539). Its origins were in fact satirical, a 'straight-faced contribution' from a Grub Street rake, one William Kenrick, 'to that body of improving literature' on which polite society in the period was conventionally reared. As pastiche it succeeded admirably, for it came to be 'read . . . as a straightforward work of edification, suitable for presentation to young ladies' (Irwin 1952: 290). In light of the fact that 'home' was regarded as a female sphere, the value of a text such as Kenrick's to any account that seeks to relate toleration to a set of domestic attitudes and behaviours learned first in private cannot be overstated. *The Whole Duty of Woman* is used in conjunction with three other texts which shed light on the home as a female sphere: *The Excellent Daughter*, first published in 1708 by the latitudinarian clergyman White Kennett; Wetenhall Wilkes' *A Letter of Genteel and Moral Advice to a Young Lady*, first published in 1740;

and Thomas Gisborne's evangelical *Enquiry into the Duties of the Female Sex*, first published in 1797.

This essay also draws extensively upon the Baptist preacher Samuel Stennett's *Discourses on Domestic Duties*. According to the introduction appended to the 1824 edition of Stennett's *Works*, the *Discourses*, first published in 1783, proved to be highly influential, and 'obtained for the author a large accession of well-earned reputation' (Jones 1824: xxxii). An advocate for toleration, Stennett was indeed a man of 'considerable public influence' (Copson 2004). Descended from a family of prominent Baptists, he enjoyed a wide influence far beyond his own denomination. Reflecting on the *Discourses*' 'unspeakable service in the world' (quoted in Jones 1824: xxvi), the *Protestant Dissenters' Magazine* described Stennett's 'connections' as being 'large and respectable, not only among Protestant dissenters of various descriptions, but with the members of the established church', too (quoted in Jones 1824: xxiii). When Stennett died in 1713, his loss 'was deeply regretted, not only by all the Baptist churches throughout the kingdom, but also by many most respectable persons of the other denominations of Protestant Dissenters, and also of the National Establishment' (Jones 1824: xx). These facts make his *Discourses on Domestic Duties* another obvious choice of source for any investigation into the homespun roots of toleration. It is to that investigation that we now turn.

If the roots of religious toleration really were struck in the eighteenth-century home, this was only possible because contemporaries regarded home and the wider world as forming a continuum. Vickery has shown that home was often seen as a refuge from the world, and the period's preoccupation with locks and thresholds certainly bears that reading out (Vickery 2008). More recently, Michael McKeon (2005) has suggested that it is the hallmark of the 'modern' mind to understand public and private as not merely 'distinct' but actually 'separable' spaces. This model of the home certainly existed in the eighteenth century. But the conduct literature examined in this essay suggests the persistence of another model: home as a microcosm of the world (Vickery 2009: 184). Contemporaries operated with an extended as well as a literal sense of home.

In Stennett's *Discourses*, the concept of home is frequently extended to various spheres and institutions beyond the doorstep. Drawing upon the Gospel of John, for instance, Stennett figures heaven as a '*house*' of '*many mansions*' (Stennett 1800: 468–69). This, indeed, is the theme of Discourse XII of Stennett's *Discourses*, 'Heaven considered as a Family' (1800: 446–76). Christ himself 'compares' heaven 'to a *house*' (1800: 452). Heaven offers 'in the highest perfection' such 'domestic pleasures' as home gives one only a 'taste' of (1800: 451). God is thus 'the great Householder of the universe' (1800: 409), and, accordingly, the 'church of Christ ... often in scripture described as a house or a family' (1800: 342–43). As with a well-run household, 'cheerfulness, mingled with seriousness' is the watchword of a church (1800: 81), so that home is a sort of church itself (1800: 79). It is our duty to welcome God among us: as 'creation' is a 'mansion . . . built' by God 'for the residence of mankind during their abode on earth' (1800: 454), so 'our hearts' ought always to be 'his residence' in us (1800: 476).

If God is 'cursed' in his children's 'hearts', they will one day find themselves cast into hell, which Stennett figures as another kind of residence: 'the abodes of darkness' (1800: 423). It is because heavenly life is seen as a household or family life in the period, and mundane domestic existence therefore a preparation for it, that any assault upon a man's domicile was seen as a sin and not only a crime. Men are left to 'their liberty' at home that they might fit themselves for heaven there; consequently, anything 'that endangers the happiness, security, and existence of domestic society, is a bold invasion on the rights of nature . . . and . . . an offence against the supreme will and authority of God' (1800: 374). If religion itself was a home, then Roman Catholic corruption of true or 'primitive' faith was likewise a kind of trespass. As Wetenhall Wilkes, the Irish Protestant author, put it in *A Letter of Genteel and Moral Advice to a Young Lady*: the reformed faith, like home, 'is a secure Refuge, in Seasons of deepest Distress' (1740: 46); 'the sovereign Purpose of the Reformation was to extirpate the superstitious Innovations, with which [it] was invaded' (1740: 43).

Like Stennett's *Discourses*, *The Whole Duty of Man* frequently extends the concept of home to spheres and institutions beyond the doorstep. Church and heaven are alike kinds of habitation, and home-life, accordingly, the principal preparation for both. The text enjoins the reader to 'be often thinking of the joyes laid up for thee in Heaven; look upon that as thy home, on this world, only as an *Inne*, where thou art fain to take up in thy passage' ([Allestree] 1659: 163). *The Whole Duty* identifies exemplars of domestic as well as religious rectitude for its readers' edification. These include King David, who is shown to have shared St. Peter's understanding of the church as a 'household of Faith' ([Allestree] 1659: 306), and drawn the corollary inference that a 'family might [also] be a kind of Church, an Assembly of godly upright persons' (1659: 327). Mankind, as the *The Whole Duty of Man* reminds its readers, properly dwells in God. It is to God, according to the 'Prayer of Intercession' recommended for receiving the sacrament, that we hope one day to be 'fetch[ed] home' (1659: 59). 'When ever' to correct or punish us God 'strikes', therefore, 'we are in all reason, not only *patiently* to lie under his *rod*, but . . . kiss it also; that is, be very *thankful* to him, that he is *pleased* not to *give us over to our own hearts lusts*, Psal. 18. 12. but still continue his *care* of us; sends *afflictions*, as so many *messengers* to call us home to himself' (1659: 39).

Just as these male-oriented texts operate with an extended sense of home, so too do those sources concerned with home specifically as a sphere of female influence. *The Excellent Daughter*, for instance, preaches the happy effects that domestic economy taught early in life might be expected to have upon women's lives, and upon a series of 'Places of Abode' which in the course of their lives women might call home: family, parish, city, nation and 'the World to come' (Kennett 1742: 21). In *A Letter of Genteel and Moral Advice to a Young Lady*, the care which a woman must take in performing 'her domestic Offices' is described as 'the trouble of the Keys'; Wilkes here draws a parallel to the power of the keys which the clergy exercise in performing the offices of the Church (1740: 120). On this reading, the church is a household which it is the duty of her sons to keep in the same way that it is the duty of a woman to keep her domicile. Thomas Gisborne's *Enquiry into the Duties of the Female Sex* also rehearses the familiar trope of home-life's radiating influence. Here, a series of 'sphere[s]' (Gisborne 1797: 11) is described (1797: 9–13) within which the 'virtuous exertion[s]' (1797: 13) of domestic womanhood are shown to have their 'real and deeply interesting effects' (1797: 11). It is a model which is also to be found in James Fordyce's popular *Sermons to Young Women,* published in 1765. In a sermon entitled 'On the Importance of the Female Sex', for instance, Fordyce speaks of the 'charming extent' of well-ordered domestic 'tenderness' (Fordyce 1809, vol. 1: 26). Fordyce figures the world as centred on home like an expanding series of concentric circles: 'I say, that the men you marry, the children you bring, and the community at large, will be all deeply interested in your' domestic 'conduct' (1809, vol. 1: 23). Through a woman's children especially the influence of home proves to be far-reaching. The virtues instilled in them – 'those lovely plants which you have reared' – 'I see spreading, from house to house, from family to family . . . diffusing virtue and happiness through the human race' (1809, vol. 1: 29). It is thus in women's 'power to communicate much happiness, or to occasion much misery' beyond their own sphere (1809, vol. 1: 23). Such sources elide the life lived behind closed doors with life lived in public spheres and institutions beyond the doorstep.

If home and the world beyond it formed a continuum in this way, we have grounds for supposing that domestic life may have contributed something significant to the period's stability. What the sources examined here suggest, I propose, is that contemporaries figured home as both a literal and a discursive space in which to cultivate various irenic habits and dispositions which are of interest to the historian of religious toleration. Histories of religious toleration have long recognized the irenic foundations of the policy promulgated in 1689, and only gradually adopted into the culture. But any suggestion that peace alone justified the policy underestimates the strength of burning religious conviction, and the lethal power of the conformist instinct. Arguments for peace had to be articulated, and contexts were required in which to articulate them. This chapter argues that eighteenth-century discourses of home and home-life gave positive expression to a spirit of Christian irenicism in ways that may help us to understand its eventual adoption.

Six domestic expressions of irenicism stand out in the sources. The first and most fundamental of these we find clearly articulated in Stennett's *Discourses*. There it takes the form of an injunction synonymous with the idea of home-life itself. In domestic life, Stennett tells his reader, habits of sound 'oeconomy' must be cultivated. On the face of it a truism, this injunction nonetheless packs a solidly irenic punch. It is therefore worth examining in detail.

Sound economy involves the execution of a number of domestic duties. But it is what these duties yield, if diligently executed, which is of most interest: sound economy of this kind guarantees what Stennett calls 'order, harmony, and devotion' (1800: 79). These are 'the three main ideas in the description of a Christian church', as Stennett explains in the third of his *Discourses*, entitled 'Family Worship' (1800: 79). For this reason, a well-run household – Stennett gives the example of Aquila and Priscilla's in Paul's Epistle to the Romans – has the character of a church. 'As their household is called a church, so we may be sure order, harmony, and devotion . . . prevailed therein' (1800: 79). The story of Aquila and Priscilla allows Stennett to detail more concretely what produced such good order in this godly couple's domestic affairs. 'Prudent management' was the answer (1800: 79). This involved much 'industry', especially on Priscilla's part, who '"looked well to the ways of her household, and [ate] not the bread of idleness"' (1800: 79). It also involved the maintenance of cordiality among members of the household: 'in so cordial and friendly a manner towards one another' did Aquila's household behave 'that their neighbours could scarce avoid saying, "How good and pleasant a thing it is for brethren to dwell together in unity"' (1800: 80). 'Every thing was conducted with regularity and decorum' (1800: 79). 'Prayer, praise, and instruction' were matters of especial concern. In these, all proper 'duty' and 'fitness' were observed (1800: 81–82). '*Priscilla* so disposed the affairs of the house as that all might attend' worship (1800: 80). It was important to Aquila and Priscilla that they did so, for 'the enjoyment of blessings, be our prudence, industry, and oeconomy what they may, depends', ultimately, 'on the favour of indulgent Providence' (1800: 89). Good things ensued as a result of astute domestic economy. 'Plenty, harmony, and cheerfulness, reigned through the house' (1800: 79). Aquila and Priscilla were able to 'live in a generous and hospitable manner' (1800: 79). 'To this virtuous and pious house all the friends of God and religion were welcome', and came (1800: 80). 'How happy were they when they had a *Paul* and an *Apollos* with them!' (1800: 80). With such men they had the pleasure 'to discourse largely of the things of God' (1800: 80). Sound management was a duty in Aquila and Priscilla's house, but it was also a pleasure and received pleasurable reward.

Stennett's instructions to his readers that at home they should cultivate 'order, harmony, and devotion' expressed a vision of Christian faith that he evidently hoped might be adopted as their own. It was an irenic vision which asked readers to recognize that order and harmony were attributes of God.

FIGURE 8.3: 'Morning Worship', *c.* 1848: A Christian family say morning prayers before their breakfast. © Hulton Archive / Getty Images.

Devotion to order and harmony in the home expressed devotion to those principles at large, as well as to God himself. To frustrate them was to frustrate what God had made. This message contained a tolerationist core: disorder and disharmony were impieties: as you would not want the peace of your home to be disturbed, so keep God's peace beyond your doorstep.

Stennett's vision of Christian faith was also resolutely practical. As William Kenrick explained to his readers in *The Whole Duty of a Woman*, to follow such instructions as these is no unpleasant task, and ought even to be our natural inclination. 'God never lays on us a greater Task than what he affords us both Ability and Opportunities to perform' ([Kenrick] 1737: 12). Stennett does not hold with the 'austerities' of 'visionaries' who preach 'indifference and contempt' for the world and for those 'earthly good[s]' – chiefly, 'bodily health and worldly prosperity' – which, if well managed, bring order and harmony into our lives (Stennett 1800: 18). With moderates of all denominations, he takes the view that it is one of the glories of the Christian religion that God requires of us nothing that is incompatible with a proper regard to 'our *temporal interests*' (1800: 17). This anti-ascetic, anti-enthusiast position has an obvious irenic payoff. From *it is sound to mind your business* to *be sure to mind your business* is but a step. Christ is quoted to this effect: '"study to be quiet," says our apostle, "and to do your own business"' (1800: 18).

Stennett's claim is that his practical vision of Christian faith is a liveable vision. Working with the grain of human nature rather than against it, it augments 'our power to make multitudes of our fellow-creatures happy' (Stennett 1800: 18). By contrast, 'enthusiasm, under the specious pretence of piety', is designed to please only the enthusiast (1800: 17). It is a 'boasted mortification', an 'affected self-denial', which is 'only a bartering two sorts of earthly good, namely ease and wealth, for a third, fame' (1800: 17). Fame itself is not ignoble: '... if bodily health and worldly prosperity may be lawfully desired and pursued, so may reputation and honour likewise'; indeed, 'no virtuous man can be indifferent to his reputation' (1800: 18–19). It is, rather, the hypocrisy of fame-seeking which *scorns* fame that for Stennett is a kind of disorder or disharmony in itself. In the end it serves its own vaunted cause no more than it serves any other, and is soon found out. Those who practise it finally 'retire from society into silence and inactivity', and, 'amidst all their splendid professions' of faith, give others cause to ask 'whether they have any just idea of the nature of religion, or have ever entered into the genuine spirit of it' at all (1800: 16–17). 'Enthusiasm' thus ends by defeating itself. In these damning terms do the *Discourses*' pronouncements on the orderliness and harmony of home-life articulate an abhorrence of what is astringent, asocial and uncompromising.

If these things are unattractive in general, they are the more particularly regrettable in those whose responsibility it is to govern the home and to set the tone of home-life for its inhabitants. As Cicero warned Mark Antony to be rather loved than feared, so eighteenth-century conduct manuals admonished householders to rule gently and not with force. This represents a second motif of advice literature by means of which authors like those examined here articulated an identifiably irenic vision of the Christian faith. *The Whole Duty of Man*, for instance, advises: 'The *Master*' of the house 'in all affairs ... is to give reasonable and *moderate commands*, not laying greater burdens on his servants than they are able to bear' ([Allestree] 1659: 328). He is likewise 'to give' those under his command '*encouragement* in well doing, by using them with that bounty and kindness which their faithfulness and diligence and piety deserves' (1659: 328). 'Finally[,] in all his dealing with them, he is to remember that himself hath, as the Apostle saith, *Ephes.* 6 9. *A Master in heaven*, to whom he must give an account of the usage of his meanest servant on earth' (1659: 328).

The logic of the admonition to rule gently is that what is reasonable and tolerable to human nature will best induce dependents to undertake their duties. As God in his mercy induces mankind to faith by conforming religion to human nature, making attachment to it a matter of 'interest' and not simply of obligation, so 'it is the duty of *Masters*' to superintend – including, when necessary, 'to admonish and reprove their servants' ([Allestree] 1659: 326) – 'in a *due manner*, that is so as may be most likely to do good' (1659: 327). Religious toleration, too, was a form of admonition and reproof delivered gently so as to do good. *The Whole Duty* could have offered no clearer model than that of kindly domestic authority for the spirit of gentle inducement to conformity that animated the policy.

Stennett's *Discourses*, too, rehearse the argument that gentleness in authority is more effective than force. As Vickery (2009: 8, 184) has noted it often was, the example of the prophet Joshua is given – tellingly, since the free vote Joshua gave to the Israelites to 'choose you this day whom you will serve' was often cited by tolerationists in support of toleration. Stennett invites the reader to imagine 'the Christian *presiding in his family*, and see how happily the fear of God assists him in the exercise of that authority with which nature has invested him (1800: 57). 'His object', Stennett avers – and it is instruction as much as observation – 'will be to make all under his care happy. But domestic happiness is not to be enjoyed where the master is churlish, morose, and severe. Set on the gratification of his peevish humours, and the making all about him submit obsequiously to his contemptible idea of despotic power, he may be feared, but he cannot be loved' (1800: 57). If he wishes to be loved, he 'will value his authority, as a parent and a master, no further than as it is a means to promote the welfare of those entrusted to his care' (1800: 57). 'And if on any occasion the resolute exertion of it becomes necessary' – as the Church of England's defence of the truth of its teachings was necessary – 'he' who is truly Christian 'will not forget to blend prudence, forbearance, and good nature' – tolerationist qualities all – 'with it' (1800: 57).

'Domestic happiness is not to be enjoyed where the master is churlish, morose, and severe': much the same kind of advice as is offered to male householders is offered also to women in positions of domestic authority. In the female case, unsurprisingly, this advice often centres on the management of children. In chapter 13 of *The Whole Duty of a Woman*, for instance – entitled 'Of the House, Family and Children' – Kenrick writes that: 'She should keep them more in Awe of her Kindness than of her Power' ([Kenrick] 1737: 138). Indeed, Kenrick is clear that 'she must begin early to make them love her, that they may obey her' (1737: 137). 'She should deny them [anything they may want] as seldom as she can, and when there is no avoiding it, she must do it gently' (1737: 137). 'A Mother is not to expect Returns of Kindness' from her children 'without Grains of Allowance' (1737: 137). For a happy life, Kenrick encourages his female readers to appeal to a child's sense of their 'Interest', in the same way that Stennett would bring order and harmony to society by leaving each in his private sphere to the pursuit of his temporal interests (1737: 137). 'When there is no avoiding' chastising children, a mother 'must flatter away their ill-Humour' as soon as possible, 'and take the next opportunity of pleasing them in some other thing, before they either ask or look for it: This will strengthen her Authority, by making it soft to them, and confirm their Obedience, by making it their Interest' (1737: 137). Deploying language taken directly from the toleration debate, Kenrick urges: 'The kind and severe Part must have their several Turns seasonably applied; but your Indulgence is to have the broader Mixture, that Love, rather than Fear, may be the Root of their Obedience' (1737: 138).

As Kenrick's text proceeds to explain, much the same maxim applies to a woman's treatment of her servants. 'Returns of Kindness and good Usage, are

FIGURE 8.4: 'The Diligent Mother', 1740 (1885). Engraving based on an original painting by Jean Simeon Chardin. A mother examines the sub-standard piece of cloth produced by her daughter. Scissors hang from a length of ribbon at the mother's waist. © The Print Collector / Print Collector / Getty Images.

as much due to such of them as deserve it, as their Service is due to us when we require it' ([Kenrick] 1737: 139). A woman in domestic authority 'will be so much the more obey'd as she is less imperious' (1737: 139). Kindness and good usage are also figured as the proper foundation of marital obeisance. In chapter 11 of *The Whole Duty of a Woman*, entitled 'Of Wives', Kenrick observes that the married state without love is mere lordliness in a man and abasement in a woman: 'Love ... is the most essential Requisite', he writes; 'without this [marriage] is only a Bargain and Compact: a Tyranny, perhaps, on the Man's Part, and a Slavery on the Woman's' (1737: 109). What is unloving is unliveable, for heartfelt 'Union' is that which 'facilitates all other Duties of Marriage; makes the Yoke sit so lightly, that it rather pleases than galls' (1737: 109).

An atmosphere of 'order, harmony, and devotion', as well as a set of relationships maintained upon a basis of 'Kindness and good Usage', were evidently taken to be essentials of happy home-life in the eighteenth century. More than this, they expressed an irenic sensibility the articulation of which, we may suppose, gained force from the domestic terms in which it was couched. A further such set of terms was furnished, our sources suggest, by another recurrent theme of the conduct literature: neighbourliness. Often the theme of neighbourliness was elided in such sources with that of 'charity', commonly in the period a synonym for religious toleration.

Stennett's *Discourses* explicitly figure neighbourliness as a training in the virtues underpinning 'Charity'. It is a training undertaken in the home. 'Charity, we usually say, begins at home' (Stennett 1800: 23). Stennett thinks this obvious: 'it is', he remarks, 'a plain dictate of nature, that offices of benevolence should originate among our most intimate connections, and so proceed, by gradual progression, to those at the remotest distance from us' (1800: 23). Neighbours form a crucial link in the chain between family and the world at large, where 'Charity' and 'benevolence' have their proper application (1800: 23). 'Men eminent for a disinterested and public spirit, have generally given distinguished proofs of a humane and friendly disposition' nearer to home (1800: 23). Little is 'to be expected from those, however warm their professions of zeal for the public good may be, who pay little or no attention to the important obligations of consanguinity, neighbourhood, and private friendship' (1800: 23).

Stennett calls the 'offices of benevolence' he advocates 'obligations', but in the spirit of a practical faith he hastens to observe that they are also pleasant to perform. Indeed, in Stennett's words, 'This is an argument addressed to a passion which every one feels, a passion which cannot be eradicated from the human breast, and which, when duly regulated' – for all passions may be carried to excess – 'will not fail to operate to the general good' (1800: 38). Stennett dwells upon the point, recognizing that 'Charity' can take many forms: 'Here let us advert a moment to the refined and exalted pleasure, which results from the idea of being the instruments of communicating happiness to our fellow creatures – What a gratification must it be to a man of a generous spirit, to rescue a family from poverty and wretchedness, and to restore cheerfulness and joy to the gloomy mansion of the widow and fatherless! How exquisite must be the sensations of an affectionate parent, whilst he realizes, in all the future honour, happiness, and usefulness of his rising offspring, the rich and lasting fruits of his unwearied attention to their best interests!' (1800: 38). The happy effects of charity are not only felt on the domestic scale; the spirit of charity, according to Stennett, also undergirds our relations with one another in society. In just the same way as to recognize the 'interests' of others might lead 'a man of a generous spirit' to acts of philanthropy, so it forms the basis also of the respect that we owe to our neighbours in leaving each to the enjoyment of his 'civil and religious rights and liberties' (1800: 23–26).

In the *Discourses*, neighbourliness is cognate with 'hospitality', which Stennett figures as a prime expression of a neighbourly spirit. The reception we extend to one another creates an opportunity not only for Christian fellowship but also to fulfil our duty of 'acknowledging the bounty of heaven, in the presence of . . . guests' (Stennett 1800: 399). To God 'you owe your substancy, houses, families, servants, leisure, and all your opportunities of shewing kindness to others in this pleasing way' (1800: 392). Consequently, to him 'who hath given you ability and hearts to be hospitable' you owe it to 'be prudent in the management of your concerns' so that these gifts may duly be shared (1800: 392). This means avoiding wantonness as well as miserliness in your distribution of them. 'In order to our acquiring an ability to be hospitable, it is necessary that we should be prudent as well as industrious. Extravagance is very nearly as inimical to this duty as sloth: this prevents our obtaining the means of generosity, that deprives us of them as soon as we possess them. Oeconomy, therefore, is to be strictly regarded, [but] here the line is to be drawn between profusion and parsimony'; the one no more to be recommended than the other (1800: 383–84). Thus: 'take heed that generosity does no precipitate you into extravagance. Do not affect splendour, and be cautious how you aspire to an equality with those whom Providence has placed in a superiour rank to yourselves. This is a vanity to which mankind are very prone, and, if it be indulged, will not only displease God, but lessen you in the opinion of all wide and discerning people' (1800: 392).

The irenic character of Stennett's advice on hospitality is twofold. On the one hand, to do kindness to another is a fitting return to God for the kindness he has shown to each of his creatures. On the other hand, in showing mankind that kindness God has placed individuals in a particular station, and it is the individual's duty to affirm the dispensations of providence by acting kindly within his station. Stennett returns a number of times to this last point; inequality of station clearly subtends hospitality, which depends for such value as it has on the condescension of one person to another. Indeed, he presses his readers to recognize the superior strength of kindness that emanates from an uncompelled heart as compared with social relations founded upon a principle of 'wanton . . . meddling with the characters and affairs of other people' (Stennett 1800: 441). 'Mutual freedom, confidence, and good nature, are necessary to the right management of [our] business. Nothing should be forced, but all flow on with ease and pleasantry' (1800: 441).

Stennett's is not the only text to articulate an irenic vision of the Christian faith in terms of domestic hospitality. Wetenhall Wilkes' *A Letter of Genteel and Moral Advice to a Young Lady* also figures the anti-enthusiast as one who repays the blessings of providence by modeling in her own life the 'wise and reasonable' spirit which the creator exemplifies in establishing order and harmony in creation (Wilkes 1740: 120). In mankind, Wilkes proposes, and in women especially, that spirit is expressed best in acts of beneficence and hospitality: 'As whatever worldly Substance you enjoy, is the Gift of Providence; make it, in all Cases, serve the wise and reasonable Ends of a beneficent, hospitable Life' (1740: 120). Wilkes is even prepared to allow that 'Though gaming is an Amusement, which, in general Terms, ought to be avoided', the dictates of hospitality are such that if it is 'sparingly practised, to entertain Company . . . it may be innocent' (1740: 122). Indeed, it is a test of the Christian's 'wise and reasonable' disposition, for as 'All Pleasures are abus'd, if not regulated, with Moderation and Prudence' (1740: 122), so if undertaken 'to be complaisant . . . and to comply with the Amusements of [one's] Company' (1740: 122) – that is, like the well-regulated 'Stage', 'made an useful Entertainment' (1740: 122) – then they may in fact prove the very expression of a Christian disposition.

Maintaining a hospitable home entails a number of duties: 'Never keep any more Servants, than you can very well afford to maintain' (Wilkes 1740: 120); 'It is a great Art, in House-keeping, to have the Furniture always clean' (1740: 120); and so on. Attending to these duties readies the home for any visitor. They serve the end of socialization, for 'The Mind never unbends itself more agreeably, than in the Enjoyment of discreet and virtuous Friends. Their Conversation clears, and improves the Understanding; eases and unloads the Mind; sooths and allays the Passions' (1740: 124). In later editions of Wilkes' *Letter*, these easings and unloadings, soothings and allayings are said to yield a number of virtuous dispositions: 'Clemency' (Wilkes 1746: 188), 'Lenity' (1746: 188) and 'Generosity' (1746: 188), as well as the aversion of a moderate and reasonable mind to the 'Spleen' (1746: 189), 'Panicks' (1746: 188) and 'Alarms' (1746: 188) of those wont to let 'Passions get the better of . . . Reason' (1746: 192).

The Whole Duty of a Woman draws the link between hospitality and toleration explicitly. Hospitality opens our hearts, for it exposes us in our homes, where we are most vulnerable, to others. 'We . . . feel' keenly 'the

Wrongs done to ourselves and [our] Families' there, and we 'are as much sensible of the Benefits we enjoy from the just and kind Dealings of those with whom we are concern'd' ([Kenrick] 1737: 11). 'Hereby we are in the shortest and plainest way admonish'd of our Behaviour to others' (1737: 11). This is a version of the golden rule. It is a crucial admonition, for if we could but open our hearts as fully as we ought, 'There would be no private Quarrels and Uneasiness among Neighbours, since by this Rule of doing as we would be done unto, all rash Censures, sharp Reflections, ungrounded Suspicions and Jealousies, which are the Seeds of private Animosities, are taken away' (1737: 11). Moreover, could we but learn to open our hearts beyond the doorstep as fully as we are admonished to open them at home, 'All persecutions for Consciences sake, which have occasion'd such violent Disorders and vast Effusion of Blood, would be at an End' (1737: 11). Kenrick is unequivocal: 'To compel Men by Fire and Faggot to partake even of a delicious Entertainment, is a savage sort of Hospitality' (1737: 11). The reference to the history of religious persecution in this section of Kenrick's text is overt, making toleration the obvious backdrop against which to read it.

Kenrick's account of hospitality's tendency to lay one open to 'Wrongs' and 'kind Dealings' alike reveals home to be a morally fragile place. It is understood by writers of conduct literature to be a site of human propinquity; a space within which, by a process of moral diffusion, attitudes and dispositions either pious or impious might extend their influence. Far from shying away from this fact, the writers examined here embraced it. They evidently saw home and home-life as essential training in the art of getting things right. If communal living thus represented a lesson in Christian socialization, so, too, did writers' exhortations to readers to embrace this fact of home-life. This forms a fourth motif in the conduct literature examined here. Bringing home to men and women the horrors of disorder, what propinquity promised to teach them was piety with peace. It was therefore another opportunity for writers like ours to articulate a spirit of Cristian irenicism in terms that were homespun and familiar.

It is the model of moral diffusion which informs the many exhortations in conduct literature to exemplary leadership on the part of male heads of household. This is Stennett's tack, for instance, in the *Discourses*. Having enumerated various Christian duties to be observed in family life, Stennett tells his reader: 'Although the duties just recommended were discharged, in regard of the external expressions of them, with the greatest punctuality, yet their ends would in all probability be defeated, if the heads of families were wholly inattentive to their own tempers and conduct' (1800: 70). 'It is religion that lays the ax at the root of vice, and enables a master, feeling the force of it in his own heart, to take such measures as will effectually prevent, with the blessings of God, the seeds of immorality from growing up in his house, and spreading their noxious influence all around him' (1800: 60). Elsewhere in the *Discourses*, 'noxious influence' is rendered as 'spread[ing] gloom' (1800: 347).

In such passages, Stennett is conscious of how easily given to ill-use is that which God intends for our edification. Citing salutary examples from the Bible, he observes: 'These family associations might . . . if properly managed, have been innocent, useful and commendable' (Stennett 1800: .417); yet, 'They unhappily became the *occasions* of sin' (1800: 417). In *The Whole Duty of Man* it is not so much the male householder's headship as the physical and spiritual proximity into which those in his care are thrown that is Allestree's concern in this respect. For instance, the 'Kindness and *love* between *Brethren* and *Sisters* ought to be very firmly grounded in their hearts', Allestree writes, for 'if it be not, they will be of all others in most danger of disagreeing; for the continual conversation that is among them, whilst they are at home in the fathers house, will be apt to minister some occasion of jar' ([Allestree] 1659: 306). In a plea that has obvious application to the situation of a country divided by confession, Allestree begs: 'let all who have brethren and sisters, possess their minde with a great and real kindness to them, look on them as parts of themselves, and then they will never think fit either to quarrel with them, or to envie them any advantage, any more then one part of the body does another of the same body' (1659: 307).

This corporate vision of the household identifies male headship of dependents, as well as 'continual conversation' between siblings, as vectors for the diffusion either of piety or sin. But other such vectors also attract our writers' attention. The system of ranks and orders is another, as is the dependence of servants upon masters (Stennett 1800: 249–53). The duty of 'the wise to instruct the ignorant', of 'the strong to help the weak', of the teacher to 'teach . . . the scholar', of the 'mature' to 'cherish the young': these, too, are vectors for the diffusion either of good or ill (1800: 248–49). In texts concerned specifically with women's roles in the home, wives and daughters are also figured as such vectors. We see this particularly clearly in two texts: White Kennett's *The Excellent Daughter* and Thomas Gisborne's *Enquiry into the Duties of the Female Sex*.

In *The Excellent Daughter*, Kennett draws attention to the fact that female qualities which might be deemed the finest adornment of a home – chiefly, 'Modesty', 'Meekness' and 'Industry' – might also cost the home its reputation entirely if not cultivated to godly purposes (1742: 4). As *The Excellent Daughter* puts it: 'Those Endowments we before mentioned, must be sanctified by Religion, or else they may be useless, or perhaps pernicious, common, or unclean' (1742: 13). '*Modesty* without a Principle of Conscience may be Bashfulness unbred' (1742: 13); '*Meekness* and Quietness of Mind, without Religion, may be no better than a Softness or Heaviness of Temper' (1742: 14); and '*Industry* and Diligence, if they are never so great in prophane and irreligious Women, what are they but Art and Craft, and the Sordid Humour of a worldly Mind' (1742: 15). Gisborne's *Enquiry* focuses on the role of the housewife, though preaches to the same effect: 'Among the most important of the duties peculiar to the situation of a married woman', he writes, 'are to be placed those arising from the influence which she will naturally possess over the conduct and character of her husband. If it be scarcely possible for two persons connected by the ties of common friendship, to live constantly together ... without gradually approaching nearer and nearer in their sentiments and habits' – whether for better or for worse – 'still less probably is it, that from the closest and most attractive of all bands of union', marriage, 'a similar effect should not be the result' (Gisborne 1797: 245).

Such attitudes yielded beliefs shocking to modern eyes, such as the presumption that good women had a duty to remain with bad husbands in an effort to reform their waywardness (Vickery 2009, ch. 7; [Kenrick] 1737, chs. 11 and 12; Gisborne 1797, ch. 12). For our purposes, the interest of these attitudes lies in how strongly they testify to a sense of home as a morally precarious place: an incubator of virtue but also of vice. In this respect, home taught a lesson about national life of which it was evidently a microcosm. As it is 'happy', in Stennett's word, to see virtue fostered in the home by such close 'friendship and harmony' as home-life enables, so it is happy 'to see all ... public bodies of men, particularly religious societies or churches', in a like condition (1800: 328). Best of all is to see 'the subjects of one kingdom, at peace among themselves' (1800: 328).

References to biblical 'civil war' suggest that the seventeenth century is the proper backdrop against which to read such comments: in 'the civil war, which so long prevailed between the two houses of *Saul* and *David*', Stennett explains, the men of these houses wanted 'the character of brethren' and thus were unable 'to enjoy the sweets of internal peace and prosperity' (1800: 328). As in all divided tribes, 'Civil feud and animosities were excited, the laws trampled underfoot, public authority treated with contempt, the nerves of government relaxed, the national counsels infatuated, mutual confidence broken, and the horrors of inhumanity, oppression, and violence, spread far and wide' (1800: 193–94). The message of writers like Stennett, White Kennett and Thomas Gisborne is plain: all this was avoidable. Had 'the character of brethren' been cultivated at home, 'peace' rather than war might have prevailed at large. Home-life proffers the same stark choice that human beings thrown together in civil society face: choose 'friendship and harmony' or make yourself a prey to 'feud and animosities'. A clearer statement than this of the spirit of religious toleration it is difficult to imagine.

Friendship and harmony require assistance, of course, and writers of conduct guides do not fail to suggest how they might best be cultivated. Various proposals are offered to readers. But among the most important of these – it forms the fifth of the six motifs examined in this chapter – is the insistence that inhabitants of Christian homes adopt a proportionate attitude to piety. Important as it is to carry Christ in one's heart, a puritanical refusal to relax the vital sinews of faith risks taxing them to the point of exhaustion. The texts examined here deploy a very particular language – that of Christian 'prudence' – to underscore the need both to observe and to manage the latitude to which, inevitably, injunctions to relax faith's sinews will lead. When Allestree, for instance, discourses at length on men's duties in connection with sleep, it is this lesson that he repeatedly draws.

Sleep being the ultimate in the relaxation of *all* sinews, including those of faith, Allestree evidently regards it as a test-case for the virtue he calls 'temperance' ([Allestree] 1659: 177–206). Like piety, sleep must be neither too much nor too little practiced. Anything but 'temperance' in the use of it is enervating. Allestree points up the irony of enervation of this kind: 'the end for which *sleep* was ordained by God is the refreshing and supporting of our frail bodies' (1659: 197). Our bodies 'being of such a temper that continual labour and toil wearies them out, *Sleep* comes as a Medicine to that weariness, as a repairer of that decay, so that we may be enabled to such labours as the duties of Religion or works of our Calling require of us' (1659: 197). Since '*Sleep* was intended to make us more profitable, not more idle', it must therefore be taken in moderation: 'we give rest to our breasts; not that we are pleased with their doing nothing, but that they may do us' – and God – 'the better service' (1659: 197). 'A moderate degree' thus 'serves best' (1659: 197).

The principle of moderation being the keynote here, *The Whole Duty* refuses any more definitively than that to lay down the law with its readers. Observing the rule of many an eighteenth-century conduct guide that proportionality in piety is best, Allestree writes that in what concerns rest from labours and devotion 'you may judge what is *temperate sleeping*' ([Allestree] 1659: 197). 'It will be impossible to set down just how many hours is that moderate degree, because as in *eating* so in *sleep*, some constitutions require more than others' (1659: 197–98). It is an expression of the spirit of latitude that 'Every mans own experience must in this judge for him'; Allestree's only stipulation is 'let him judge uprightly and not consult with his sloth in the case, for that will still, with *Solomon's sluggard*, cry, *A little more sleep, a little more slumber, a little more folding of the hands to sleep*' (1659: 198). Other matters of domestic routine Allestree similarly leaves to the exercise of discretionary judgement. It is both a householder's right and his duty to determine such matters for himself and his dependents.

Both the injunction to rest itself, and the instruction to exercise discretionary judgement in determining the appropriate amount of it, expressed an anti-puritanical, essentially irenic spirit of faith. That spirit also found expression in the admonitions of conduct guides to heads of household to proportion piety most carefully of all to children. No person's faith ought to be too hard to bear. But children especially are a salutary case, reminding the Christian that the taste of faith ought generally to be sweet rather than bitter. Stennett's *Discourses* articulate this position in discussing rules to be observed on the Sabbath.

Rules, especially on that day, matter. Accordingly, 'as every pious man will feel himself obliged to pay a due regard to public worship, so they who have families must be sensible it is their duty, too, to oblige their children and servants to attend regularly upon it' (Stennett 1800: 68). Advice follows about attendance at 'divine service', and about the 'watch' that a head of household must keep over his dependents' 'demeanour' at the two services that ought to be the business of a Sunday (1800: 68). They should be 'serious and attentive' (1800: 68).

But 'at the close of the two stated services', when 'the whole family should retire to their own home', the *Discourses*' instructional tone shifts gear, with the emphasis now falling on the householder's prerogative to do as he sees fit (Stennett 1800: 68). 'Visits . . . should be interdicted', Stennett makes clear, 'except where offices of mercy are required' (1800: 68). 'And all social intercourses for the purpose of mere amusement' should be 'avoided' (1800: 68). But otherwise discretion is the keynote: 'Opportunity should be given every one to recollect seriously by himself what he has been about' (1800: 68). A head of household may feel that 'a suitable exercise in the evening, wherein the younger part of the family may have an opportunity of giving an account of what they have heard' at church 'will happily and usefully close the day' (1800: 68–69). But 'Religion, I am sensible, should not be made a burden: and young minds especially should not be held too long to one subject' (1800: 69). Stennett's preference is for a faith that is liveable and even congenial rather than heavy-duty: 'As therefore two public services in the day will be sufficient, so prudence will teach the master of a family to direct his discourse in the intervals of worship, and to diversify the evening exercise in such a manner, as that, with the agreeable refreshments nature has provided, no one may have cause to say that this is the most unpleasant day in the week' (1800: 69).

The language of 'prudence' we find deployed across the sources examined here. It is a language that was intimately associated with toleration. No wonder: it was a version of 'discretion'. Edward Stillingfleet, an early latitudinarian, used it to approve St. Paul's policy of not foisting on new churches particular forms of worship: Paul, Stillingfleet emphasizes, left the precise details to the 'prudence' of the converts he made (Stillingfleet 1662: 4, 10, 170–71, 186). Similarly, in *The Protestant Religion Vindicated*, John Tillotson from a later generation of latitudinarian churchmen showed that it is a mark of Joshua's prudence – as well as the root of his success – that he left it to his people's judgement to 'choose you this day whom you will serve' (Tillotson 1680: 4–6). When Stennett advises that whilst it is the Christian household's duty to gather daily for private worship, 'the exact time is left to every ones prudence to determine', it is a plea for toleration that he is issuing (Stennett 1800: 88–89). 'Rules' that might be 'propose[d]' ought only to be 'of a prudential kind, and [should] therefore . . . be submitted, with all due caution and deference, to the judgment and discretion of those who preside in families . . . Some of them will be founded on intimations thrown out occasionally in scripture: and, if the scriptures are silent as to the rest, it will not be wondered at, since the circumstances of families widely differ, and of consequence what is merely accidental to this duty, must be left to conscience and prudence to adjust, according to the nature of the case' (1800: 93).

In *A Letter of Genteel and Moral Advice to a Young Lady*, too, the same essentially latitudinarian spirit is to be detected. Like Allestree in *The Whole Duty of Man* and Stennett in the *Discourses*, Wilkes in his *Letter* urges prudential management of domestic life so as not to substitute bitterness for sweetness in the conduct of religious duty. Being active in domestic piety is important, Wilkes notes, and indeed it suits human nature. But he is also keen to emphasize that we must be permitted to relax 'in the Intervals of those devout Offices' (Wilkes 1740: 120). 'The mind cannot be always screw'd up to a pitch of Virtue' (1740: 121); in fact, it must be allowed to 'unbend . . . itself' (1740: 124). The payoff is peace, both within oneself and with others. The mind screwed up to a pitch of virtue is a bossy, puritanical mind, and 'it is an Error, subversive of Christian Charity and of Public Peace, to be rigid in condemning the Opinions, and Professions of others' (1740: 128).

Amidst the advice Wilkes has for young ladies as they seek to unbend their minds 'in the Intervals of Piety, and good Offices', his only absolute insistence is that they ensure that such 'Diversions' as they pursue be 'innocent' rather than sinful or frivolous (1740: 121). This means being careful to structure the time between worship. We are a prey to sinful and frivolous activities when we allow ourselves to become idle and undisciplined in our use of the hours. Such activities diminish our sense of the finitude of our time on earth, for we wallow in them as if death and judgement will not soon be upon us. Thus, the 'innocent Diversions of Life' recommended in domestic conduct manuals such as Wilkes' had as their aim to furnish men and women with means of so conducting themselves as that they should 'lengthen Time in general, and prevent any Part of it to be useless, or tedious' (1740: 121). As Wilkes explains to his readers, 'of all the Methods of unbending the Mind, and of finding Employment for those retir'd Hours, in which we are altogether left to ourselves, destitute of Compony [*sic*] and Business, that is the most noble which places us in the Contemplation of our Divine Original, and the Prospect of being admitted into his beatific Presence' (1740: 124). Wilkes' message is one of moderation: neither virtue screwed up to an insufferable pitch nor vice given free rein by open frivolity. This was the even-tempered spirit in which the Church promulgated toleration in 1689, in preference to a much-mooted policy of comprehension (Spurr 1989). In Wilkes' language, the Church's aim was to check the insufferable pitch to which high-church intolerance had risen but without substituting for it a tolerance so open as to be frivolous. The connections between toleration and discourses of home and home-life were many and intimate.

The spirit of Christian irenicism evoked by authors like Allestree, Stennett, Kenrick and the others would have been half as powerful as it was if not for a further injunction, and a sixth motif, contained within these texts. This injunction made use of the position of the domestic sphere – connected to public life but distinct from it – to urge readers to be the person behind closed doors that they wished to be thought beyond their doorsteps. Many a reputation is undeserved, for reputation is more readily acquired than the authentic and thoroughgoing goodness of which private life is the real test. Domestic conduct guides seized upon the opportunity afforded them by the threshold between public and private to insist on one supreme necessity of home-life: moral consistency as between the public and private self. In all the texts examined here, the dangers of moral *inconsistency* loom large. It is our writers' wish to give peace a solid and secure foundation which preoccupies them.

The Whole Duty of Man has much to say on this score. Among the duties identified in the text as pertaining to men is that of private prayer. '*Private* or *secret Prayer* is that which is used by a man *alone* apart from all others, wherein we are to be more *particular*, according to our *particular* needs, then in *publick* it is fit to be' ([Allestree] 1659: 117). A pious disposition in public must be matched by a pious disposition at home. 'This of *private Prayer* is a duty which will not be excused by the performance of the other of *publick*. They are *both* required, and one must not be taken in *exchange* for the other' (1659: 117). The danger when things are otherwise *The Whole Duty* spells out for the reader: 'whoever is diligent in *publick* prayers, and yet negligent in *private*, it is much to be feared he rather seeks to *approve* himself to *men* then to *God*' (1659: 117).

To offer regular and heartfelt private prayers is one way in which to practise piety at home of the kind one might hope to be known for abroad. Another is to keep the ungodly from one's door, and to 'endeavour to advance piety and godliness among all those that are under [one's] charge' ([Allestree] 1659: 326). Allestree figures this as the extension into the heart of domestic life of the '*spiritual . . . Brotherhood*' which we enjoy publicly among 'those who profess the same Faith with us' (1659: 307). Between the two spheres ought to be no disjuncture; the spirit of the life out of doors and the spirit of the life indoors ought to align. At the heart of this injunction, according to *The Whole Duty*, is the Christian virtue of truth-telling. The truth, Allestree instructs, must be prized in private as fully as in public; pursued as eagerly where the pursuit is not spectated as where it is. Allestree turns to the Bible for an example: 'Of this *David* was so careful, that we see he professes, *Psal.* 101 7. *That no deceitful*

FIGURE 8.5: Queen Anne at prayer in an intimate space by Michael van der Gutch, 1702–14. Note the inscription 'Liturgia Ecclesia Anglicana'. © Hulton Archive / Getty Images.

person should dwell in his house, that he that told lies should not tarry in his sight; so much he thought himself bound to provide that his family might be a kind of Church' (1659: 327).

The text's lengthy discussion of sleep likewise offers Allestree an opportunity to emphasize the necessity of sincerity. As we have seen, *'temperate sleeping'* – neither too much nor too little – is what *The Whole Duty* recommends to readers. Too little leaves one without sufficient energy for 'such labours as the

Duties of Religion or works of our Calling' ([Allestree] 1659: 197). But too much leads one 'into several sins', which Allestree lists 'under this general one of sloth' (1659: 198). One of these sins is the 'waste . . . [of] time', and such 'precious talent [as] was committed to [each] by God to improve' (1659: 198). Another is that 'he injures his body'; 'immoderate *sleep* fills [it] full of diseases, [and] makes it a very sink of humours' (1659: 198). '*Thirdly*, he injures his Soul also, and that not only in robbing it of the service of the body, but in dulling its proper faculties, making them useless and unfit for those imployments to which God hath designed them; of all which ill husbandry the poor Soul must one day give account' (1659: 198). The spectre of hypocrisy – of patent misalignment between the public and outward profession of faith and a private and domestic indifference to it – hovers over these comments. Indeed, as *The Whole Duty* goes on to explain, 'he that *sleeps* away his life' necessarily 'affronts and despises God . . . by crossing the very end of his creation, which was to serve God in an active obedience' (1659: 198–99). Such a man may in his 'outward estate' repeat the pious mantra that 'God saith, *Man is born to labour*', but if that man shall be 'slothful', then 'his practice saith the direct contrary, that man *was born to rest*' (1659: 199). Hypocrisy heaps sin upon sin. Allestree's advice to the reader is to 'take heed therefore of giving thy self to immoderate *sleep*, which is the committing of so many sins in one' (1659: 199).

If it can reasonably be expected of men and women that they should be the same pious Christians in private as they would wish to appear in public, it is only because, in the words of Kenrick quoted above, 'God never lays on us a greater Task than what he affords us both Ability and Opportunities to perform' ([Kenrick] 1737: 12). That being so, and 'the greatest Part of Mankind being necessarily employ'd in making daily Provisions for themselves and their Families', God can have made it no less our 'interest' to practise piety behind closed doors than to practise it among other men and women beyond the doorstep (1737: 12). *The Whole Duty of a Woman* thus joins its male-oriented counterpart in suggesting that we should regard private hypocrisy as an affront to God's plan of creation.

In the *Discourses on Domestic Duties*, too, the spectre of hypocrisy leads Stennett to envisage home-life as a litmus test of faith's sincerity. This expresses itself in Stennett's concern about the likely effects of insincere faith on the part of the head of household in particular. It is not his own soul alone which is ill-served by his moral hypocrisy. His dependents' spiritual health, too, must suffer: 'zeal for certain principles in religion, they will, in such care, let down to the account of narrowness, bigotry, and hypocrisy. The religious order observed in the family, they will consider as a mere form, the effect of education and custom. And the duties of public worship itself. . .they will treat with indifference, if not contempt' (Stennett 1800: 71). Stennett's only consolation, faced with this dispiriting possibility, is that 'such wretchedly inconsistent characters as these, are, I hope, rarely to be met with' (1800: 71). For there is such a force of 'truth in religion' that 'as it will impel those masters of families, who really possess it, to the observance of the duties we have been recommending, so it will infallibly secure them' – and, by extension, their dependents – 'from those gross evils, which tend to defeat their effect' (1800: 71).

Once again, Joshua is the example to which writers like Stennett turn. Joshua is the model of moral sincerity: of well-aligned inner and outer selves. The force of his example upon his own people drew from them all that made for peace and good order, as Stennett hopes the same example might draw from his readers. 'Here permit me to hold up to your view the temper and conduct of a *Joshua*', Stennett writes, 'who, as he spake ... with unfeigned fervour and sincerity, so, we may be bold to affirm, walked within his house with a perfect heart ... While, in familiar and expressive language, he recommended to [his children and servants] the duties of truth, integrity, modesty, meekness, and benevolence' – irenic and tolerationist dispositions all – 'the native beauty of these virtues, was still more strikingly exhibited to their view in his own countenance and actions' (1800: 71). The happy effects of his sincerity were profound. In describing them, and quoting from Deuteronomy, Stennett's prose rises to its most florid: 'the truths of revealed religion which he taught them, were the genuine sentiments of his own heart: and while his doctrine dropped as the rain, and distilled as the dew, he felt the influence of those divine hopes which the promise made to the fathers of the Messiah was adapted to produce. Deeply impressed himself with the greatness and goodness of God, he daily offered the prayers and praises of his family to Heaven, with a fervour and affection that could scarce fail to excite and enflame their devotion' (1800: 71–72). Crucially, it was the specifically irenic qualities in Joshua which excited and enflamed his people's devotion, and home where he fashioned those qualities: his 'cheerfulness' and 'the benevolence which mingled itself with all his domestic behaviour' (1800: 72).

The sources analysed here articulate an irenic vision of the Christian faith. That vision, if not this articulation of it, has been documented elsewhere by historians interested in the pacific, ethics-oriented version of Christianity that emerged in England in the late-seventeenth century (Rivers 1991, ch. 2; Champion 1992, ch. 7). The texts examined in this chapter chime with that version of Christianity. Practicability forms the core of their moral vision. The emphasis they place on orderliness and harmony; the preference they express for love over fear, especially in what concerns authority; the high importance they accord to neighbourliness and hospitality; the relaxation from piety that they prescribe as an antidote to enthusiasm; the exercise of prudence that they recommend in matters on which to lay down the law would jar: all these are intended to make for a liveable domestic environment. At the same time, all have obvious benefits beyond the home. This essay has argued that it is noteworthy how closely recommendations of this kind for a happy home-life accord with tolerationist recommendations for a happy national life. Understanding that contemporaries saw life behind closed doors as a microcosm of life beyond the doorstep helps us to understand why we might expect this to be so. The texts examined here figure home as the first and best place for learning the lessons germane to a happy national life. Accordingly, the domestic space is one to be prized. Readers are urged to ensure that the private self which reigns at home accords at all times with the public self which enjoys esteem beyond the doorstep. They are also admonished to remember that sin may as readily flourish as virtue in conditions of human propinquity.

The irenic spirit of this advice suggests a tolerationist connection. But it is the spirit in which it is offered as much as the advice itself which points in that direction. Like the policy of toleration, these texts' purpose is to cultivate a liveable environment. But as litanies of *dos* and *don'ts*, patently, their aim is not to fulfil their purposes by withdrawing authority. On the contrary, they seek to promote authority – albeit a peaceable rather than authoritarian authority. The goal is muscular even if the means are gentle: to conquer the spirit of 'magisterialism' that had loosed such bloodshed in the seventeenth century (Klein 1999: xiii–xiv). They are another instance of 'moderation' conceived as 'rule' (Shagan 2011). For William Bulman, this was the essence of eighteenth-century 'Enlightened Anglicanism'. 'Toleration . . . was usually an Enlightened move', Bulman reports, 'and typically defended with calls for peace, moderation, civility, humanity, latitude, and charity' (2015: 210). But it was also a strategy for rule, no less a 'programme' than persecution was 'for achieving political stability and shepherding humans along the path set by God' (2015: 211). That is the idiom in which the domestic prescriptions examined in this essay are written.

It is always difficult to be certain that advocacy translated into action. Given the programmatic character of the domestic advice examined here, it is not to the triumph of anti-prescriptive liberalism in the nineteenth century that we should look for proof of our authors' impact. The better indicator of impact, besides the texts' popularity, is the purchase of languages like 'politeness' and 'enlightenment' in the eighteenth century: languages with which the Christian irenicism articulated in our sources was consonant, and even cognate.

Indeed, the degree of consonance between our texts' vision of Christian moderation and the precepts of 'polite' and 'enlightened' living offers a salutary reminder of how little the achievement of stability in the eighteenth century owed to the retreat of religion (Clark 2012; Haakonssen 1996, Gregory 2009; Shaw 2006). How fully faith remained at the centre of everyday life, customary though it has sometimes been to insist that 'liveability' necessitated a trade-off with faith (Gay 1967). Even Tony Claydon (2006), in a recent review of work by Alexandra Walsham, has written that advocates for toleration 'weighed the demands of spiritual purity against the sometimes opposed considerations of social order, neighbourliness, and kinship'. This 'calculation', Claydon observes, 'explain[s] . . . the persistent reluctance of local magistrates and populations to proceed against those at the heart of settled communities'. What this essay has shown is that spiritual best practice was not so much *weighed against* considerations of order, neighbourliness and kinship as *redefined* – or *defined anew* – in light of them. There was no trade-off for the writers examined here. Rather, home and home-life gave such writers a vocabulary with which to articulate an enlightened spiritual and social vision in which God and good living were powerfully fused.

NOTES

Chapter 1

1. For more information on the development of the concept of home and domesticity in the eighteenth century, see, for example, Amanda Vickery, *Behind Closed Doors: At Home in Georgian England* (New Haven, CT: Yale University Press, 2009), esp. 2–5; Karen Harvey, *The Little Republic: Masculinity and Domestic Authority in Eighteenth-Century Britain* (Oxford: Oxford University Press, 2012), Ch. 1; Karen Lipsedge, *Domestic Space in Eighteenth-Century British Novels* (Basingstoke: Palgrave Macmillan, 2012); Karen Lipsedge and Melinda McCurdy, 'The Interior and the Arts', in Stacey Slaboda (ed.), *A Cultural History of Interiors in the Age of Enlightenment* (London: Bloomsbury Academic, forthcoming).
2. Judith Lewis, 'When a House Is Not a Home: Elite English Women and the Eighteenth-Century Country House', *Journal of British Studies*, 48: 2 (2009), 359.
3. For a detailed account of the representation of the domestic interior in early novels published in the late seventeenth and early eighteenth centuries, see, for instance, C. Wall, *The Prose of Things: Transformations of Description in the Eighteenth Century* (Chicago, IL: University of Chicago Press, 2006).
4. Janet E. Aikins, 'Richardson's "Speaking Pictures"', in Margaret Anne Doody and Peter Sabor (eds.), *Samuel Richardson: Tercentenary Essays* (Cambridge: Cambridge University Press, 1989), 146–66; and Lynn Shepherd, *Clarissa's Painter: Portraiture, Illustration, and Representation in the Novels of Samuel Richardson* (Oxford: Oxford University Press, 1989), 58–111.
5. Aikins, 'Richardson's "Speaking Pictures"', 355.
6. Ellen G. D'Oench, *The Conversation Piece: Arthur Devis and his Contemporaries* (New Haven, CT: Yale Center for British Art, 1980), 1.
7. Carolyn Steedman, *Master and Servant: Love and Labour in the English Industrial Age* (Cambridge: Cambridge University Press, 2007), 196.

8. I. Watt, *The Rise of the Novel* (London: Hogarth Press, 1957). For later, but equally influential works, see Christina Marsden Gillis, *The Paradox of Privacy: Epistolary Form in 'Clarissa'* (Florida: University Presses of Florida, 1984); Nancy Armstrong, *Desire and Domestic Fiction: A Political History of the Novel* (Oxford: Oxford University Press, 1987); Philippa Tristram, *Living Space in Fact and Fiction* (London: Routledge, 1989); Simon Varey, *Space and the Eighteenth-Century English Novel* (Cambridge: Cambridge University Press, 1990); and, more recently, Michael McKeon, *The Secret History of Domesticity: Public, Private, and the Division of Knowledge* (Baltimore, MD: Johns Hopkins University Press, 2005); Wall, *The Prose of Things*.
9. Ruth Perry, *Novel Relations: The Transformation of Kinship in English Literature and Culture, 1748–1818* (Cambridge: Cambridge University Press, 2006), 5.
10. See Lipsedge, *Domestic Space in Eighteenth-Century British Novels*, Ch. 1.
11. A. Ashley Cooper, *Characteristics of Men, Manners, Opinions, Times*, ed. J.M. Robertson (London: G. Richards, [1711] 1900), vol. I, 179.
12. Ibid., 245.
13. Charles Saumarez Smith, *Eighteenth-Century Decoration: Design and the Domestic Interior in England* (London: Weidenfeld & Nicolson, 1993), 53.
14. Ibid., 245.
15. See Karen Lipsedge, '"At Home": The Representation of the Domestic Interior in the Novels of Samuel Richardson and Fanny Burney', in Francesca Sagginni and Anna Enrichetta Soccio (eds.), *The House of Fiction as the House of Life: Representations on the House from Richardson to Woolf* (Cambridge: Cambridge Scholars, 2012), 30–32.
16. Samuel Richardson, *Clarissa; or, The History of a Young Lady*, ed. Angus Ross (Harmondsworth: Penguin, [1747–48] 1985). From now on references to this novel will be included in the main body of the chapter, and the title will be reduced to *Clarissa*.
17. Samuel Richardson, *Pamela; or, Virtue Rewarded*, ed. Peter Sabor (Harmondsworth: Penguin, [1740] 1985) and Frances Sheridan, *The Memoirs of Miss Sidney Bidulph*, ed. P. Koster and J. Coates Clearly, vol. 1 (Oxford: Oxford University Press, 1995). From now on references to these novels will be included in the main body of the chapter, and the title will be reduced to *Pamela* and *Memoirs*, respectively.
18. See *Pamela*, Letter IV.
19. Robert Folkenflik, '*Pamela*: Domestic Servitude, Marriage, and the Novel', *Eighteenth-Century Fiction*, 5: 3 (1993), 254.
20. This is from Sheridan's Dedication for her *Memoirs of Miss Sidney Bidulph* in which she writes: 'The Editor of the following sheets takes this opportunity of paying the tribute due to exemplary Goodness and distinguished Genius, when found united in One Person, by inscribing these Memoirs to The Author of *Clarissa* and *Sir Charles Grandison*' (*Memoirs*). For more on the similarities between the novels of Sheridan and Richardson, see Anna M. Fitzer, 'Mrs. Sheridan's Active Demon: *Memoirs of Miss Sidney Bidulph* and the Sly Rake in Petticoats', *Eighteenth-Century Ireland Society*, 18 (2003), 39–62; and Janet M. Todd, *The Sign of Angelica: Women, Writing and Fiction, 1660–1800* (London: Virago, 1989), 160–75.
21. Charles Saumarez Smith, *The Rise of Design: Design and the Domestic Interior in Eighteenth-Century England* (London: Pimlico, 2000), 167.

22. Margaret Anne Doody, 'Frances Sheridan: Morality and Annihilated Time', in Mary Anne Schofield and Cecilia Macheski (eds.), *Fetter'd or Free? British Women Novelists, 1670–1815* (Athens, OH: Ohio University Press, 1986), 333.
23. Ibid., 338 n.10.
24. Ibid., 345.
25. Edward Copeland and Juliet McMaster, eds., *The Cambridge Companion to Jane Austen* (Cambridge: Cambridge University Press, 2006), 108.
26. Lipsedge, '"At Home", 26–39.
27. See, for instance, Patricia Meyer Spacks, *Privacy: Concealing the Eighteenth-Century Self* (Chicago, IL: University of Chicago Press, 2003), esp. 197; and John Paul Hunter, 'The World as Stage and Closet', in Shirley Strum Kenny (ed.), *British Theatre and the Other Arts, 1600–1800* (Washington, DC: Folger Books, 1984), 282.
28. See Watt, *The Rise of the Novel*.
29. Jonathan Swift, 'A Description of a Morning' (1709), lines 7–8, 3–4.
30. Jonathan Swift, 'A Beautiful Nymph Going to Bed' (1734), lines 9–12.
31. Penelope Wilson, 'Feminism and the Augustans: Some Readings and Problems', in Claude Rawson (ed.), *Jonathan Swift: A Collection of Critical Essays* (London: Pearson, 1994), 790. See also Stacey Sloboba, 'Porcelain Bodies: Gender, Acquisitiveness, and Taste in Eighteenth-Century England', in Alla Myzelev and John Potvin (eds.), *Material Cultures 1740–1920: The Meanings and Pleasures of Collecting* (Burlington, VT: Ashgate, 2009), 19–36; and Elizabeth Kowaleski-Wallace, 'Women, China and Consumer Culture in Eighteenth-Century England', *Eighteenth-Century Studies*, 29: 2 (1996), 153–67.
32. For instance, see Carole Shammas, 'The Domestic Environment in Early Modern England and America', *Journal of Social History*, 14: 1 (1980), 3–24; Margaret Ponsonby, *Stories from Home: English Domestic Interiors, 1750–1850* (Aldershot: Ashgate, 2007), esp. 13; and Leonore Davidoff and Catherine Hall, *Family Fortunes: Men and Women of the English Middle Class 1780–1850*, revised edition (London: Routledge, 2002).
33. Shammas, 'The Domestic Environment', 5.
34. Karen Harvey, 'Men Making Home: Masculinity and Domesticity in Eighteenth-Century Britain', *Gender and History*, 21: 3 (2009), 527.
35. Harvey, *The Little Republic*; David Hussey, 'Guns, Horses and Stylish Waistcoats? Male Consumer Activity and Domestic Shopping in Late-Eighteenth- and Early-Nineteenth-Century England', in David Hussey and Margaret Ponsonby (eds.), *Buying for the Home: Shopping for the Domestic from the Seventeenth Century to the Present* (Aldershot: Ashgate, 2008), 47–72; Shawn Lisa Maurer, *Proposing Men: Dialectics of Gender and Class in the Eighteenth-Century English Periodical* (Stanford, CA: Stanford University Press, 1998); Philip Carter, *Men and the Emergence of Polite Society, Britain 1660–1800* (Harlow: Longman, 2001); and Vickery, *Behind Closed Doors*, esp. Ch. 2.
36. Maurer, *Proposing Men*, 2.
37. Oliver Goldsmith, *The Vicar of Wakefield* (Harmondsworth: Penguin, 1982), 50.
38. Samuel Richardson, *The History of Sir Charles Grandison*, ed. Jocelyn Harris (Oxford: Oxford University Press, [1753] 1986), Charles Grandison, I.xxvii.191;

I.xxxvi.254. From now on references to this novel will be included in the main body of the chapter, and the title will be reduced to *Sir Charles Grandison*.

Chapter 2

1. See Amy Froide, *Never Married: Single Women in Early Modern England* (Oxford: Oxford University Press, 2007), 60, 71, 75; Naomi Tadmor, 'Early Modern English Kinship in the Long Run: Reflections on Continuity and Change', *Continuity and Change*, 25:1 (2010), 31.
2. See Lawrence Stone, *The Family, Sex and Marriage 1500–1800*, abridged edition (London: Penguin, 1990); Randolph Trumbach, *The Rise of the Egalitarian Family: Aristocratic Kinship and Domestic Relations in Eighteenth-Century England* (New York: Academic Press, 1978).
3. See Naomi Tadmor, *Family and Friends in the Eighteenth Century: Household, Kinship, and Patronage* (Cambridge: Cambridge University Press, 2007); Joanne Bailey (Begiato), *Unquiet Lives: Marriage and Marriage Breakdown in England, 1660–1800* (Cambridge: Cambridge University Press, 2003); Helen Berry and Elizabeth Foyster, 'Childless Men in Early Modern England', in Helen Berry and Elizabeth Foyster (eds.), *The Family in Early Modern England* (Cambridge: Cambridge University Press, 2010), 158–83.
4. See the collection of essays in Berry and Foyster, eds. (2010); Karen Harvey, *The Little Republic: Masculinity and Domestic Authority in Eighteenth-Century Britain* (Oxford: Oxford University Press, 2012); Keith Wrightson, 'The Family in Early Modern England: Continuity and Change', in Stephen Taylor, Richard Connors and Clyve Jones (eds.), *Hanoverian Britain and Empire: Essays in Memory of Philip Lawson* (Woodbridge: Boydell Press, 1998), 1–22.
5. This research is the focus of my PhD thesis, see Helen Metcalfe, 'The Social Experience of Bachelorhood in Late-Georgian England, *c.* 1760–1830', PhD dissertation (University of Manchester, 2016).
6. See also Amanda Vickery, *Behind Closed Doors: At Home in Georgian England* (New Haven, CT: Yale University Press, 2009).
7. Froide (2007) is an exception to this exclusion.
8. Accounts that have associated bachelors' lifestyles with feckless behaviour include: Alexandra Shepard, *Meanings of Manhood in Early Modern England* (Oxford: Oxford University Press, 2008); Paul Griffiths, *Youth and Authority: Formative Experiences in England, 1560–1640* (Oxford: Clarendon Press, 1996); Elizabeth Foyster, *Manhood in Early Modern England: Honour, Sex and Marriage* (London: Longman, 1999); Anthony Fletcher, *Gender, Sex and Subordination in England, 1500–1800* (New Haven, CT: Yale University Press, 1999a); Vickery (2009).
9. Dod's and Cleaver's passage can be found in their treatise. See J. Dod and R. Cleaver, *A Godlie Forme of Household Government: for the Ordering of Private Families, according to the Direction of God's Word* (London, 1612), 87–88.
10. The equivalent advice can be found in Dod and Cleaver (1612), 16.
11. See Tara Hamling and Catherine Richardson, *A Day at Home in Early Modern England: Material Culture and Domestic Life, 1500–1700* (New Haven, CT: Yale

University Press, 2017); Amanda Flather, *Gender and Space in Early Modern England* (Woodbridge: Boydell Press, 2007).
12. Original emphasis.
13. See, for example, William Fleetwood, *The Relative Duties of Parents and Children, Husbands and Wives, Masters and Servants; Consider'd in Sixteen Practical Discourses*, 2nd edition (London: John Hooke, 1716), 133, 235.
14. Original emphasis.
15. See James Woodforde, in *The Diary of James Woodforde*, 17 vols., ed. R. L. Winstanley, P. Jameson and H. Edwards (Beeston: The Parson Woodforde Society, [1759–1802] 1985–2013); William Bagshaw Stevens, in *The Journal of the Rev. William Bagshaw Stevens*, ed. Georgina Gailbraith (Oxford: Clarendon Press, 1965); John Ingamells and John Edgcumbe (eds.), *The Letters of Sir Joshua Reynolds* (New Haven, CT: Yale University Press, 2000); Susan Neave and David Neave (eds.), *The Diary of a Yorkshire Gentleman: John Courtney of Beverley, 1759–1768* (Otley: Smith Settle, 2001).
16. See Anthony Fletcher, 'Manhood, the Male Body, Courtship and the Household in Early Modern England', *History*, 84:275 (1999b), 431, 432; Harvey (2012a), 189; Hannah Barker, 'Soul, Purse and Family: Middling and Lower-Class Masculinity in Eighteenth-Century Manchester', *Social History*, 33:1 (2008), 17.
17. Mary killed their mother in 1796 in what has been described as a 'violent fit of insanity'. See Jane Aaron, 'Lamb, Mary Anne (1764–1847)', *Oxford Dictionary of National Biography* (Oxford: Oxford University Press, 2004). Available online: http://www.oxforddnb.com/view/article/15918.
18. See D.A. Kent, 'Ubiquitous but Invisible: Female Domestic Servants in Mid-Eighteenth Century London', *History Workshop Journal*, 28:1 (1989), 111.
19. For further details of sibling animosities, see Amy Harris, *Siblinghood and Social Relations in Georgian England: Share and Share Alike* (Manchester: Manchester University Press, 2012), ch. 3, esp. 87–96.
20. John remained at The Lower House once Woodforde moved into Ansford parsonage following the death of their father two years later.
21. Original emphasis.
22. See also Sheila McIsaac Cooper, 'Service to Servitude? The Decline and Demise of Life-Cycle Service in England', *The History of the Family*, 10:4 (2005), 368–72.
23. Woodforde discharged Luke on 6 April 1768 and hired a George Hutchins on the same day.
24. For shifting notions of service into the nineteenth century, see Tim Meldrum, *Domestic Service and Gender, 1660–1750: Life and Work in the London Household* (Abingdon: Routledge, 2014); McIsaac Cooper (2005).
25. Original emphasis.

Chapter 3

1. My calculations are based on Philip Jenkins, *The Making of a Ruling Class: The Glamorgan Gentry, 1640–1790* (Cambridge: Cambridge University Press, 1983), Appendices 2 and 3, 292–93.

Chapter 5

1. Leonore Davidoff and Catherine Hall, *Family Fortunes: Men and Women of the English Middle Class, 1780–1850* (London: Routledge, 2002); Irene Cieraad, *At Home: An Anthropology of Domestic Space* (Syracuse, NY. Syracuse University Press, 1999); Amanda Vickery, *Behind Closed Doors: At Home in Georgian England* (New Haven, CT: Yale University Press, 2009); Margaret Ponsonby, *Stories from Home: English Domestic Interiors, 1750–1850* (Aldershot: Ashgate, 2007); Jane Hamlett, *Material Relations: Domestic Interiors and Middle-class Families in England, 1850–1910* (Manchester: Manchester University Press, 2014).
2. Most famously in Mark Girouard's *Life in the English Country House: A Social and Architectural History* (New Haven, CT: Yale University Press, 1978), but also Hannah Greig and Giorgio Riello, 'Eighteenth-Century Interiors – Redesigning the Georgian: Introduction', *Journal of Design History*, 20:4 (2007), 273–89.
3. Jurgen Habermas, *The Structural Transformation of the Public Sphere: An Inquiry into a Category of Bourgeois Society*, trans. Thomas Burger (Cambridge, MA: MIT Press, 1989).
4. Amanda Vickery, 'Golden Age to Separate Spheres? A Review of the Categories and Chronology of English Women's History', *The Historical Journal* 36:2 (1993): 383–414. See also, Laura Gowing, '"The Freedom of the Streets": Women and Social Space, 1560–1640', in M.S.R. Jenner and P. Griffiths (eds.), *Londinopolis: A Social and Cultural History of Early Modern London, 1500–1750* (Manchester: Manchester University Press, 2000), 130–52; Vickery, *Behind Closed Doors*, 23–48.
5. Vickery, *Behind Closed Doors*, 27.
6. Michael McKeon, *The Secret History of Domesticity: Public, Private, and the Division of Knowledge* (Baltimore, MD: John Hopkins University Press, 2005).
7. Carolyn Steedman, *Labours Lost: Domestic Service and the Making of Modern England* (Cambridge: Cambridge University Press, 2009).
8. James Krasner, *Home Bodies: Tactile Experience in Domestic Space* (Columbus, OH: Ohio State University Press, 2010), 5.
9. Ibid.
10. Elizabeth Shove, *Comfort, Cleanliness and Convenience: The Social Organization of Normality* (Oxford: Berg, 2003), 20.
11. Dorothy Marshall, *The English Domestic Servant in History* (London: Historical Association, 1949); J. Jean Hecht, *The Domestic Servant Class in Eighteenth-Century England* (London: Routledge & Kegan Paul, 1956); Bridget Hill, *Servants: English Domestics in the Eighteenth Century* (Oxford: Clarendon Press, 1996).
12. Tim Meldrum, *Domestic Service and Gender, 1660–1750: Life and Work in the London Household* (London: Pearson Education, 2000).
13. Steedman, *Labours Lost*, 14.
14. Carolyn Steedman on Adam Smith and John Locke's interpretations of labour in *Labours Lost*, 41, 53.
15. For example, Bridget Hill, *Women, Work and Sexual Politics in Eighteenth-Century England* (Oxford: Basil Blackwell, 1989); I. Baudino, J. Carré and C. Révauger (eds.), *The Invisible Woman: Aspects of Women's Work in Eighteenth-Century Britain* (Aldershot: Ashgate, 2005); Nicola Phillips, *Women in Business, 1700–1850*

(Woodbridge: Boydell and Brewer, 2006); Karen Harvey, *The Little Republic: Masculinity and Domestic Authority in Eighteenth-Century Britain* (Oxford: Oxford University Press, 2012).

16. Leonore Davidoff and Catherine Hall, *Family Fortunes: Men and Women of the English Middle Class, 1780–1850* (London: Hutchinson, 1987).
17. For example, middle-class women's involvement in the anti-slavery campaign of the late eighteenth and early nineteenth centuries.
18. Vickery, 'Golden Age to Separate Spheres?'.
19. See Kathryn Gleadle, 'Revisiting *Family Fortunes*: Reflections on the Twentieth Anniversary of the Publication of L. Davidoff and C. Hall (1987) *Family Fortunes: Men and Women of the English Middle Class, 1780–1850* (London: Hutchinson)', *Women's History Review*, 16:5 (2007): 773–82 for a critical appraisal of this work's contribution and reception.
20. Jane Whittle has published an excellent article on how domestic work has been categorized and understood: 'A Critique of Approaches to "Domestic Work": Women, Work and the Pre-industrial Economy', *Past and Present*, 243 (2019), 35–70; see also Jeanne Boydston, *Home and Work: Housework, Wages, and the Ideology of Labor in the Early Republic* (New York: Oxford University Press, 1990) and for current statistics on women's unpaid work, see http://visual.ons.gov.uk/the-value-of-your-unpaid-work/ (accessed 9 January 2017).
21. Although valuable studies such as Naomi Tadmor, '"In the even my wife read to me": Women, Reading and Household Life in the Eighteenth Century', in J. Raven, H. Small and N. Tadmor (eds.), *The Practice and Representation of Reading in Britain* (Cambridge: Cambridge University Press, 1996), 162–74 have illuminated intellectual practices within middling sort households.
22. Matthew Dimmock, Andrew Hadfield and Margaret Healy (eds.), *The Intellectual Culture of the English Country House* (Manchester: Manchester University Press, 2015).
23. Maurice Howard, '"The Lordship of the Eye": Country Houses as the Setting for Intellectual Enquiry in the Early Modern Period', in Dimmock, Hadfield and Healy, *Intellectual Culture*, 11.
24. Elaine Chalus, 'Elite Women, Social Politics, and the Political World of Late Eighteenth-Century England', *The Historical Journal*, 43:3 (2000), 669–97. See also Carole Shammas, 'The Domestic Environment in Early Modern England and America', *Journal of Social History*, 14:1 (1980), 3–24.
25. Howard, '"The Lordship of the Eye"', 11.
26. Tita Chico, *Designing Women: The Dressing Room in Eighteenth-Century English Literature and Culture* (Lewisburg, PA: Bucknell University Press, 2005). See also Karen Lipsedge, '"Enter into Thy Closet": Women, Closet Culture and the Eighteenth-Century English Novel', in John Styles and Amanda Vickery (eds.), *Gender, Taste, and Material Culture in Britain and North America, 1700–1830* (New Haven, CT: Yale University Press, 2006), 107–22.
27. Bedfordshire and Luton Archive (BLA), Lucas Papers, L 30/9a/3, f. 64: Jemima Grey to Catherine Talbot, 6 June 1741 [copy].
28. Sarah Hutton, 'Damaris Cudworth, Lady Masham: Between Platonism and Enlightenment', *British Journal for the History of Philosophy*, 1:1 (1993), 29–54.

29. Leonie Hannan, 'Scholarship on the Margins: An Epistolary Network', *Women's Writing*, 21:3 (2014), 290–315.
30. Rosemary Sweet, *Antiquaries: The Discovery of the Past in Eighteenth-Century Britain* (London: Hambledon & London, 2004), 310.
31. Elizabeth Eger (ed.), *Bluestockings Displayed: Portraiture, Performance and Patronage* (Cambridge: Cambridge University Press, 2013), 1.
32. Ibid., 8.
33. Amy Prendergast, '"The drooping genius of our Isle to raise": The Moira House Salon and its Role in Gaelic Cultural Revival', *Eighteenth-Century Ireland*, 26 (2011), 95–114.
34. Steven Shapin, 'The House of Experiment in Seventeenth-Century England', *Isis*, 79:3 (1988), 373–404.
35. Deborah E. Harkness, 'Managing an Experimental Household: The Dees of Mortlake and the Practice of Natural Philosophy', *Isis*, 88:2 (1997), 247–62.
36. Clare Hickman, 'The Garden as a Laboratory: The Role of Domestic Gardens as Places of Scientific Exploration in the Long 18th Century', *Post-Medieval Archaeology*, 48:1 (2014), 229–47.
37. Simon Werrett, *Thrifty Science: Making the Most of Materials in the History of Experiment* (Chicago, IL: University of Chicago Press, 2019).
38. Elaine Leong, *Recipes and Everyday Knowledge: Medicine, Science, and the Household in Early Modern England* (Chicago, IL: University of Chicago Press, 2018).
39. Harvey, *The Little Republic*.
40. John Rylands Library (JRL), Stamford Papers, Household Consumption Account Book, GB 133 EGR7/1/1.
41. Margaret Hunt, *The Middling Sort: Commerce, Gender, and the Family in England, 1680–1780*, Berkeley, CA: University of California Press, 1996), 58.
42. Beverly Lemire, *The Business of Everyday Life: Gender, Practice and Social Politics in England, c. 1600–1900* (Manchester: Manchester University Press, 2005), 195, 200. This is issue is also discussed by Harvey, *The Little Republic*, 72–77.
43. Sara Pennell, *The Birth of the English Kitchen, 1600–1850* (London: Bloomsbury Academic, 2016).
44. See Pamela A. Sambrook and Peter Brears (eds.), *The Country House Kitchen, 1650–1900* (Stroud: The History Press, 2010).
45. Carol Barstow, *In Grandmother Gell's Kitchen: A Selection of Recipes Used in the Eighteenth Century* (Nottingham: Nottingham County Council, 2009), 4-5.
46. Shropshire Archives (SA), Styche Hall inventory, 552/12/153 (1825).
47. John Brewer and Roy Porter (eds.), *Consumption and the World of Goods* (London: Routledge, 1993).
48. For an illuminating account of the importance of thrift and recycling in natural philosophy, see Simon Werrett, 'Recycling in Early Modern Science', *British Journal for the History of Science*, 46:4 (2013): 627–46.
49. Harvey, *The Little Republic*, 101.
50. Ibid.
51. See Lisa Jardine, *Ingenious Pursuits: Building the Scientific Revolution* (London: Abacus, 1999), esp. 42–89.

NOTES 211

52. British Library (BL), Evelyn Papers, Add MS 78539, Mary Evelyn to Ralph Bohun, 23 November 1674.
53. C. Anne Wilson, 'Stillhouses and Stillrooms', in Sambrook and Brears (eds.), *Country House Kitchen*, 129.
54. R. Simpson, 'Sir Thomas Smith's Stillhouse at Hill Hall: Books, Practice, Antiquity and Innovation', in Dimmock, Hadfield and Healy (eds.), *Intellectual Culture*, 101–16. See also, P. J. Drury (with a major contribution by R. Simpson), *Hill Hall: A Singular House Devised by a Tudor Intellectual* (London: Society of Antiquaries, 2009).
55. Simpson, 'Sir Thomas Smith's Stillhouse', 103.
56. Wilson, 'Stillhouses and Stillrooms', 129, 136. Diet and health were closely related concepts in the eighteenth century.
57. British Library (BL), Evelyn Papers, Add MS 78539, Mary Evelyn to Ralph Bohun, 4 January 1674.
58. Shropshire Archives (SA), Styche Hall inventory, 552/12/153 (1825).
59. Christina Hardyment, *Home Comfort: A History of Domestic Arrangements* (London: Viking, 1992), 82.
60. Ibid., 83.
61. See Peter Brears, 'Behind the Green Baize Door', in Sambrook and Brears (eds.), *Country House Kitchen*, 30–76, esp. 48, 52.
62. For a detailed description, see Hardyment, *Home Comfort*, 82–89.
63. See Pamela Sambrook, 'Household Beer and Brewing', in Sambrook and Brears (eds.), *Country House Kitchen*, 239.
64. Hardyment, *Home Comfort*, 85.
65. Earlier refrigerator designs used *gutta percha* coils, later ones were made from metal, see Sambrook, 'Household Beer and Brewing', 249–50.
66. Sambrook, 'Household Beer and Brewing', 251.
67. Ibid., 253.
68. Peter Brears, 'The Ideal Kitchen in 1864', in Sambrook and Brears (eds.), *Country House Kitchen*, 15.
69. Julie Day, 'Elite Women's Household Management: Yorkshire 1680–1810', unpublished PhD thesis (2007), 225.
70. Christina Hardyment (ed.), *The Housekeeping Book of Susanna Whatman* (London: The National Trust, 1992), 45.
71. Brears, 'Behind the Green Baize Door', 40–45.
72. British Library (BL), Trumbull Papers, Add MS 72516, Anne Dormer to Elizabeth Trumbull, 10 September *c.* 1687.
73. Ibid., Anne Dormer to Elizabeth Trumbull, 22 June *c.* 1687.
74. Royal Society of Arts (RSA), PR/GE/110/5/18, 18 June 1756.
75. Ibid.
76. Royal Society of Arts (RSA), PR/GE/110/11/2, 1761.
77. Ibid.
78. Royal Society of Arts (RSA), PR/GE/110/11/25, 13 April 1761.
79. Royal Society of Arts (RSA), PR/MC/015/10/469, 21 April 1799.
80. Ibid.
81. Ibid.

82. Royal Society of Arts (RSA), PR/MC/015/10/470, 20 July 1800.
83. Ibid.
84. Ibid.
85. Royal Society of Arts (RSA), PR/GE/110/5/51, 1765.
86. Ibid. For Cornhill fire, see http://www.british-history.ac.uk/old-new-london/vol2/pp170-183 (accessed 7 February 2017).
87. Ibid.
88. Ibid.
89. Ibid.
90. Ibid.
91. Ibid.
92. Elizabeth Wyndham, in 'Papers in Mechanicks', *Transactions of the Society for the Encouragement of Arts, Manufactures and Commerce*, XIV (1796), 295–98.
93. Ibid., 295–96.
94. Ibid., 297.
95. Alison McCann, 'A Private Laboratory at Petworth House, Sussex, in the Late Eighteenth Century', *Annals of Science*, 40:6 (1983), 635–55.
96. Royal Society of Arts (RSA), PR/MC/101/10/468, 26 May 1791.
97. Ibid.
98. Shropshire Archives (SA), C20/2629/1, 'A List of Patents granted under the old law 1617 to 1852'.
99. Ibid.
100. Ibid.

Chapter 6

1. Madrid's Royal Economic Society of Friends of the Country.

Chapter 7

1. Felicity Heal, *Hospitality in Early Modern England* (Oxford: Clarendon Press, 1990), 23–90, 223–56.
2. Ibid., 141–91, 300–88.
3. Hans Conrad Peyer, *Von der Gastfreundschaft zur Gasthaus: Studien zur Gastlichkeit in Mittelalter* (Hannover: Hansche Buchhandlung, 1987); Anna Bryson, *From Courtesy to Civility: Changing Codes of Conduct in Early Modern England* (Oxford: Clarendon Press, 1998).
4. Heal, *Hospitality*, 389–403.
5. Ibid., 1.
6. Raffaella Sarti, *Europe at Home: Family and Material Culture, 1500–1800*, trans. Allan Cameron (New Haven, CT: Yale University Press, 2002), 75–85. Because of the restricted length of the present chapter, it focuses mainly, although not entirely, on Britain.
7. Woodruff D. Smith, *Consumption and the Making of Respectability, 1600–1800* (New York: Routledge, 2002), 210–15.

8. See Neil McKendrick, John Brewer and J.H. Plumb, *The Birth of a Consumer Society: The Commercialization of Eighteenth Century England* (Bloomington, IN: Indiana University Press, 1982), 286–315; Larry Wolff, 'Childhood and the Enlightenment: The Complications of Innocence', in Paula Fass (ed.), *The Routledge History of Childhood in the Western World* (London: Routledge, 2013), 78–99; Sarti, *Europe at Home*, 86–147; Richard L. Bushman, *The Refinement of America: Persons, Houses, Cities* (New York: Knopf, 1992), 100–38, 238–79.
9. Smith, *Consumption and the Making of Respectability*, 189–91.
10. *Oxford English Dictionary*, 2nd edition, 20 vols. (Oxford: Clarendon Press, 1989), 13: 734.
11. Paul Robert, *Dictionnaire alphabétique et analogique de la Langue Française*, 6 vols. (Paris: Littre, 1966), 3: 510–11, 6: 851; Keith Spalding, *An Historical Dictionary of German Figurative Usage*, 5 vols. (Oxford: Blackwell, n.d.), 1: 61–62.
12. This analysis of respectability is developed more fully in Woodruff D. Smith, *Respectability as Moral Map and Public Discourse in the Nineteenth Century* (New York: Routledge, 2018), 23–104 and, in a much more limited way, in Woodruff D. Smith, 'Respectability and the Social Question in the Mid-Nineteenth Century: Constructing a Space of Moral Contestation', in I. van den Broek, C. Smit and D.J. Wolffram (eds.), *Commitment and Imagination: Representations of the Social Question* (Leuven: Peeters, 2010), 1–18.
13. A.M. Wilberforce, ed., *Private Papers of William Wilberforce* (New York: Burt Franklin, [1897] 1968), 45–81.
14. Ibid., 55.
15. The dinner, which occurred in October 1783, was widely publicized at the time. See Noel B. Gerson, *Statue in Search of a Pedestal: A Biography of the Marquis de Lafayette* (New York: Dodd, Mead, 1976), 69–70, and Olivier Bernier, *Lafayette: Hero of Two Worlds* (New York: E.P. Dutton, 1983), 150–51.
16. Wilberforce, ed., *Private Papers*, 57.
17. Gerson, *Statue*, 68; Bernier, *Lafayette*, 150–51.
18. Bernier, *Lafayette*, 144.
19. Ibid., 150. See also (mainly for a later period) Lloyd Kramer, *Lafayette in Two Worlds: Popular Culture and Personal Identities in an Age of Revolutions* (Chapel Hill, NC: University of North Carolina Press, 1996), 92–97.
20. Jacques Gélis, 'The Child: From Anonymity to Individuality', in Roger Chartier (ed.), *A History of Private Life, vol. III: Passions of the Renaissance* (Cambridge, MA: Harvard University Press, 1989), 309–25.
21. Gerson, *Statue*, 73–74.
22. The generic eighteenth-century image of English tea is discussed in greater depth in Smith, *Consumption and the Making of Respectability*, 171–75.
23. Thomas Short, M.D., *Discourses on Tea, Sugar, Milk, Made-Wines, Spirits, Punch, Tobacco, etc., with Plain and Useful Rules for Gouty People* (London: T. Longman, 1750), 32, makes this point explicitly. See Maggie Lane, *Jane Austen and Food* (London: Hambleton Press, 1995), 25–54, for English tea in general.
24. Smith, *Consumption and the Making of Respectability*, 178–81.

25. Patterns of evening entertainment of house guests are described frequently in novels. See, for example, Jane Austen, *Pride and Prejudice* (London: Penguin, [1813] 1972), 81–86, 93–98.
26. See Sidney Mintz, *Sweetness and Power: The Place of Sugar in Modern History* (New York: Penguin, 1989), 112–50.
27. Austen, *Pride and Prejudice*, 58–60.
28. Ibid., 58.
29. Ibid., 132–45.
30. Ibid., 71, 142, 207–10.
31. Ibid., 142.
32. Jean-Louis Flandrin, 'Distinction through Taste', in Roger Chartier (ed.), *A History of Private Life, vol. III: Passions of the Renaissance* (Cambridge, MA: Harvard University Press, 1989), 265–69.
33. Hannah More, *Strictures on the Modern System of Female Education*, 2 vols. (Oxford: Woodstock Books, [1799] 1995), 2: 254–77.
34. Austen, *Pride and Prejudice*, 71, 207–10.
35. Ibid., 191–245.
36. Ibid., 200.
37. Ibid., 204.
38. Ibid., 203.
39. Ibid., 361–68.
40. Bryson, *From Courtesy to Civility*, 203–5.
41. Austen, *Pride and Prejudice*, 361–68.
42. Ibid., 366.
43. For one example out of many that could be cited, see George L. Mosse, *The Culture of Western Europe: The Nineteenth and Twentieth Centuries*, 3rd edition (Boulder, CO: Westview Press, 1988), 17–24.
44. Smith, *Consumption and the Making of Respectability*, 204–10.
45. Frances Burney, *Evelina, or the History of a Young Lady's Entrance into the World* (London: Oxford University Press, [1778] 1968).
46. Ibid., 294.
47. Margaret Anne Doody, *Frances Burney: The Life in the Works* (Cambridge: Cambridge University Press, 1988), 11–34.
48. Burney, *Evelina*, 173–79.

BIBLIOGRAPHY

Archives

Bedfordshire and Luton Archive (BLA), Lucas Papers, L 30/9a/3, f. 64: Jemima Grey to Catherine Talbot, 6 June 1741 [copy].
British Library (BL), Charles Lamb, Add MS 35256, Letters of Charles Lamb to Bernard Barton.
British Library (BL), Evelyn Papers, Add MS 78539, Mary Evelyn to Ralph Bohun, 4 January 1674.
British Library (BL), Evelyn Papers, Add MS 78539, Mary Evelyn to Ralph Bohun, 23 November 1674.
British Library (BL), Gibbon Papers, vol. X, Add MS 34883, Original Letters of Edward Gibbon.
British Library (BL), Gibbon Papers, vol. XI, Add MS 34884, Original Letters of Edward Gibbon.
British Library (BL), Gibbon Papers, vol. XII, Add MS 34885, Original Letters of Edward Gibbon.
British Library (BL), Original Letters of Anne, Countess of Strafford, Add MS 22226, f.135, Anne Strafford, 23 July 1712.
British Library (BL), Trumbull Papers, Add MS 72516, Anne Dormer to Elizabeth Trumbull, 10 September *c.* 1687.
Gillow Archives, Gillow's Letter Books, 1778–81, 344/169.
Gloucestershire Archives (GA), D45/E14, 'An Estimate for Alterations at Gen. Whitmore's' (n.d., 1760s).
Gloucestershire Archives (GA), D45/F4, 'Inventories of goods, linen, etc., belonging to Elizabeth Whitmore of Slaughter House', 1724–35.
John Rylands Library (JRL), Stamford Papers, Household Consumption Account Book, GB 133 EGR7/1/1.
Lewis Walpole Library (LWL), MSS 2/Box 25/Folder 1, Correspondence, Thomas Adams to Elizabeth Adams, his mother, 1758–1782, 30 December 1758, TA, Greys Inn, to EA.

Lewis Walpole Library (LWL), MSS 2/Box 25/Folder 1, Correspondence, Thomas Adams to Elizabeth Adams, his mother, 1758–1782, 11 March 1760.
Lewis Walpole Library (LWL), MSS 2/Box 25/Folder 1, Correspondence, Thomas Adams to Elizabeth Adams, his mother, 1758–1782, 16 May 1761.
Royal Society of Arts (RSA), PR/GE/110/5/18, 18 June 1756.
Royal Society of Arts (RSA), PR/GE/110/11/2, 1761.
Royal Society of Arts (RSA), PR/GE/110/11/25, 13 April 1761.
Royal Society of Arts (RSA), PR/GE/110/5/51, 1765.
Royal Society of Arts (RSA), PR/MC/101/10/468, 26 May 1791.
Royal Society of Arts (RSA), PR/MC/015/10/469, 21 April 1799.
Royal Society of Arts (RSA), PR/MC/015/10/470, 20 July 1800.
Shropshire Archives (SA), C20/2629/1, 'A List of Patents granted under the old law 1617 to 1852'.
Shropshire Archives (SA), Styche Hall inventory, 552/12/153 (1825).
The National Archives (TNA), London, PRO 30/29/4/2, Letter from Frances, Lady Ingram, Temple Newsam, to Susan Stafford, 16 March, n.y.
West Yorkshire Archive Service (WYAS), Pawson MSS, Ac 1038, vols. 6–8.

Primary sources

Adam, Robert and James Adam (1773), *The Works in Architecture of Robert and James Adam, Esquires*, London: Printed for the authors.
Allestree, Richard ([1659] 1704), *The Whole Duty of Man*, London: E. & R. Pawlet.
Angell James, John (1830), *The Family Monitor; or, a Help to Domestic Happiness*, Boston, MA: Crocker & Brewster.
Anon. (1706), *The House-Keeper's Guide, in the Prudent Managing of their Affairs. Being Several Observations relating to the Orderly and Discreet Government of Private Families, Grounded upon Reason, Experience and the Word of God*, London: A Bosvile.
Anon. [Kenrick, W.] (1737), *The Whole Duty of a Woman*, London: T. Read.
Anon. (c. 1790), *Virtue in a Cottage; Or, a Mirror for Children in Humble Life*, London: John Marshall.
Anon. [Lewis, Sarah] (1839), *Woman's Mission*, 4th edition, London: John W. Parker.
Ashley Cooper, A. ([1711] 1900), *Characteristics of Men, Manners, Opinions, Times*, 2 vols., ed. J.M. Robertson, London: G. Richards.
Austen, Jane ([1817] 2006), "Northanger Abbey", in Barbara M Benedict and Dierdre Le Faye (eds.), *The Cambridge Edition of the Works of Jane Austen*, Cambridge: Cambridge University Press.
Bagshaw Stevens, William (1965), *The Journal of the Rev. William Bagshaw Stevens*, ed. Georgina Gailbraith, Oxford: Clarendon Press.
Barbon, Nicholas (1685), *An Apology for the Builder, or a Discourse Shewing the Cause and Effects of the Increase of Building*, London: Cave Pullen.
Beckford, William (1957), *Life at Fonthill 1807–1822*, ed. and trans. Boyd Alexander, London: Rupert Hart-Davies.
Bulbring, Karl D., ed. (1890), *The Compleat English gentleman by Daniel Defoe. Edited for the First Time from the Author's Autograph Manuscript in the British Museum, with Introduction, Notes, and Index by Karl D. Bülbring, M.A., Ph.D.*, London: David Nutt.
Burney, Frances ([1778] 1968), *Evelina, or the History of a Young Lady's Entrance into the World*, London: Oxford University Press.

Campbell, Colen (1715–25), *Vitruvius Britannicus; or, the British Architect*, 3 vols., London.
Carlisle, Isabella Howard (1789), *Thoughts in the Form of Maxims Addressed to Young Ladies, on Their First Establishment in the World, By the Countess Dowager of Carlisle*, London: T. Cornell.
Chippendale, Thomas (1754), *The Gentleman and Cabinet-Maker's Director*, London.
Cotton, Dr. (1796), *Domestic Happiness Exhibited in The Fireside. A Poem*, Glasgow.
Cowper, William ([1784] 1852), The *Poetical Works of William Cowper*, London: T. Nelson.
Defoe, Daniel (1722), *Journal of the Plague Year*, London: E. Nutt.
Defoe, Daniel (1724–27), *A tour thro' the whole island of Great Britain, divided into circuits or journies*, 3 vols., London.
Dod, J. and R. Cleaver (1612), *A Godlie Forme of Household Government: for the Ordering of Private Families, according to the Direction of God's Word*, London.
Edgeworth, Maria (1894), *The Life and Letters of Maria Edgeworth*, 2 vols., ed. Augusta J.C. Hare, London: Edward Arnold.
Fielding, Henry (1749), *Tom Jones*, Book 8, London.
Fleetwood, William (1716), *The Relative Duties of Parents and Children, Husbands and Wives, Masters and Servants; Consider'd in Sixteen Practical Discourses*, 2nd edition, London: John Hooke.
Fordyce, James (1809), *Sermons to Young Women*, 2 vols., 13th edition, London: T. Cadell & W. Davies.
Gibbs, James (1728), *A Book of Architecture containing Designs of Buildings and Ornaments*, London.
Gisborne, Thomas (1797), *An Enquiry into the Duties of the Female Sex*, London: T. Cadell & W. Davies.
Hepplewhite, George (1788), *The Cabinet-Maker and Upholsterer's Guide*, London.
Ince, William and John Mayhew (1762), *The Universal System of Household Furniture*, London: Robt. Sayer.
Ingamells, John and John Edgcumbe, eds. (2000), *The Letters of Sir Joshua Reynolds*, New Haven, CT: Yale University Press.
Jones, William (1824), 'Some Account of the Life and Writings of the Author', in *The Works of Samuel Stennett, D.D.*, London: Thomas Tegg.
Kennett, White (1742), *The Excellent Daughter*, 4th edition, London: J. Wilford.
Lamb, Charles (1935), *The Letters of Charles Lamb: to which are Added those of his Sister Mary Lamb*, 3 vols., ed. E.V. Lucas, London: J.M. Dent.
Lamb, Charles (1975), *The Letters of Charles and Mary Anne Lamb*, 3 vols., ed. Edwin W. Marrs, Jr., Ithaca, NY: Cornell University Press.
La Roche, Sophie von (1933), *Sophie in London, 1786; being the diary of Sophie v. la Roche*, trans. Clare Williams. London: J. Cape.
Loudon, J.C. (1839), *An Encyclopedia of Cottage, Farm and Villa Architecture and Furniture*, revised edition, London: Longmans.
Malthus, Thomas R. ([1803] 1992), *An Essay on the Principle of Population: Or a View of Its Past and Present Effects on Human Happiness: with an Inquiry into Our Prospects Respecting the Future Removal or Mitigation of the Evils Which It Occasions*, selected and introduced by Donald Winch using the text of the 1803 edition, as prepared by Patricia James for the Royal Economic Society, 1990, Cambridge: Cambridge University Press.
Mandeville. Bernard ([1714] 1970), *The Fable of the Bees: or, Private Vices Publick Benefits*, Harmondsworth: Penguin.

Montesquieu, Charles de Secondat, Baron de ([1721] 1973), *Persian Letters*, ed. and trans. C.J. Betts, Harmondsworth: Penguin.

Neave, Susan and David Neave, eds. (2001), *The Diary of a Yorkshire Gentleman: John Courtney of Beverley, 1759–1768*, Otley: Smith Settle.

Nourse, Timothy (1700), *Campania Fœlix; or, A Discourse of the Benefits and Improvements of Husbandry: etc*, London: Tho. Bennet.

Repton, Humphrey (1816), *Fragments on the Theory and Practice of Landscape Gardening,* London: T. Bensley.

Reynolds, Sir Joshua ([1778] 1997), *Discourses on Art*, ed. Robert R. Wark, New Haven, CT: Yale University Press.

Richardson, Samuel ([1740] 1985), *Pamela; or, Virtue Rewarded*, ed. Peter Sabor, Harmondsworth: Penguin.

Richardson, Samuel ([1747–48] 1985), *Clarissa; or, The History of a Young Lady*, ed. Angus Ross, Harmondsworth: Penguin.

Richardson, Samuel ([1753] 1986), *The History of Sir Charles Grandison*, ed. Jocelyn Harris, Oxford: Oxford University Press.

Rochefoucauld, François de la (1933), *A Frenchman in England, 1784: Being the* Mélanges sur L'Angleterre *of François de la Rochefoucauld*, ed. Jean Marchand, trans. S.C. Roberts, Cambridge: Cambridge University Press.

Sheraton, Thomas (1802), *The Cabinet-Maker and Upholsterer's Drawing-Book*, London: T. Bensley.

Sheraton, Thomas ([1803] 1970), *Cabinet Dictionary*, New York: Praeger.

Sheridan, Frances ([1761] 1995), *The Memoirs of Miss Sidney Bidulph*, ed. P. Koster and J. Coates Clearly, 3 vols., Oxford: Oxford University Press.

Short, Thomas, M.D. (1750), *Discourses on Tea, Sugar, Milk, Made-Wines, Spirits, Punch, Tobacco, etc., with Plain and Useful Rules for Gouty People*, London: T. Longman.

Single (Henry Ward), Simon (1772), 'A Map of the Island of Matrimony', in Henry Carey and T.B., *Cupid and Hymen; A Voyage to the Isles of Love and Matrimony*, 4th edition, London: S. Bladon.

Stennett, Samuel (1800), *Discourses on Domestic Duties*, Edinburgh: J. Ogle.

Stillingfleet, Edward (1662), *A Discourse Concerning the Power of Excommunication in a Christian Church, by way of appendix to the Irenicum*, London: Henry Mortlock.

Swift, Jonathan (1709), 'A Description of a Morning'.

Swift, Jonathan (1734), 'A Beautiful Nymph Going to Bed'.

The Book of Trades: Or, Library of The Useful Arts (1804), London: B. & R. Crosby.

Tillotson, John (1680), *The Protestant Religion Vindicated, from the Charge of Singularity and Novelty: In a Sermon Preached before the King at White-Hall, April 2nd 1680*, London: Brabazon Aylmer.

Trussler, John (1785), 'On Domestic Happiness', A Sermon, Enfield, nr. London. British Library 4477.d.120.

Tryon, Thomas (1691), *The Way to Health, Long Life and Happiness*, London: R. Baldwin.

Upcott, William (1825), *The Miscellaneous Writings of John Evelyn, Esq. F.R.S.*, London: Henry Colburn.

Ware, Sir Isaac (1756), *A Complete Body of Architecture. Adorned with Plans and Elevations, from Original Designs*, London: T. Osborne & J. Shipton.

Wilkes, Wetenhall (1740), *A Letter of Genteel and Moral Advice to a Young Lady*, London: E. Jones.

Wilkes, Wetenhall (1746), *A Letter of Genteel and Moral Advice to a Young Lady*, 4th edition, London: C. Hitch.
Wollstonecraft, Mary (1790), *A Vindication of the Rights of Men*, London: J. Johnson.
Wood, John (1765), *A Description of Bath*, vol. II, London.
Woodforde, James ([1759–1802] 1985–2013), *The Diary of James Woodforde*, 17 vols., ed. R. L. Winstanley, P. Jameson and H. Edwards, Beeston: The Parson Woodforde Society.
Wootton, Sir Henry (1624), *The Elements of Architecture*. London: Iohn Bill. Available online: https://archive.org/details/architectureelem00wott/page/n4 (accessed 24 September 2019).
Wyndham, Elizabeth (1796), in 'Papers in Mechanicks', *Transactions of the Society for the Encouragement of Arts, Manufactures and Commerce*, XIV: 295–98.

Secondary sources

Aaron, Jane (2004), 'Lamb, Mary Anne (1764–1847)', *Oxford Dictionary of National Biography*, Oxford: Oxford University Press. Available online: http://www.oxforddnb.com/view/article/15918 (accessed 15 August 2019).
Ackerman, James S. (1990), *The Villa: Form and Ideology of Country Houses*, London: Thames & Hudson.
Aikins, Janet E. (1989), 'Richardson's "Speaking Pictures"', in Margaret Anne Doody and Peter Sabor (eds.), *Samuel Richardson: Tercentenary Essays*, 146–66, Cambridge: Cambridge University Press.
Alblas, J.B.H. (1991), 'Richard Allestree's *The Whole Duty of Man* (1658) in Holland: The Denominational and Generic Transformations of an Anglican Classic', *The Dutch Review of Church History*, 71 (1): 92–104.
Arciszewska, Barbara and Elizabeth McKellar, eds. (2004), *Articulating British Classicism: New Approaches to Eighteenth-Century Architecture*, Aldershot: Ashgate.
Armstrong, Nancy (1987), *Desire and Domestic Fiction: A Political History of the Novel*, Oxford: Oxford University Press.
Arnold, Dana (1998a), 'Defining Femininity: Women and the Country House', in Dana Arnold (ed.), *The Georgian Country House: Architecture, Landscape and Society*, 79–99, Stroud: Sutton Press.
Arnold, Dana, ed. (1998b), *The Georgian Villa*, Stroud: History Press.
Aspin, Richard (2000), 'Who was Elizabeth Okeover?', *Medical History*, 44 (4): 531–40.
Austen, Jane ([1813] 1972), *Pride and Prejudice*, London: Penguin.
Austen, Jane ([1815] 2003), *Emma*, ed. F. Strafford, Harmondsworth: Penguin.
Ayres, James (1998), *Building the Georgian City*, New Haven, CT: Yale University Press.
Bachelard, Gaston (1994), *The Poetics of Space,* trans. Maria Jolas, Boston, MA: Beacon Press.
Bailey (Begiato), Joanne (2003), *Unquiet Lives: Marriage and Marriage Breakdown in England, 1660–1800*, Cambridge: Cambridge University Press.
Bailey (Begiato), Joanne (2012), *Parenting in England, 1760–1830: Emotion, Identity, & Generation*, Oxford: Oxford University Press.
Barker, Hannah (2008), 'Soul, Purse and Family: Middling and Lower-Class Masculinity in Eighteenth-Century Manchester', *Social History*, 33 (1): 12–35.
Barker, Hannah (2017), *Family and Business during the Industrial Revolution*, Oxford: Oxford University Press.

Barker, Hannah and Elaine Chalus (1997), 'Introduction', in Hannah Barker and Elaine Chalus (eds.), *Gender in Eighteenth-Century England: Roles, Representations and Responsibilities*, 1–28, London: Longman.

Barker-Benfield, G.J. (1992), *The Culture of Sensibility: Sex and Society in Eighteenth-Century Britain*, Chicago, IL: Chicago University Press.

Barnard, Toby (2008), *Improving Ireland: Projector, Prophets and Profiteers, 1641–1786*, Dublin: Four Courts Press.

Barstow, Carol (2009), *In Grandmother Gell's Kitchen: A Selection of Recipes Used in the Eighteenth Century*, Nottingham: Nottingham County Council.

Baudino, Isabelle, Jacques Carré and Cécile Révauger, eds. (2005), *The Invisible Woman: Aspects of Women's Work in Eighteenth-Century Britain*, Aldershot: Ashgate, 2005.

Beggs, Courtney (2014), 'Writing from the Road: Space and the Spectacle of Hortense Mancini, Duchess of Mazarin', in Karen B. Gevirtz and Mona Narain (eds.), *Gender and Space in Britain 1660–1820*, 117–31, Farnham: Ashgate.

Benhamou, Reed (1991), 'Imitation in the Decorative Arts of the Eighteenth Century', *Journal of Design History*, 4 (1): 1–13.

Berg, Maxine (1985), *The Age of Manufactures: Industry, Innovation and Work in Britain, 1700–1820*, London: Routledge.

Berg, Maxine (1999), 'New Commodities, Luxuries and their Consumers in Eighteenth Century England', in Maxine Berg and Helen Clifford (eds.), *Consumers and Luxury: Consumer Culture in Europe, 1650–1850*, 000–000, Manchester: Manchester University Press.

Bermingham, Ann (2005), 'The Simple Life: Cottages and Gainsborough's Cottage Doors', in Peter De Bolla, Nigel Leask and David Simpson (eds.), *Land, Nation and Culture, 1740–1840*, 37–62, London: Palgrave Macmillan.

Bernier, Olivier (1983), *Lafayette: Hero of Two Worlds*, New York: E.P. Dutton.

Berry, Helen and Elizabeth Foyster (2010), 'Childless Men in Early Modern England', in Helen Berry and Elizabeth Foyster (eds.), *The Family in Early Modern England*, 158–83, Cambridge: Cambridge University Press.

Borsay, Peter (1989), *The English Urban Renaissance: Culture and Society in the Provincial Town, 1660–1770*, Oxford: Oxford University Press.

Boydston, Jeanne (1990), *Home and Work: Housework, Wages, and the Ideology of Labor in the Early Republic*, New York: Oxford University Press.

Bray, Alan (2003), *The Friend*, London: University of Chicago Press.

Brears, Peter (2010a), 'Behind the Green Baize Door', in *The Country House Kitchen, 1650–1900*, Pamela Sambrook and Peter Brears, 30–76, Stroud: The History Press.

Brears, Peter (2010b), 'The Ideal Kitchen in 1864', in *The Country House Kitchen, 1650–1900*, Pamela Sambrook and Peter Brears, 11–29, Stroud: The History Press.

Bremner, G.A., ed. (2016), *Architecture and Urbanism in the British Empire*, Oxford: Oxford University Press.

Brewer, John (1997), *The Pleasures of the Imagination: English Culture in the Eighteenth Century*, Chicago, IL: University of Chicago Press.

Brewer, John and Roy Porter, eds. (1993), *Consumption and the World of Goods*, London: Routledge.

Broomhall, Susan (2008), 'Emotions in the Household', in Susan Broomhall (ed.), *Emotions in the Household, 1200–1900*, 1–37, Basingstoke: Palgrave Macmillan.

Bryden, Inga and Janet Floyd (1999), 'Introduction', in Inga Bryden and Janet Floyd (eds.), *Domestic Space: Reading the Nineteenth-Century Interior*, 1–17, Manchester: Manchester University Press.

Bryson, Anna (1998), *From Courtesy to Civility: Changing Codes of Conduct in Early Modern England*, Oxford: Clarendon Press.
Bulman, William J. (2015), *Anglican Enlightenment: Orientalism, Religion and Politics in England and its Empire 1648–1715*, Cambridge: Cambridge University Press.
Bush, Michael (1988), *Rich Noble, Poor Noble*, Manchester, Manchester University Press.
Bushman, Richard L. (1992), *The Refinement of America: Persons, Houses, Cities*, New York: Knopf.
Campbell, Colin (1993), 'Understanding Traditional and Modern Patterns of Consumption in Eighteenth-Century England: A Character-Action Approach', in John Brewer and Roy Porter (eds.), *Consumption and the World of Goods*, 40–57, London: Routledge.
Campbell Orr, Clarissa (2002), 'Introduction: Court Studies, Gender and Women's History, 1660–1837', in Clarissa Campbell Orr (ed.), *Queenship in Britain 1660–1837: Royal Patronage, Court Culture and Dynastic Politics*, 1–52, Manchester: Manchester University Press.
Campbell Orr, Clarissa (2009), 'Introduction: Court Studies, Gender and Women's History, 1660–1837', in Clarissa Campbell Orr (ed.), *Queenship in Britain 1660–1837: Royal Patronage, Court Culture and Dynastic Politics*, 1–52, paperback edition, Manchester: Manchester University Press.
Carson, Cary and Carl Lounsbury (2013), *The Chesapeake House: Architectural Investigations by Colonial Williamsburg*, Chapel Hill, NC: University of North Carolina Press.
Carter, Philip (2001), *Men and the Emergence of Polite Society, Britain 1660–1800*, Harlow: Longman.
Chalus, Elaine (2000), 'Elite Women, Social Politics, and the Political World of Late Eighteenth-Century England', *The Historical Journal*, 43 (3): 669–97.
Chalus, Elaine (2005), *Elite Women in English Political Life, c. 1754–1790*, Oxford: Oxford University Press.
Champion, J.A.I. (1992), *The Pillars of Priestcraft Shaken: The Church of England and its Enemies, 1660–1730*, Cambridge: Cambridge University Press.
Chappell, Edward A. (1986), 'Acculturation in the Shenandoah Valley: Rhenish Houses of the Massanutten Settlement', in Dell Upton and John Michael Vlach (eds.), *Common Places: Readings in American Vernacular Architecture*, 27–57, Athens, GA: University of Georgia Press.
Chico, Tita (2005), *Designing Women: The Dressing Room in Eighteenth-Century English Literature and Culture*, Lewisburg, PA: Bucknell University Press.
Cieraad, Irene (1999), *At Home: An Anthropology of Domestic Space*, Syracuse, NY: Syracuse University Press.
Clark, J.C.D. (2000), *English Society 1660–1832: Religion, Ideology and Politics During the Ancien Regime*, Cambridge: Cambridge University Press.
Clark, J.C.D. (2012), 'Secularization and Modernization: The Failure of a 'Grand Narrative'', *The Historical Journal*, 55 (1): 161–94.
Claydon, Tony (2006), 'Reviews in History: *Charitable Hatred: Tolerance and Intolerance in England 1500–1700*' (review no. 568). Available online: https://reviews.history.ac.uk/review/568 (accessed 24 September 2019).
Cockayne, Emily (2007), *Hubbub: Filth, Noise, and Stench in England, 1600–1770*, New Haven, CT: Yale University Press.
Colley, Linda (1992), *Britons: Forging the Nation 1707–1837*, New Haven, CT: Yale University Press.

Connell, David (1998), 'The Grand Tour of William and Winifred Constable 1769–1771', in A.G. Credland (ed.), *Burton Constable Hall: The Eighteenth and Nineteenth Centuries*, 38–55, Beverly: East Yorkshire Local History Series.
Connell, R.W. and James W. Messerschmidt (2005), 'Hegemonic Masculinity: Rethinking the Concept', *Gender and Society*, 19 (6): 829–59.
Cooper, Nicholas (1999), *The Houses of the Gentry, 1480–1680*, New Haven, CT: Yale University Press.
Cooper, Nicholas (2007), 'The English Villa: Sources, Forms and Functions', in Malcolm Airs and Geoffrey Tyack (eds.), *The Renaissance Villa in Britain, 1500–1700*, 9–24, Reading: Spire Books.
Copeland, Edward and Juliet McMaster, eds. (2006), *The Cambridge Companion to Jane Austen*, Cambridge: Cambridge University Press.
Copson, S.L. (2004), 'Stennett, Joseph (1663–1713)', in *The Oxford Dictionary of National Biography*, Oxford: Oxford University Press.
Corfield, Penelope (1995), 'Georgian England: One State, Many Faiths', *History Today*, 45 (4): 14–21.
Cousins, A.D. and Geoffrey Payne (2015), *Home and Nation in British Literature from the English to the French Revolutions*, Cambridge: Cambridge University Press.
Crane, Mary Thomas (2000), '"Players in your huswifery, and huswives in your beds": Conflicting Identities of Early Modern English Women', in Naomi J. Miller and Naomi Yavneh (eds.), *Maternal Measures: Figuring Caregiving in the Early Modern Period*, 212–23, Aldershot: Ashgate.
Craske, Matthew (2004), 'From Burlington Gate to Billingsgate: James Ralph's Attempt to Impose Burlingtonian Classicism as a Canon of Public Taste', in Barbara Arciszewska and Elizabeth McKellar (eds.), *Articulating British Classicism: New Approaches to Eighteenth-Century Architecture*, 97–118, Aldershot: Ashgate.
Cressy, David (1986), 'Kinship and Kin Interaction in Early Modern England', *Past and Present*, 113 (1): 38–69.
Crowley, John E. (2001), *The Invention of Comfort: Sensibilities and Design in Early Modern Britain and Early America*, Baltimore, MD: Johns Hopkins University Press.
Csikszentmihalyi, Mihaly, and Eugene Halton (1981), *The Meaning of Things: Domestic Symbols and the Self*, Cambridge: Cambridge University Press.
Cunningham, Colin (1994), '"An Italian house my lady": Some Aspects of the Definition of Women's Role in the Architecture of Robert Adam', in Gill Perry and Michael Rossington (eds.), *Femininity and Masculinity in Eighteenth-Century Art and Culture*, 63–77, Manchester: Manchester University Press.
D'Oench, Ellen G. (1980), *The Conversation Piece: Arthur Devis and his Contemporaries*, New Haven, CT: Yale Center for British Art.
Dadabhoy, A. (2014), '"Going native": Geography, Gender, and Identity in Lady Mary Wortley Montagu's Turkish Embassy Letters', in Karen B. Gevirtz and Mona Narain (eds.), *Gender and Space in Britain 1660–1820*, 49–66, Farnham: Ashgate.
Davidoff, Leonore and Catherine Hall (1987), *Family Fortunes: Men and Women of the English Middle Class, 1780–1850*, London: Hutchinson.
Davidoff, Leonore and Catherine Hall (2002), *Family Fortunes: Men and Women of the English Middle Class, 1780–1850*, revised edition, London: Routledge.
Day, Julie (2007), 'Elite Women's Household Management: Yorkshire 1680–1810', unpublished PhD thesis, University of Leeds.
De Bellaigue, Christina, ed. (2016), *Home Education in Historical Perspective: Domestic Pedagogies in England and Wales 1750–1900*, London: Routledge.

DeJean, Joan (2009), *The Age of Comfort: When Paris Discovered Casual and the Modern Home Began*, New York: Bloomsbury.
Desmahis, Joseph-François-Édouard de Corsembleu de ([1756] 2004), 'Woman', in *The Encyclopedia of Diderot & d'Alembert Collaborative Translation Project*, trans. Naomi J. Andrews. Ann Arbor, MI: Michigan Publishing, University of Michigan Library. Available online: http://hdl.handle.net/2027/spo.did2222.0000.287 (accessed 27 November 2018). Originally published as 'Femme', in *Encyclopédie ou Dictionnaire raisonné des sciences, des arts et des métiers*, vol. 6, 472–75, Paris.
Deutsch, Phyllis (1996), 'Moral Trespass in Georgian London: Gaming, Gender, and Electoral Politics in the Age of George III', *The Historical Journal*, 39 (3): 637–56.
De Vries, Jan (2008), *The Industrious Revolution: Consumer Behavior and the Household Economy, 1650 to the Present*, Cambridge: Cambridge University Press.
Dickie, Simon (2011), *Cruelty and Laughter: Forgotten Comic Literature and the Unsentimental Eighteenth Century*, Chicago, IL: University of Chicago Press.
Dimmock, Matthew, Andrew Hadfield and Margaret Healy, eds. (2015), *The Intellectual Culture of the English Country House*, Manchester: Manchester University Press.
Doody, Margaret Anne (1986), 'Frances Sheridan: Morality and Annihilated Time', in Mary Anne Schofield and Cecilia Macheski (eds.), *Fetter'd or Free? British Women Novelists, 1670–1815*, 324–58, Athens, OH: Ohio University Press.
Doody, Margaret Anne (1988), *Frances Burney: The Life in the Works*, Cambridge: Cambridge University Press.
Douglas, Mary (1991), 'The Idea of a Home: A Kind of Space', *Social Research*, 58 (1): 287–307.
Douglas, Mary (1992), 'Why Do People Want Goods?', in Shaun Hargreaves Heap and Angus Ross (eds.), *Understanding the Enterprise Culture: Themes in the Work of Mary Douglas*, Edinburgh: Edinburgh University Press.
Douglas, Mary and Baron Isherwood (1996), *The World of Goods: Towards an Anthropology of Consumption*, London: Routledge.
Drury, P. J. (with a major contribution by R. Simpson) (2009), *Hill Hall: A Singular House Devised by a Tudor Intellectual*, London: Society of Antiquaries.
Dwyer, John (1987), *Virtuous Discourse: Sensibility and Community in Late Eighteenth-Century Scotland*, Edinburgh: John Donald.
Eger, Elizabeth, ed. (2013), *Bluestockings Displayed: Portraiture, Performance and Patronage*, Cambridge: Cambridge University Press.
Ellis, Markman (2004), *Politics of Sensibility: Race, Gender and Commerce in the Sentimental Novel*, Cambridge: Cambridge University Press.
Elmen, Paul (1951), 'Richard Allestree and *The Whole Duty of Man*', in *The Library*, s5-VI (1): 19–27.
Faherty, Duncan (2007), *Remodeling the Nation: The Architecture of American Identity, 1776–1858*, Durham, NH: University of New Hampshire Press.
Fennetaux, Ariane (2009), 'Female Crafts: Women and Bricolage in Late Georgian Britain 1750–1820', in Maureen Daly Goggin and Beth Fowkes Tobin (eds.), *Women and Things, 1750–1950*, 91–108, Farnham: Ashgate.
Finn, Margot (2000), 'Men's Things: Masculine Possession in the Consumer Revolution', *Social History*, 25 (2): 133–55.
Fitzer, Anna M. (2003), 'Mrs. Sheridan's Active Demon: *Memoirs of Miss Sidney Bidulph* and the Sly Rake in Petticoats', *Eighteenth-Century Ireland Society*, 18: 39–62.

Flandrin, Jean-Louis (1989), 'Distinction through Taste', in Roger Chartier (ed.), *A History of Private Life, vol. III: Passions of the Renaissance*, 267–307, Cambridge, MA: Harvard University Press.

Flather, Amanda (2007), *Gender and Space in Early Modern England*, Woodbridge: Boydell Press.

Fletcher, Anthony (1999a), *Gender, Sex and Subordination in England, 1500–1800*, New Haven CT: Yale University Press.

Fletcher, Anthony (1999b), 'Manhood, the Male Body, Courtship and the Household in Early Modern England', *History*, 84 (275): 419–36.

Flint, Christopher (1998), *Family Fictions: Narrative and Domestic Relations in Britain, 1688–1798*, Stanford, CA: Stanford University Press.

Folkenflik, Robert (1993), '*Pamela*: Domestic Servitude, Marriage, and the Novel', *Eighteenth-Century Fiction*, 5 (3): 253–68.

Foyster, Elizabeth (1999), *Manhood in Early Modern England: Honour, Sex and Marriage*, London: Longman.

French, Henry and Mark Rothery (2012), *Man's Estate: Landed Gentry Masculinities, 1660–1900*, Oxford: Oxford University Press.

Froide, Amy (2007), *Never Married: Single Women in Early Modern England*, Oxford: Oxford University Press.

Fussell, Paul, Jr. (1951), 'William Kenrick's "Courtesy" Book', in *PMLA*, 66 (4): 538–40.

Gallet, Michel (1972), *Stately Mansions: Eighteenth Century Paris Architecture*, New York: Praeger.

Gatrell, Vic (2007), *City of Laughter: Sex and Satire in Eighteenth-Century London*, London: Atlantic Books.

Gay, Peter (1967), *The Enlightenment: An Interpretation*, 2 vols., London: Weidenfeld & Nicholson.

Gélis, Jacques (1989), 'The Child: From Anonymity to Individuality', in Roger Chartier (ed.), *A History of Private Life, vol. III: Passions of the Renaissance*, 309–25, Cambridge, MA: Harvard University Press.

Gerson, Noel B. (1976), *Statue in Search of a Pedestal: A Biography of the Marquis de Lafayette*, New York: Dodd, Mead.

Girouard, Mark (1978), *Life in the English Country House: A Social and Architectural History*, New Haven, CT: Yale University Press.

Girouard, Mark (1985), 'The Power House', in Gervase Jackson-Stops (ed.), *The Treasure Houses of Britain: Five Hundred Years of Private Patronage and Art Collecting*, 22–39, New Haven, CT: Yale University Press.

Glassie, Henry (1986), 'Eighteenth-Century Cultural Process in Delaware Valley Folk Building', in Dell Upton and John Michael Vlach (eds.), *Common Places: Readings in American Vernacular Architecture*, 394–425, Athens, GA: University of Georgia Press.

Gleadle, Kathryn (2007), 'Revisiting *Family Fortunes*: Reflections on the Twentieth Anniversary of the Publication of L. Davidoff and C. Hall (1987) *Family Fortunes: Men and Women of the English Middle Class, 1780–1850* (London: Hutchinson)', *Women's History Review*, 16 (5): 773–82.

Glennie, Philip (1995), 'Consumption within Historical Studies', in Daniel Miller (ed.), *Acknowledging Consumption: A Review of New Studies*, 164–203, London: Routledge.

Goffman, Erving (1971) *The Presentation of Self in Everyday Life*, London: Penguin.

Goldsmith, Oliver (1982), *The Vicar of Wakefield*, Harmondsworth: Penguin.

Gowing, Laura (2000), '"The Freedom of the Streets": Women and Social Space, 1560–1640', in M.S.R. Jenner and P. Griffiths (eds.), *Londinopolis: A Social and Cultural History of Early Modern London, 1500–1750*, 130–52, Manchester: Manchester University Press.
Grant, Charlotte (2005), 'Reading the House of Fiction: From Object to Interior 1720–1920', *Home Cultures*, 2 (3): 233–49.
Green, Adrian (2010), 'The Polite Threshold in Seventeenth- and Eighteenth-Century Britain', *Vernacular Architecture*, 41 (1): 1–9.
Greene, Donald (1970), *The Age of Exuberance: Backgrounds to Eighteenth-Century English Literature*, New York, McGraw-Hill.
Gregory, Jeremy (1999), '"*Homo Religiosus*": Masculinity and Religion in the Long Eighteenth Century', in Tim Hitchcock and Michéle Cohen (eds.), *English Masculinities, 1660–1800*, 85–110, London: Longman.
Gregory, Jeremy (2009), 'Introduction: Transforming "the Age of Reason" into "an Age of Faiths": or, Putting Religions and Beliefs (Back) into the Eighteenth Century', *The Journal for Eighteenth-Century Studies*, 32 (3): 287–305.
Greig, Hannah and Giorgio Riello (2007), 'Eighteenth-Century Interiors – Redesigning the Georgian: Introduction', *Journal of Design History*, 20 (4): 273–89.
Grell, Ole Peter, Jonathan I. Israel and Nicholas Tyacke, eds. (1991), *From Persecution to Toleration: The Glorious Revolution and Religion in England*, Oxford: Oxford University Press.
Griffin, Ben, Lucy Delap and Abigail Wills (2009), 'Introduction: The Politics of Domestic Authority in Britain Since 1800', in Lucy Delap, Ben Griffin and Abigail Wills (eds.), *The Politics of Domestic Authority in Britain since 1800*, 1–24, London: Palgrave Macmillan.
Griffiths, Paul (1996), *Youth and Authority: Formative Experiences in England, 1560–1640*, Oxford: Clarendon Press.
Guillery, Peter (2004), *The Small House in Eighteenth-Century London: A Social and Architectural History*, New Haven, CT: Yale University Press.
Haakonssen, Knud, ed. (1996), *Enlightenment and Religion: Rational Dissent in Eighteenth-Century Britain*, Cambridge: Cambridge University Press.
Habermas, Jurgen (1989), *The Structural Transformation of the Public Sphere: An Inquiry into a Category of Bourgeois Society*, trans. Thomas Burger, Cambridge, MA: MIT Press.
Hague, Stephen G. (2015), *The Gentleman's House in the British Atlantic World, 1680–1780*, London: Palgrave Macmillan.
Hall, Catherine (1979), 'The Early Formation of Victorian Domestic Ideology', in Sandra Burman (ed.), *Fit Work for Women*, 15–32, London: Croom Helm.
Hall, Catherine (1992), *White, Male and Middle Class: Explorations in Feminism and History*, Cambridge: Polity Press.
Hall, Linda (1991), 'Yeoman or Gentleman? Problems in Defining Social Status in Seventeenth- and Eighteenth-Century Gloucestershire', *Vernacular Architecture*, 22: 2–19.
Halliday, Paul D. (1998), *Dismembering the Body Politic: Partisan Politics in England's Towns, 1650–1730*, Cambridge: Cambridge University Press.
Hamlett, Jane (2014), *Material Relations: Domestic Interiors and Middle-Class Families in England, 1850–1910*, Manchester: Manchester University Press.
Hamling, Tara and Catherine Richardson (2017), *A Day at Home in Early Modern England: Material Culture and Domestic Life, 1500–1700*, New Haven, CT: Yale University Press.

Hannan, Leonie (2014), 'Scholarship on the Margins: An Epistolary Network', *Women's Writing*, 21 (3): 290–315.
Hardyment, Christina, ed. (1992a), *The Housekeeping Book of Susanna Whatman*, London: The National Trust.
Hardyment, Christina (1992b), *Home Comfort: A History of Domestic Arrangements*, London: Viking.
Hareven, Tamara K. (1991a), 'The History of the Family and Complexity of Social Change', *The American Historical Review*, 96 (1): 95–124.
Hareven, Tamara K. (1991b), 'The Home and the Family in Historical Perspective', *Social Research*, 58 (1): 253–85.
Harkness, Deborah E. (1997) 'Managing an Experimental Household: The Dees of Mortlake and the Practice of Natural Philosophy', *Isis*, 88 (2): 247–62.
Harris, Amy (2012), *Siblinghood and Social Relations in Georgian England: Share and Share Alike*, Manchester: Manchester University Press.
Harris, Bob and Charles McKean (2015), *The Scottish Town in the Age of Enlightenment, 1740–1820*, Edinburgh: Edinburgh University Press.
Hartman, Mary S. (2007), *The Household and the Making of History: A Subversive View of the Western Past*, Cambridge: Cambridge University Press.
Harvey, Karen (2005), 'The History of Masculinity, circa 1650–1800', *Journal of British Studies*, 44 (2): 296–311.
Harvey, Karen (2009), 'Men Making Home: Masculinity and Domesticity in Eighteenth-Century Britain', *Gender and History*, 21 (3): 520–40.
Harvey, Karen (2012a), *The Little Republic: Masculinity and Domestic Authority in Eighteenth-Century Britain*, Oxford: Oxford University Press.
Harvey, Karen (2012b), 'Ritual Encounters: Punch Parties and Masculinity in the Eighteenth Century', *Past and Present*, 214 (1): 165–203.
Harvey, Karen (2014), 'Oeconomy and the Eighteenth-Century House', *Home Cultures*, 11 (3): 375–389.
Heal, Felicity (1990), *Hospitality in Early Modern England*, Oxford: Clarendon Press.
Hecht, J. Jean (1956), *The Domestic Servant Class in Eighteenth-Century England*, London: Routledge & Kegan Paul.
Heller, Benjamin (2010), 'Leisure and the Use of Domestic Space in Georgian London', *The Historical Journal*, 53 (3): 623–45.
Hellmann, Mimi (1999), 'Furniture, Sociability, and the Work of Leisure in Eighteenth-Century France', *Eighteenth Century Studies*, 32 (4): 415–445.
Herman, Bernard L. (1987), *Architecture and Rural Life in Central Delaware 1700–1900*, Knoxville, TX: University of Tennessee Press.
Herman, Bernard L. (2005), *Townhouse: Architecture and Material Life in the Early American City, 1780–1830*, Chapel Hill, NC: University of North Carolina Press.
Herman, Bernard L. (2006), 'Tabletop Conversations: Material Culture and Everyday Life in the Eighteenth-Century Atlantic World', in John Styles and Amanda Vickery (eds.), *Gender, Taste, and Material Culture in Britain and North America, 1700–1830*, 37–59, New Haven, CT: Yale University Press.
Hewitt, Martin (1999), 'District Visiting and the Constitution of Domestic Space in the Mid-Nineteenth Century', in Inga Bryden and Janet Floyd (eds.), *Domestic Space: Reading the Nineteenth-Century Interior*, 121–41, Manchester: Manchester University Press.
Hickman, Clare (2014), 'The Garden as a Laboratory: The Role of Domestic Gardens as Places of Scientific Exploration in the Long 18th Century', *Post-Medieval Archaeology*, 48 (1): 229–47.

Higgs, Emma (1983), 'Domestic Servants and Households in Victorian England', *Social History*, 8 (2): 201–10.
Hill, Bridget (1989), *Women, Work and Sexual Politics in Eighteenth-Century England*, Oxford: Basil Blackwell.
Hill, Bridget (1996), *Servants: English Domestics in the Eighteenth Century*, Oxford: Clarendon Press.
Hilton, Boyd (1993), *The Age of Atonement: The Influence of Evangelicalism on Social and Economic Thought 1785–1865*, Oxford: Oxford University Press.
Hilton, Boyd (2006), *A Mad, Bad, and Dangerous People? England 1783–1846*, Oxford: Oxford University Press.
Hilton, Mary and Jill Shefrin, eds. (2009), *Educating the Child in Enlightenment Britain: Beliefs, Cultures, Practices*, Abingdon: Routledge.
Hoppit, Julian (2000), *A Land of Liberty? England 1689–1727*, Oxford: Oxford University Press.
Houston, Rab and K.D.M. Snell (1984), 'Proto-Industrialization? Cottage Industry, Social Change and Industrial Revolution', *The Historical Journal*, 27 (2): 473–92.
Howard, Maurice (2015), '"The Lordship of the Eye": Country Houses as the Setting for Intellectual Enquiry in the Early Modern Period', in Matthew Dimmock, Andrew Hadfield and Margaret Healy (eds.), *The Intellectual Culture of the English Country House, 1500–1700*, 11–24, Manchester: Manchester University Press.
Hudson, Pat (1981) 'Proto-Industrialisation: The Case of the West Riding Wool Textile Industry in the 18th and Early 19th Centuries', *History Workshop Journal*, 12 (1): 34–61.
Hufton, Olwen (1995), *The Prospect Before Her: A History of Women in Western Europe, vol. 1, 1500–1800*, London: HarperCollins.
Hunt, Lyn (1992), *The Family Romance of the French Revolution*, London: Routledge.
Hunt, Margaret (1996), *The Middling Sort: Commerce, Gender, and the Family in England, 1680–1780*, Berkeley, CA: University of California Press.
Hunter, John Paul (1984), 'The World as Stage and Closet', in Shirley Strum Kenny (ed.), *British Theatre and the Other Arts, 1600–1800*, 271–87, Washington, DC: Folger Books.
Hussey, David (2008), 'Guns, Horses and Stylish Waistcoats? Male Consumer Activity and Domestic Shopping in Late-Eighteenth- and Early-Nineteenth-Century England', in David Hussey and Margaret Ponsonby (eds.), *Buying for the Home: Shopping for the Domestic from the Seventeenth Century to the Present*, 47–69, Aldershot: Ashgate.
Hutton, Sarah (1993), 'Damaris Cudworth, Lady Masham: Between Platonism and Enlightenment', *British Journal for the History of Philosophy*, 1 (1): 29–54.
Ilmakunnas, Johanna (2016), 'Embroidering Women and Turning Men', *Scandinavian Journal of History*, 41 (3): 306–31.
Irwin, W.R. (1952), 'William Kenrick: Volunteer Moralist', *PMLA*, 67 (2): 288–91.
Jardine, Lisa (1999), *Ingenious Pursuits: Building the Scientific Revolution*, London: Abacus.
Jenkins, Philip (1983), *The Making of a Ruling Class: The Glamorgan Gentry, 1640–1790*, Cambridge: Cambridge University Press, 1983.
Jeong-Oh, Kim (2014), 'Anne Finch's Strategic Retreat into the Country House', in Karen B. Gevirtz and Mona Narain (eds.), *Gender and Space in Britain 1660–1820*, 147–63, Farnham: Ashgate.
Johnson, Matthew (2010), *English Houses 1300–1800: Vernacular Architecture, Social Life*, Harlow: Pearson Education.

Johnson, Samuel (1755), 'Family', in *A Dictionary of the English Language: A Digital Edition of the 1755 Classic by Samuel Johnson*. Available online: https://johnsonsdictionaryonline.com/ (accessed 24 September 2019).

Joy, Edward (1968), in Ralph Edwards and L.G.G. Ramsey (eds.), *The Connoisseur's Complete Period Guides to the Houses, Decoration, Furnishing and Chattels of the Classic Periods*, London: The Connoisseur.

Kelly, Clare Lise (2011), *Places from the Past: The Tradition of Gardez Bien in Montgomery County, Maryland*, Silver Spring, MD: The Maryland-National Capital Park and Planning Commission, 10th Anniversary Edition. Available online: http://montgomeryplanning.org/wp-content/uploads/2017/12/Places-from-the-Past-web_with_cover.pdf (accessed 24 September 2019).

Kent, D. A. (1989), 'Ubiquitous but Invisible: Female Domestic Servants in Mid-Eighteenth Century London', *History Workshop Journal*, 28 (1): 111–28.

Kerber, Linda (1976), 'The Republican Mother: Women and the Enlightenment – An American Perspective', *American Quarterly*, 28 (2): 187–205.

Kerber, Linda (1988), 'Separate Spheres, Female Worlds, Woman's Place: The Rhetoric of Women's History', *Journal of American History*, 75 (1): 9–39.

Klein, Lawrence E. (1994), *Shaftesbury and the Culture of Politeness: Moral Discourse and Cultural Politics in Early Eighteenth-Century England*, Cambridge: Cambridge University Press).

Klein, Lawrence E., ed. (1999), *Anthony Ashley Cooper, Third Earl of Shaftesbury: Characteristics of Men, Manners, Opinions, Times*, Cambridge: Cambridge University Press.

Kniffen, Fred B. (1936), 'Louisiana House Types', *Annals of the Association of American Geographers*, 26 (4): 179–93.

Kowaleski-Wallace, Elizabeth (1996), 'Women, China and Consumer Culture in Eighteenth-Century England', *Eighteenth-Century Studies*, 29 (2): 153–67.

Kramer, Lloyd (1996), *Lafayette in Two Worlds: Popular Culture and Personal Identities in an Age of Revolutions*, Chapel Hill, NC: University of North Carolina Press.

Krasner, James (2010), *Home Bodies: Tactile Experience in Domestic Space*, Columbus, OH: Ohio State University Press.

Ladd, Heather Ann (2014), 'Invaded Spaces in Charlotte Smith's *The Banished* Man (1794)', in Karen B. Gevirtz and Mona Narain (eds.), *Gender and Space in Britain 1660–1820*, 179–91, Farnham: Ashgate.

Lane, Maggie (1995), *Jane Austen and Food*, London: Hambleton Press.

Langford, Paul (1989), *Polite and Commercial People: England 1727–1783*, Oxford: Oxford University Press.

Langford, Paul (2002), 'The Uses of Eighteenth-Century Politeness', *Transactions of the Royal Historical Society*, 12: 311–31.

LeGates, Marlene (1976), 'The Cult of Womanhood in Eighteenth-Century Thought', *Eighteenth-Century Studies*, 10 (1): 21–39.

Lemire, Beverly (2005), *The Business of Everyday Life: Gender, Practice and Social Politics in England, c. 1600–1900*, Manchester: Manchester University Press.

Leong, Elaine (2018), *Recipes and Everyday Knowledge: Medicine, Science, and the Household in Early Modern England*, Chicago, IL: University of Chicago Press.

Lewis, Judith S. (2003), *Sacred to Female Patriotism: Gender, Class, and Politics in Late Georgian Britain*, London: Routledge.

Lewis, Judith S. (2009), 'When a House Is Not a Home: Elite English Women and the Eighteenth-Century Country House', *Journal of British Studies*, 48 (2): 336–63.

Lipsedge, Karen (2006), '"Enter into Thy Closet": Women, Closet Culture and the Eighteenth-Century English Novel', in John Styles and Amanda Vickery (eds.), *Gender, Taste, and Material Culture in Britain and North America, 1700–1830*, 107–22, New Haven, CT: Yale University Press.

Lipsedge, Karen (2012a), *Domestic Space in Eighteenth-Century British Novels*, Basingstoke: Palgrave Macmillan.

Lipsedge, Karen (2012b) '"At Home": The Representation of the Domestic Interior in the Novels of Samuel Richardson and Fanny Burney', in Francesca Sagginni and Anna Enrichetta Soccio (eds.), *The House of Fiction as the House of Life: Representations on the House from Richardson to Woolf*, 26–39. Cambridge: Cambridge Scholars.

Lipsedge, Karen and Melinda McCurdy (forthcoming, 2020), 'The Interior and the Arts', in J. Turpin (ed.), *Cultural Interiors*, London: Bloomsbury Academic.

Lloyd, Sarah (2004), 'Cottage Conversations: Poverty and Manly Independence in Eighteenth-Century England', *Past and Present*, 184 (1): 69–108.

Locock, Martin (1994), 'Meaningful Architecture', in Martin Locock (ed.), *Meaningful Architecture: Social Interpretations of Buildings*, 1–13, Aldershot: Avebury Press.

Lougee, Carolyn C. (1974), 'Noblesse, Domesticity, and Social Reform: The Education of Girls by Fénelon and Saint-Cyr', *History of Education Quarterly*, 14 (1): 87–113.

Lund, Roger D. (2012), *Ridicule, Religion and the Politics of Wit in Augustan England*, London: Routledge.

Mack, Phyllis (2008), *Heart Religion in the British Enlightenment: Gender and Emotion in Early Methodism*, Cambridge: Cambridge University Press.

Mallett, Shelley (2004), 'Understanding Home: A Critical Review of the Literature', *The Sociological Review*, 52 (1): 62–89.

Mander, Nicholas (2008), *Country Houses of the Cotswolds*, London: Arum.

Maples Dunn, Mary (1979), 'Women of Light', in Carol Ruth Berkin and Mary Beth Norton (eds.), *Women of America: A History*, 114–38, Boston, MA: Houghton Mifflin.

Marsden Gillis, Christina (1984), *The Paradox of Privacy: Epistolary Form in 'Clarissa'*, Gainesville, FL: University Presses of Florida.

Marshall, Dorothy (1949), *The English Domestic Servant in History*, London: Historical Association.

Massey, Doreen (1994), *Space, Place, and Gender*, London: Polity Press.

Maudlin, Daniel (2012), 'Telling Stories: Myths and Memoires of the 'Blackhouse' in the Scottish National Narrative', in Olivia Horsfall Turner (ed.), *'The Mirror of Great Britain': National Identity in Seventeenth-Century British Architecture*, 261–80, Reading: Spire Books.

Maurer, Shawn Lisa (1998), *Proposing Men: Dialectics of Gender and Class in the Eighteenth Century English Periodical*, Stanford, CA: Stanford University Press.

McCann, Alison (1983), 'A Private Laboratory at Petworth House, Sussex, in the Late Eighteenth Century', *Annals of Science*, 40 (6): 635–55.

McCormack, Matthew (2005), *The Independent Man: Citizenship and Gender Politics in Georgian England*, Manchester: Manchester University Press.

McCormack, Matthew (2007), '"Married Men and Fathers of Families": Fatherhood and Franchise Reform in Britain', in Trev Lynn Broughton and Helen Rogers (eds.), *Gender and Fatherhood in the Nineteenth Century*, 43–54, Basingstoke: Palgrave.

McCracken, Grant (1990), *Culture and Consumption*, Bloomington, IN: Indiana University Press.

McDonagh, Briony (2018), *Elite Women and the Agricultural Landscape, 1700–1830*, Abingdon: Routledge.

McIsaac Cooper, Sheila (2005), 'Service to Servitude? The Decline and Demise of Life-Cycle Service in England', *The History of the Family*, 10 (4): 367–86.

McKendrick, Neil, John Brewer and J.H. Plumb (1982), *The Birth of a Consumer Society: The Commercialization of Eighteenth Century England*, Bloomington, IN: Indiana University Press.

McKeon, Michael (2005), *The Secret History of Domesticity: Public, Private, and the Division of Knowledge*, Baltimore, MD: Johns Hopkins University Press.

Meldrum, Tim (2000), *Domestic Service and Gender, 1660–1750: Life and Work in the London Household*, London: Pearson Education.

Meldrum, Tim (2014), *Domestic Service and Gender, 1660–1750: Life and Work in the London Household*, Abingdon: Routledge.

Metcalfe, Helen (2016) 'The Social Experience of Bachelorhood in Late-Georgian England, *c.* 1760–1830', PhD dissertation, University of Manchester.

Miller, Daniel (1995), 'Consumption as the Vanguard of History: A Polemic by Way of Introduction', in Daniel Miller (ed.), *Acknowledging Consumption: A Review of New Studies*, 1–57, London: Routledge.

Millon, Henry A., ed. (2006), *Circa 1700: Architecture in Europe and the Americas*, New Haven, CT: Yale University Press.

Mingay, Gordon Edmund (1976), *The Gentry: The Rise and Fall of a Ruling Class*, London: Longman.

Mintz, Sidney (1989), *Sweetness and Power: The Place of Sugar in Modern History*, New York: Penguin.

More, Hannah ([1799] 1995), *Strictures on the Modern System of Female Education*, 2 vols., Oxford: Woodstock Books.

Morris, Marilyn (1996), 'The Royal Family and Family Values in Late Eighteenth-Century England', *Journal of Family History*, 21(4): 519–32.

Mosse, George L. (1988), *The Culture of Western Europe: The Nineteenth and Twentieth Centuries*, 3rd edition, Boulder, CO: Westview Press.

Muldrew, Craig (1998), *The Economy of Obligation: The Culture of Credit and Social Relations in Early Modern England*, Basingstoke: Macmillan.

Mullan, John (1988), *Sentiment and Sociability. The Language of Feeling in the Eighteenth Century*, Oxford: Clarendon Press.

Nenadic, Stana (1994), 'Middle-Rank Consumers and Domestic Culture in Edinburgh and Glasgow 1720–1840', *Past and Present*, 145 (1): 122–56.

North, Roger (1981), *Of Building: Roger North's Writings on Architecture*, ed. H. Colvin and J. Newman, Oxford: Oxford University Press.

Norton, Mary Beth (1979), 'A Cherished Spirit of Independence: The Life of an Eighteenth-Century Boston Businesswoman', in Carol Ruth Berkin and Mary Beth Norton (eds.), *Women of America: A History*, 48–67, Boston, MA: Houghton Mifflin.

Okin, Susan Moller (1982), 'Women and the Making of the Sentimental Family', *Philosophy and Public Affairs*, 11 (1): 65–88.

Ottoway, Susannah (2007), *The Decline of Life: Old Age in Eighteenth-Century England*, Cambridge: Cambridge University Press.

Outram, Dorinda (1989), *The Body and the French Revolution: Sex, Class, and Political Culture*, New Haven, CT: Yale University Press.

Oxford English Dictionary (OED) (1989), 2nd edition, 20 vols., Oxford: Clarendon Press.

Pardailhé-Galabrun, Annik (1991), *The Birth of Intimacy: Privacy and Domestic Life in Early Modern Paris*, Philadelphia, PA: University of Pennsylvania Press.

Parker, Rozsika (1984), *The Subversive Stitch: Embroidery and the Making of the Feminine*, London: Women's Press.

Pavlik, Milan and Vladimir Uher (1998), *Prague Baroque Architecture*, Amsterdam: Pepin Press.

Pearsall, Sarah (2010), *Atlantic Families: Lives and Letters in the Later Eighteenth Century*, Oxford: Oxford University Press.

Pennell, Sara (1999), 'Consumption and Consumerism in Early Modern England', *The Historical Journal*, 42 (2): 549–64.

Pennell, Sara (2009), 'Mundane Materiality, or Should Small Things Still Be Forgotten? Material Culture, Micro-histories and the Problem of Scale', in Karen Harvey (ed.), *History and Material Culture*, 173–91, London: Routledge.

Pennell, Sara (2016), *The Birth of the English Kitchen, 1600–1850*, London: Bloomsbury Academic, 2016.

Perry, Ruth (2006), *Novel Relations: The Transformation of Kinship in English Literature and Culture, 1748–1818*, Cambridge: Cambridge University Press.

Peyer, Hans Conrad (1987), *Von der Gastfreundschaft zur Gasthaus: Studien zur Gastlichkeit in Mittelalter*, Hannover: Hansche Buchhandlung.

Phillips, Nicola (2006), *Women in Business, 1700–1850*, Woodbridge: Boydell & Brewer, 2006.

Platt, Colin (1994), *The Great Rebuildings of Tudor and Stuart England: Revolutions in Architectural Taste*, London: UCL Press.

Ponsonby, Margaret (2007), *Stories from Home: English Domestic Interiors, 1750–1850*, Aldershot: Ashgate.

Porter, Roy (1990), *English Society in the Eighteenth Century*, London: Penguin.

Porter, Roy (2001), *Enlightenment: Britain and the Creation of the Modern World*, London: Penguin.

Prendergast, Amy (2011), '"The Drooping Genius of Our Isle to Raise": The Moira House Salon and its Role in Gaelic Cultural Revival', *Eighteenth-Century Ireland*, 26: 95–114.

Price, Richard (1999), *British Society 1680–1880: Dynamism, Containment, and Change*, Cambridge: Cambridge University Press.

Reinberger, Mark (1991), 'Graeme Park and the Three-Cell Plan: A Lost Type in Colonial Architecture', in Thomas Carter and Bernard Herman, eds., *Perspectives in Vernacular Architecture*, vol. 4, 146–54, Columbia, MO: University of Missouri Press.

Rendall, Jane (1985), *The Origins of Modern Feminism: Women in Britain, France and the United States 1780–1860*, Basingstoke: Macmillan.

Rendall, Jane (1999), 'Women and the Public Sphere', *Gender and History*, 11 (3): 475–88.

Retford, Kate (2006), *The Art of Domestic Life: Family Portraiture in Eighteenth-Century England*, London: Yale University Press.

Reynolds, K.D. (1998), *Aristocratic Women and Political Society in Victorian Britain*, Oxford: Clarendon Press.

Richardson, R.C. (2010), *Household Servants in Early Modern England*, Manchester: Manchester University Press.

Richardson, Sarah (1996), 'The Role of Women in Electoral Politics in Yorkshire during the Eighteen-Thirties', *Northern History*, 32: 133–51.

Rivers, Isabel (1991), *Reason, Grace, and Sentiment: A Study of the Language of Religion and Ethics in England, 1660–1780*, vol. I: *Whichcote to Wesley*, Cambridge: Cambridge University Press.

Robert, Paul (1966), *Dictionnaire alphabétique et analogique de la Langue Française*, 6 vols., Paris: Littre.

Rogers, Katharine (1982), *Feminism in Eighteenth-Century England*, Brighton: Harvester Press.

Rosenwein, Barbara H. (2007), *Emotional Communities in the Early Middle Ages*, London: Cornell University Press.

Rosenwein, Barbara H. (2010), 'Problems and Methods in the History of Emotions', *Passions in Context: Journal of the History and Philosophy of the Emotions*, 1 (1): 1–32.

Rybczynski, Witold (1986), *Home: A Short History of an Idea*, New York: Penguin.

Sambrook, Pamela A. (2010), 'Household Beer and Brewing', in Pamela A. Sambrook and Peter Brears (eds.), *The Country House Kitchen, 1650–1900*, Stroud: The History Press.

Sambrook, Pamela A. and Peter Brears, eds. (2010), *The Country House Kitchen, 1650–1900*, Stroud: The History Press.

Sarti, Raffaella (2002), *Europe at Home: Family and Material Culture, 1500–1800*, trans. Allan Cameron, New Haven, CT: Yale University Press.

Saumarez Smith, Charles (1993), *Eighteenth-Century Decoration: Design and the Domestic Interior in England*, London: Weidenfeld & Nicolson.

Saumarez Smith, Charles (2000), *The Rise of Design: Design and the Domestic Interior in Eighteenth-Century England*, London: Pimlico.

Saunders, Peter and Peter Williams (1988), 'The Constitution of the Home: Towards a Research Agenda', *Housing Studies*, 3 (2): 81–93.

Schubert, Ernst (1996), 'Daily Life, Consumption, and Material Culture', in Sheilagh Ogilvie (ed.), *Germany: A New Social and Economic History, vol. 2: 1630–1800*, 350–75, London: Edward Arnold.

Sebastiani, Silvia (2013), *The Scottish Enlightenment. Race, Gender, and the Limits of Progress*, trans. Jeremy Carden, London: Palgrave.

Sedda, Julia (2009), 'Reading Circles, Crafts and Flower Arranging: Everyday Items in the Silhouettes of Luise Duttenhofer (1776–1829)', in Maureen Daly Goggin and Beth Fowkes Tobin (eds.), *Women and Things, 1750–1950*, 109–28, Aldershot: Ashgate.

Shagan, Ethan H. (2011), *The Rule of Moderation: Violence, Religion and the Politics of Restraint in Early Modern England*, Cambridge: Cambridge University Press.

Shammas, Carole (1980), 'The Domestic Environment in Early Modern England and America', *Journal of Social History*, 14 (1): 3–24.

Shapin, Steven (1988), 'The House of Experiment in Seventeenth-Century England', *Isis*, 79 (3): 373–404.

Shaw, Jane (2006), *Miracles in Enlightenment England*, New Haven, CT: Yale University Press.

Shepard, Alexandra (2008), *Meanings of Manhood in Early Modern England*, Oxford: Oxford University Press.

Shepard, Alexandra (2015), *Accounting for Oneself: Worth, Status, and the Social Order in Early Modern England*, Oxford: Oxford University Press.

Shepherd, Lynn (1989), 'Richardson's First Novel: Images of *Pamela* from Carwitham to Highmore', in *Clarissa's Painter: Portraiture, Illustration, and Representation in the Novels of Samuel Richardson*, 58–111, Oxford: Oxford University Press.

Shevelow, Kathryn (1989), *Women and Print Culture: The Construction of Femininity in the Early Periodical*, London: Routledge.
Shorter, Edward (1976), *The Making of the Modern Family*, London: Collins.
Shove, Elizabeth (2003), *Comfort, Cleanliness and Convenience: The Social Organization of Normality*, Oxford: Berg.
Simpson, Richard (2015), 'Sir Thomas Smith's Stillhouse at Hill Hall: Books, Practice, Antiquity and Innovation', in Matthew Dimmock, Andrew Hadfield and Margaret Healy (eds.), *The Intellectual Culture of the English Country House, 1500–1700*, 101–16, Manchester: Manchester University Press.
Skinner, Quentin (1998), *Liberty Before Liberalism*, Cambridge: Cambridge University Press.
Sloboda, Stacey (2009), 'Porcelain Bodies: Gender, Acquisitiveness, and Taste in Eighteenth-Century England', in Alla Myzelev and John Potvin (eds.), *Material Cultures 1740–1920: The Meanings and Pleasures of Collecting*, 19–36, Burlington, VT: Ashgate.
Smith, Billy G. (1990), *The 'Lower Sort': Philadelphia's Laboring People, 1750–1800*, Ithaca, NY: Cornell University Press.
Smith, Theresa Ann (2006), *The Emerging Female Citizen: Gender and Enlightenment in Spain*, Berkeley, CA: University of California Press.
Smith, Woodruff D. (2002), *Consumption and the Making of Respectability, 1600–1800*, New York: Routledge.
Smith, Woodruff D. (2010), 'Respectability and the Social Question in the Mid-Nineteenth Century: Constructing a Space of Moral Contestation', in I. van den Broek, C. Smit and D.J. Wolffram (eds.), *Commitment and Imagination: Representations of the Social Question*, 1–18, Leuven: Peeters.
Smith, Woodruff D. (2018), *Respectability as Moral Map and Public Discourse in the Nineteenth Century*, New York: Routledge.
Solkin, David (1993), *Painting for Money: The Visual Arts and the Public Sphere in Eighteenth-Century England*, New Haven, CT: Paul Mellon Centre for Studies in British Art.
Spacks, Patricia Meyer (2003), *Privacy: Concealing the Eighteenth-Century Self*, Chicago, IL: University of Chicago Press.
Spalding, Keith (n.d.), *An Historical Dictionary of German Figurative Usage*, 5 vols., Oxford: Blackwell.
Spershott, James (1962), *The Memoirs of James Spershott*, ed. Francis W. Steer, Chichester: Chichester City Council.
Spurr, John (1989), 'The Church of England, Comprehension and the Toleration Act of 1689', *The English Historical Review*, 104: (413): 927–46.
Staves, Susan (1990), *Married Women's Separate Property in England, 1660–1833*, Cambridge, MA: Harvard University Press.
Steedman, Carolyn (2007), *Master and Servant: Love and Labour in the English Industrial Age*, Cambridge: Cambridge University Press.
Steedman, Carolyn (2009), *Labours Lost: Domestic Service and the Making of Modern England*, Cambridge: Cambridge University Press.
Stewart, Rachel (2009), *The Town House in Georgian London*, London, CT: Yale University Press.
Stobart, Jon and Mark Rothery (2016), *Consumption and the Country House*, Oxford: Oxford University Press.
Stone, Lawrence (1977), *The Family, Sex and Marriage in England 1500–1800*, London: Harper & Row.

Stone, Lawrence (1990), *The Family, Sex and Marriage 1500–1800*, abridged edition, London: Penguin.
Stranks, C.J. (1961), *Anglican Devotion: Studies in the Spiritual Life of the Church of England between the Reformation and the Oxford Movement*, London: SCM Press.
Styles, John and Amanda Vickery (2006), *Gender, Taste, and Material Culture in Britain and North America, 1700–1830*, New Haven, CT: Yale Center for British Art.
Summerson, John (1986), *The Architecture of the Eighteenth Century*, London: Thames & Hudson.
Sweet, Rosemary (2004), *Antiquaries: The Discovery of the Past in Eighteenth-Century Britain*, London: Hambledon & London.
Tadmor, Naomi (1996), '"In the even my wife read to me": Women, Reading and Household Life in the Eighteenth Century', in J. Raven, H. Small and N. Tadmor (eds.), *The Practice and Representation of Reading in Britain*, 162–74, Cambridge: Cambridge University Press.
Tadmor, Naomi (2007), *Family and Friends in the Eighteenth Century: Household, Kinship, and Patronage*, Cambridge: Cambridge University Press.
Tadmor, Naomi (2010), 'Early Modern English Kinship in the Long Run: Reflections on Continuity and Change', *Continuity and Change*, 25 (1): 15–48.
Tague, Ingrid H. (2002), *Women of Quality: Accepting and Contesting Ideals of Femininity in England, 1690–1760*, Woodbridge: Boydell Press.
Tague, Ingrid H. (2007), 'Aristocratic Women and the Ideas of Family in the Early Eighteenth Century', in Helen Berry and Elizabeth Foyster (eds.), *The Family in Early Modern England*, 184–208, Cambridge: Cambridge University Press.
Taylor, Barbara (2004), 'Feminists Versus Gallants: Manners and Morals in Enlightenment Britain', *Representations*, 87 (1): 125–48.
Thomas, Keith (1976), 'Age and Authority in Early Modern England', *Proceedings of the British Academy*, 62: 205–48.
Thomas, Keith (2009), *The Ends of Life: Roads to Fulfilment in Early Modern England*, Oxford: Oxford University Press.
Thomas, Keith (2018), *In Pursuit of Civility: Manners and Civilization in Early Modern England*, Waltham, MA: Brandeis University Press.
Thompson, E.P. (1963), *The Making of the English Working Class*, London: Gollancz.
Todd, Janet M. (1989), *The Sign of Angelica: Women, Writing and Fiction, 1660–1800*, London: Virago.
Tomaselli, Sylvana (2001), 'The Most Public Sphere of All: The Family', in Elizabeth Eger, Charlotte Grant, Cliona O Gallchoir and Penny Warburton (eds.), *Women, Writing and the Public Sphere, 1700–1830*, 239–56, Cambridge: Cambridge University Press.
Tosh, John (1999), *A Man's Place: Masculinity and the Middle Class Home in Victorian England*, New Haven, CT: Yale University Press.
Tristram, Philippa (1989), *Living Space in Fact and Fiction*, London: Routledge.
Trumbach, Randolph (1978), *The Rise of the Egalitarian Family: Aristocratic Kinship and Domestic Relations in Eighteenth-Century England*, New York: Academic Press.
Ulrich, Laurel Thatcher (1995), 'Furniture as Social History: Gender, Property, and Memory in the Decorative Arts', *American Furniture*, 3: 35–64.
Upton, Dell and John Michael Vlach, eds. (1986), *Common Places: Readings in American Vernacular Architecture*, Athens, GA: University of Georgia Press.
Valenze, Deborah (1991), 'The Art of Women and the Business of Men: Woman's Work and the Dairy Industry, c. 1740–1840', *Past and Present*, 130: 142–69.

Varey, Simon (1990), *Space and the Eighteenth-Century English Novel*, Cambridge: Cambridge University Press.
Vickery, Amanda (1993a), 'Golden Age to Separate Spheres? A Review of the Categories and Chronology of English Women's History', *The Historical Journal*, 36 (2): 383–414.
Vickery, Amanda (1993b), 'Women and the World of Goods: A Lancashire Consumer and Her Possessions, 1751–1781', in John Brewer and Roy Porter (eds.), *Consumption and the World of Goods*, 274–301, London: Routledge.
Vickery, Amanda (1998), *The Gentleman's Daughter: Women's Lives in Georgian England*, New Haven, CT: Yale University Press.
Vickery, Amanda (2008), 'An Englishman's Home is his Castle? Thresholds, Boundaries and Privacies in the Eighteenth-Century London House', *Past and Present*, 199: 147–73.
Vickery, Amanda (2009), *Behind Closed Doors: At Home in Georgian England*, New Haven, CT: Yale University Press.
Vickery, Amanda and John Styles (2006), 'Introduction', in John Styles and Amanda Vickery (eds.), *Gender, Taste, and Material Culture in Britain and North America, 1700–1830*, 1–35, New Haven, CT: Yale University Press.
Vila, Anne C. (2007), 'Elite Masculinities in Eighteenth-Century France', in Christopher E. Forth and Bertrand Taithe (eds.), *French Masculinities: History, Culture, and Politics*, 15–30, Basingstoke: Palgrave Macmillan.
von Kalnein, Wend (1995), *Architecture in France in the Eighteenth Century*, New, CT: Yale University Press.
Wahrman, Dror (1993), '"Middle-Class" Domesticity Goes Public: Gender, Class, and Politics from Queen Caroline to Queen Victoria', *Journal of British Studies*, 32 (4): 396–432.
Wahrman, Dror (1998), 'Percy's Prologue: From Gender Play to Gender Panic in Eighteenth-Century England', *Past and Present*, 159: 113–60.
Walker, Lynne (2002), 'Home Making: An Architectural Perspective', *Signs: Journal of Women in Culture and Society*, 27 (3): 823–35.
Wall, Cynthia Sundberg (2006), *The Prose of Things: Transformations of Description in the Eighteenth Century*, Chicago, IL: University of Chicago Press.
Walsh, John, Colin Haydon and Stephen Taylor, eds. (1993), *The Church of England c. 1689–c. 1833: From Toleration to Tractarianism*, Cambridge: Cambridge University Press.
Walsham, Alexandra (2006), *Charitable Hatred: Tolerance and Intolerance in England 1500–1700*, Manchester: Manchester University Press.
Watt, I. (1957), *The Rise of the Novel*, London: Hogarth Press.
Weatherill, Lorna (1988), *Consumer Behaviour and Material Culture in Britain: 1660–1760*, London: Routledge & Kegan Paul.
Weatherill, Lorna (1996), *Consumer Behaviour and Material Culture in Britain 1660–1760*, 2nd edition, London: Routledge.
Weaver, William W. (1986), 'The Pennsylvania German House: European Antecedents and New World Forms', *Winterthur Portfolio*, 21 (4): 243–64.
Weinbrot, Howard D. (1978) *Augustus Caesar in Augustan England: The Decline of a Classical Norm*, Princeton, NJ: Princeton University Press.
Weinbrot, Howard D. (1988), *Eighteenth-Century Satire: Essays on Text and Context from Dryden to Peter Pindar*, Cambridge: Cambridge University Press.
Werrett, Simon (2013), 'Recycling in Early Modern Science', *British Journal for the History of Science*, 46 (4): 627–46.

Werrett, Simon (2019), *Thrifty Science: Making the Most of Materials in the History of Experiment*, Chicago, IL: University of Chicago Press.

West, Susie (1999), 'Social Space and the English Country House', in Sarah Tarlow and Susie West (eds.), *The Familiar Past? Archaeologies of Later Historical Britain*, 103–22, London: Routledge.

White, Jerry (2012), *A Great and Monstrous Thing: London in the Eighteenth Century*, Cambridge, MA: Harvard University Press.

White, Jonathan (2006), 'The Laboring-Class Domestic Sphere in Eighteenth-Century British Social Thought', in John Styles and Amanda Vickery (eds.), *Gender, Taste, and Material Culture in Britain and North America, 1700–1830*, 247–63, New Haven, CT: Yale University Press.

Whittle, Jane (2019), A Critique of Approaches to "Domestic Work": Women, Work and the Pre-industrial Economy', *Past and Present*, 243: 35–70.

Wilberforce, A.M., ed. ([1897] 1968), *Private Papers of William Wilberforce*, reprint, New York: Burt Franklin.

Williams, Abigail (2017), *The Social Life of Books: Reading Together in the Eighteenth-Century Home*, New Haven, CT: Yale University Press.

Wills, Geoffrey (1971), *English Furniture: 1550–1760*, Enfield: Guinness Superlatives.

Wilson, C. Anne (2010), 'Stillhouses and Stillrooms', in Pamela A. Sambrook and Peter Brears (eds.), *The Country House Kitchen, 1650–1900*, 129–43, Stroud: The History Press.

Wilson, Penelope (1994), 'Feminism and the Augustans: Some Readings and Problems', in Claude Rawson (ed.), *Jonathan Swift: A Collection of Critical Essays*, 785–94, London: Pearson.

Wilson, Richard and Alan Mackley (2000), *Creating Paradise: The Building of the English Country House, 1660–1880*, London: Hambledon & London.

Wolff, Larry (2013), 'Childhood and the Enlightenment: The Complications of Innocence', in Paula Fass (ed.), *The Routledge History of Childhood in the Western World*, 78–99, London: Routledge.

Woodforde, James and John Beresford (1929), *The Diary of a Country Parson*, London: Oxford University Press.

Woodley, Sophia (2009), '"Oh Miserable and Most Ruinous Measure": The Debate between Private and Public Education in Britain, 1760–1800', in M. Hilton and J. Shefrin (eds.), *Educating the Child in Enlightenment Britain: Beliefs, Cultures, Practices*, 21–40, London: Routledge.

Woolrich, A.P., ed. (1986), *Ferner's Journal, 1759–1760: An Industrial Spy in Bath and Bristol*, Eindhoven: Die Archaeologische Pers.

Wrightson, Keith (1998), 'The Family in Early Modern England: Continuity and Change', in Stephen Taylor, Richard Connors and Clyve Jones (eds.), *Hanoverian Britain and Empire: Essays in Memory of Philip Lawson*, 1–22, Woodbridge: Boydell Press.

Wrigley, E.A. and R.S. Schofield (1989), *The Population History of England 1541–1871: A Reconstruction*, Cambridge: Cambridge University Press.

CONTRIBUTORS

Clive Edwards is Professor Emeritus of Design History at Loughborough University, UK. After a career in the furniture and interiors business, he furthered his research with a PhD at the Royal College of Art. Published works include *Encyclopaedia of Furniture Materials, Trades and Techniques*; *Victorian Furniture: Technology and Design*, and *Turning Houses into Homes: A History of the Retailing and Consumption of Domestic Furnishings*, as well as contributions to numerous academic journals and edited works. He was general editor of *The Bloomsbury Encyclopedia of Design*. Forthcoming chapters include 'Visual Representation' in *A Cultural History of Furniture* (Bloomsbury Academic, 2021) and 'Artefacts and Colour during the Eighteenth Century' in *A Cultural History of Colour* (Bloomsbury Academic, 2020).

Stephen Hague is a historian of Britain and its empire at Rowan University in New Jersey, USA. He has published widely on houses in the British Atlantic World, including *The Gentleman's House in the British Atlantic World, 1680–1780* (Palgrave Macmillan, 2015), historic buildings and community, and is co-editing a volume *At Home in the Eighteenth Century: Interrogating Domestic Space*. He holds a DPhil from Oxford University and is also a Supernumerary Fellow of Linacre College, Oxford, UK.

Leonie Hannan is Lecturer in Eighteenth-Century History at Queen's University, Belfast, UK and a social and cultural historian with interests in gender, material culture, intellectual life and histories of home. Her 2016 monograph, *Women of Letters* (Manchester University Press), situated correspondence as the central social practice in the development of female agency through intellectual life. Hannan has co-edited several collections, including *Gender and Material Culture in Britain since 1600* (with Hannah Greig and Jane Hamlett, Palgrave

Macmillan, 2015), and co-written (with Sarah Longair) a research guide entitled *History through Material Culture* (Manchester University Press, 2017).

Ruth Larsen is Senior Lecturer in History at the University of Derby, UK. Having received her PhD from the University of York, UK in 2004, she has published a range of edited books, articles and chapters on eighteenth- and nineteenth-century history, especially exploring country houses, elite women and religious history. Recent publications include 'Sisterly Guidance: Elite Women, Sorority and the Life Cycle, 1770–1860', in T. Dooley, M. O'Riordan and C. Ridgway (eds.), *Women and the Country House in Ireland and Britain* (Four Courts Press, 2018). She is co-editor (with Ian Whitehead) of *Popular Experience and Cultural Representation of the Great War 1914–1918* (Cambridge Scholars, 2017).

Karen Lipsedge is Associate Professor in English Literature at Kingston University, UK. Her research focuses on eighteenth-century domestic space, material culture and society and its representation in British eighteenth-century literature and art. Her publications include '"Enter into thy Closet": Women, Closet Culture and the Eighteenth-Century Novel', in John Styles and Amanda Vickery (eds.), *Gender, Taste, and Material Culture in Britain and North America, 1700–1830* (Yale University Press, 2006), and *Domestic Space in Eighteenth-Century British Novels* (Palgrave Macmillan, 2012). She is co-author (with Melinda McCurdy) of 'The Interior and the Arts', which is to appear in Stacey Sloboda (ed.), *A Cultural History of Interiors in the Age of Enlightenment* (Bloomsbury Academic, forthcoming), and is also co-editing *Home Is Where the Start Is: Interrogating the Eighteenth-Century Home and the Concept of Domesticity* (with Stephen Hague, forthcoming) and 'Women and Property in the Long Eighteenth Century' (with Rita Dashwood, forthcoming special issue of the *Journal for Eighteenth-Century Studies*).

Helen Metcalfe is a social, gender and family historian of late-Georgian Britain specializing in the history of masculinities, the home and domestic material culture. Her next research project seeks to interrogate experiences of grief, loss and resilience in late-Georgian society. She has published on subjects including bachelors' notions of domestic and emotional comfort, military bachelors' feelings of nostalgia, as well as single men's experiences of domesticity. Helen was awarded her AHRC-funded doctorate from the University of Manchester, UK in 2017, and is currently a Teaching Fellow at the University of York, UK.

Matthew Neal is Affiliated Lecturer in the Faculty of History at the University of Cambridge, UK, and a Bye-Fellow and Tutor at Fitzwilliam College. His doctoral dissertation examined the growth of religious toleration after 1660. He is now studying the religious roots of eighteenth-century reformist and radical movements, focusing on languages of political and religious debate, and how these shape and are shaped by historical circumstances. His interests are methodological as well as historical.

Woodruff D. Smith is Professor Emeritus of History at the University of Massachusetts Boston, USA, and Senior Research Fellow at the University of Texas at Austin, USA. He has published seven books in fields that include German history, imperialism, the history of social science, and economic and cultural history. His most recent book is *Respectability as Moral Map and Public Discourse in the Nineteenth Century* (Routledge, 2018).

INDEX

Note: Numbers in **bold** indicate figures.

A Godlie Forme of Household Government, (Dod and Cleaver), 41
Adam, Robert, **9**, 98, 136, 137
Adams, Thomas, 69
advice literature, 33, 40–3, 61
Alexander, William, 144
Allestree, Richard, 41, 177–8, **178**, 181, 185–6, 192, 194, 196, 197–9
American colonies, 66–7, **70**, 77, 81, 82
American Revolution, 2
Angell James, John Angell, 41, 42–3
Anne, Countess of Strafford, 92, 96–7
architects, 76
architectural principles, 14–5, 63–84
   city houses, 68–72, **70**
   common housing, 64–8
   elite, 65, 67–8, **67**, 71, 72–5, **74**
   France, 71
   middling houses, 75–8, **79**
   pattern books, 77
   and the public-private division, 134–6
   rationalization, 64
   vernacular buildings, 66
Arciszewska, Barbara, 76
Arkwright, Richard, 11
Armstrong, Nancy, 152
Austen, Jane, 31, 160, 172
   Emma, 171
   Northanger Abbey, 136
   Pride and Prejudice, 166–71

bachelor household, the, 39, 47–50, 61
   companionship, love and support, 57–60
   and family reputation, 54–7, 61
   financial circumstances, 56
   household management, 50–7, 61
   servants, 55–6
Bacon, Francis, 2
bakehouses, 121
balls, **167**, 168
Barbon, Nicolas, 11–2
Barton, Bernard, 59
Bath, 19, 71
bedrooms, 81, 95–7, **96**
beds, 80–1
Begiato, Joanne, 38
Behn, Aphra, 19
Bermingham, Ann, 43
Berry, Helen, 38
Beverly, William, 75
Blenheim Palace, 74, **74**
Blondel, Jacques-Francois, 73
Bluestockings, 113
Book of Trades, The, 86
Bowles, Carrington, 'The Pleasures of a Married State', 45, **47**

brewing and brewhouses, 119–22, **120**
Bristol, 71, 83
Bulman, William, 202
Bunyan, John, 19
Burney, Frances, 31
    Evelina, 31, 172–3

Cabarrús, Francisco, 131, 152
Campbell, Colen, 77
capitalist production, and gender, 134
carpets, 93
Catherine the Great of Russia, 1
centre-hall passage arrangement, 80
chairs, 94, 95, 100–1
Champion, William, 83
Chardin, Jean-Baptiste, 4–5
charity, 188–9
Charlotte, Queen, 146, **146**
Chatsworth House, 67–8, **67**, 75
Chico, Tita, 112
children, 186–7, **187**
Chinoiserie, 78, **79**
chintz craze, the, 88
Chippendale, Thomas, 95, 96
    The Gentleman and Cabinet-Maker's Director, 88, **89**
Christian masculinity, 55
Christian revivalism, 177
Church, the, 1
citizenship, 142
civil peace, 175
Clare, Richard A., 115, 125
Classicism, 78
Claydon, Tony, 202–3
cleanliness, 13
Cleaver, R., 41
closet, the, 14, 26, 31–2, 112–3
Cobb, John, 103
Cohen, Tobias, 4
comfort, 12–3, 16, 19, 75, 81, 87
companionship, love and support, the bachelor household, 57–60
conduct, codes of, 15
conduct literature, 18, 175–202
    concept of home, 180–2
    and domesticity, 183–8, **187**
    and faith, 195–200, **198**
    and harmony, 193–6
    and hospitality, 188–91
    and household leadership, 191–2
    and hypocrisy, 199–200
    moral vision, 200–2
    vision of Christian faith, 183–5, **184**
    women's roles, 192–3
consumer revolution, 76, 90, 118, 158
consumption, 10, 11–3, 85, 87, 149
    and men, 149
    women and, 14, 32–3, 148–9
cooking arrangements, 81
Cooper, Nicholas, 78
cottage, cult of the, 43–4, 68
Courtney, John, 48
Cowper, William, 94
craft and production, 150–1, **151**
craftsmen-builders, 76
Craske, Matthew, 77
credit, culture of, 54–5
Crompton, Samuel, 11
Crowley, John, 13
Cunningham, Colin, 136
curtains, 93–4
Curteen, A., 124

d'Alembert, Jean, 2
Davidoff, Leonore, 111
Day, Julie, 122
de Vries, Jan, 177
decoration, 82
Dee, John, 114–5
Defoe, Daniel, 6, 19, 64, 88
Delap, Lucy, 133
Descartes, René, 2
Devis, Arthur, 4
Deyverdun, George, 50
difference, 16
Dimmock, Matthew, 112
Discourses on Domestic Duties (Stennett), 18, 180, 180–1, 183–6, 188–90, 191–2, 195, 196, 199–200
diversity, 175–6
Dod, J., 41
domestic happiness, 42
Domestic Man, 34–5
domestic space, 24–5, 67, 79, 83, 94
    changes in attitudes to, 3
    dynamism of, 109
    feminized, 141
    fictional references, 24–32
    and men, 33–5
    naming, 101

performance of, 107
and political identity, 76
private, 30–2
public-private division, 109–10
shift in, 82–3
social, 24–30
domestic woman, 138–9, **140**, 141–3, 152
domestic work, 16–7, 109–29
and innovation, 123–8, **127**
intellectual labour, 111–5, **114**, 128–9
domesticity
changing attitudes towards, 23
culture of, 19–20
definition, 131
idealization of, 138–9, **140**, 141–3, 152
and men, 33–5
performance of, 16, 97
and religion, 183–8, **187**, 202
rise of, 10
Doody, Margaret Anne, 27–8, 29, 30
doors, 82
Dormer, Anne, 123
Douglas, Mary, 131
drapes, 93–4
drawing rooms, 26–30, **28**, 101
dressing rooms, 97–8
duty, 14, 141
Dwyer, John, 142

East India Company, 74
Edgeworth, Maria, 104
Edinburgh, 100
education, women, 152, 168–9
Edwards, Clive, 15–6
effeminacy, 145
Eger, Elizabeth, 113
Elias, Norbert, 85
Ellis, Markman, 145
Elmen, Paul, 178
embroidery, 151, **151**
emotional communities, 57–60
Encyclopédie, ou Dictionnaire raisonné des sciences, des arts et des métiers, 10–1, 73
Enlightenment, the, 1–2, 4
Enquiry into the Duties of the Female Sex (Gisborne), 180, 182, 192, 193
entertaining, 7
entertainment, 8

Evelyn, John, 90
Evelyn, Mary, 119
Excellent Daughter, The (Kennett), 179, 181–2, 192–3

façades, 82
familial affection, 3, 42, 44–5
family, 14, 37–47, 60–1, 134, 161–2
bonds, 42–3
boundaries, 37–8
composition, 37–8
conjugal idealization, 37
definition, 3
idealization of, 145–7, **146**
ideals, 40–3
instructive literature, 40–3, 60–1
normative, 39–40
reciprocity, 48
structure, 38
visual representations, 43–5, **44**, **45**, **46**, **47**
family reputation, 54–7, 61
fashion, 8
feminine occupations, social conceptions about, 26–30
femininity, constructions of, 30
Fénelon, François, 139
fictional references, 13–4, 19–35, **22**
aims, 21
detail, 19–20
furniture and furnishings, 86
hospitality, 166–73
material wealth, 32–3
men, 33–5
organization, arrangement and decorative style, 23–30, **28**
private domestic spaces, 30–2
respectability, 166–73
social domestic spaces, 24–30
women and consumption, 32–3
Fielding, Henry, 69, 86
figuration, 15, 85, 86, 107
financial circumstances, 56
Finn, Margot, 149
fireplaces, 82, 87
Flather, Amanda, 136, 138
floor plans, 23–4, 65
flooring, 93
Fordyce, James, 134, 182
Foyster, Elizabeth, 38

France, 71, 72–3, 75, 80, 81, 94, 95, 103, 139, 142, 145, 160–2
Frances, Lady Ingram, 147
Francesco Burney, Edward, 28–9, **28**
Franklin, Benjamin, 2
Frederick the Great of Prussia, 1
freedom, 3
French Revolution, 63, 83, 161
Froide, Amy, 48
furniture and furnishings, 3, 8, 15–6, 65, 85–108
   bedrooms, 95–7, **96**
   chairs, 94, 95, 100–1, 106
   changes in, 90–104
   comfort and convenience, 87
   as cultural signifier, 86, 107
   dining rooms, 98–101, **99**
   drapes, 93–4
   drawing rooms, 101
   dressing rooms, 97–8
   fashion and taste, 87–8
   fictional references, 86
   and gender, 15–6, 86–7, 107–8
   halls and vestibules, 94–5
   in the home, 91–3, **93**
   libraries/studies, 103–4
   living rooms, 101–3
   metamorphic, 103, 104
   pattern books, 88, **89**, 95–6
   performative role, 102
   press beds, 104–5
   second-hand, 106–7
   and self-consciousness, 89
   and social performance, 89–90
   special, 104–5
   and status, 91
   sub-themes, 85–6
   upholstery, 94
   vernacular and cottage, 105–6, **106**
Fussell, Paul, Jr., 179

Gainsborough, Thomas, *The Cottage Door*, 43–4, **44**
Galileo Galilei, 2
gardens, 115
gender, 17, 131–53
   and capitalist production, 134
   and domesticity, 138–9, **140**, 141–3, 152
   and duty, 141
   and furniture and furnishings, 15–6, 86–7, 107–8
   and household management, 147–51, **151**
   and politeness, 143–7, **144**, **146**, 152–3
   and the public-private division, 132–8, **137**
   separate spheres, 133
gendered space, 136–8
George IV, King, 146
Germany, 66, 80, 135
gerontocracy, 54
Gibbon, Edward, 50–1, 56
Gibbs, James, 77
Gillow, Richard, 105
Girouard, Mark, 73, 137
Gisborne, Thomas, 180, 182, 193
Goffman, Erving, 3, 92
Grand Pump Room, Bath, 19
Great Rebuilding, the, 66
Gregory, Dr John, 143, 145
Grey, Jemima, Marchioness, 112
Griffin, Ben, 133

Habermas, Jürgen, 109, 132, 133
habitus, 15, 85, 86, 107
Hadfield, Andrew, 112
Hague, Stephen, 14–5
Hales, Reverend Dr Stephen, 125–6
Hall, Catherine, 111
halls and vestibules, 94–5
Hamling, Tara, 40, 82
Hannan, Leonie, 16–7
Hardyment, Christina, 121
Hareven, Tamara K., 48, 134
Hargreaves, James, 11
Harkness, Deborah, 115
harmony, 193–6
Harris, Amy, 38, 53
Harvey, Karen, 38, 50, 118, 147
Heal, Felicity, 155, 157–8
hearth tax, 67
Heller, Benjamin, 138
Hellmann, Mimi, 102
Hepplewhite, George, 96
   The Cabinet-Maker and Upholsterer's Guide, 88, 97
Herman, Bernard, 149
Hervey, John, 107

heterosociability, 143–4, **144**
High-Life Below Stairs, **10**
Hill, Bridget, 57
Hobbes, Thomas, 2
Hogarth, William, 4
 Beer Street, 69, **70**
 Gin Lane, 69
 Marriage A-La-Mode, 5
 The Wollaston Family, 146–7
Holkham, 74
home
 definition, 1, 2, 19
 religious concept of, 180–2
home economy, and innovation, 17, 123–8, **127**
homemaking, 86–7
Honing Hall, 74
hospitality, 17–8, 155–8, 155–73, **156**
 and class, 169–72
 conduct literature and, 188–91
 representations of respectable, **163**, **164**, 166–73, **167**
 and respectability, 159–62, **159**
 respectable, 162–73, **163**, **164**, **167**
 welfare function, 156
Houghton Hall, 74
house, definition, 1, 19
house construction, 14–5, 63–84
 city houses, 68–72, **70**
 common persons, 64–8, **65**
 elite, 65, 67–8, **67**, 71, 72–5, **74**
 floor plan, 65
 improvement, 68
 middling houses, 75–8, **79**
 pattern books, 77
 polite buildings, 65–6
 and the public-private division, 134–6
 rationalization, 64
 spatial differentiation, 63
 vernacular buildings, 66
 and worldview, 64
household, the, 14, 66–7
 bachelor, 39, 47–60, 61
 boundaries, 37, 38
 co-residence, 48–9, 54–7, 57–60, 60, 61
 emotional communities, 57–60
 head, 52–3
 instructive literature, 40–3
 leadership, 191–2

 organization, arrangement and decorative style, 40
 power structures, 40
 roles, 61
 structure, 38
household accounts, 17, 115–7, 118, 121, 147–8, 149
household management, 38
 bachelor households, 50–7, 61
 and gender, 147–51, **151**
household materials, 17, 115–23, **117**, **120**, 128–9
house/home distinction, 1
House-Keeper's Guide, The, 40–1
Hufton, Olwen, 136
human nature, 2
Hume, David, 134
Hunt, Lynn, 142
Hunt, Margaret, 117
Huntingford, Thomas, 53
Hussey, David, 143, 149
Hutton, Sarah, 112–3

identity, 76
Ince, William, 95, 98
industrialization, 3, 9–11, 115, 134
innovation, and home economy, 17, 123–8, **127**
intellectual approaches, dissemination, 1–2
intellectual labour, 16–7, 111–5, **114**, 128–9
intimacy, 19
invasion narrative, 176
Irwin, Isabella, 148
Irwin, W.R., 178
Isaac Royall House, Medford, Massachusetts, 67
Isabella, fourth Countess of Carlisle, 147–8
Italian baroque, 72

Jefferson, Thomas, 2
Johnson, Matthew, 78, 84
Johnson, Samuel, 3
Joseph II of Austria, 1

Kennett, White, 179, 181–2, 192–3
Kenrick, William, 184–5, 186–8, 191, 199
Kenwood House, **99**
Kepler, Johannes, 2
Kerber, Linda, 134

keys, ownership of, 142
kinship, 22–3, 38, 203
kitchens, 81, 117–8, **117**
Kniffen, Frederick, 66
Krasner, James, 110

La Rochefoucauld, 3, 100
Lamb, Charles and Mary, 49, 57–9
land reforms, 68
Langford, Paul, 84
Larsen, Ruth, 17
Leibniz, Gottfried Wilhelm, 2
Lemire, Beverley, 117
Letter of Genteel and Moral Advice to a Young Lady (Wilkes), 179, 181, 182, 190, 196–7
Lewis, Judith, 19
Lewis, Sarah, 152
libraries/studies, 103–4, 137–8
Lipsedge, Karen, 13–4
Lisbon earthquake, 70
living rooms, 101–3
living spaces, specialization of, 13
Locke, John, 2
London, 68–71, 82, 82–3, 84, 133
    Great Fire of, 70–1
    Vauxhall pleasure gardens, 19
London Building Acts, 71
Louis XIV, King of France, 73
love, 3, 14, 42, 43, 44–5, 60
luxury, 11–3
    demand for, 148

McCormack, Matthew, 133
McCracken, Grant, 91
Mack, Phyllis, 177
McKellar, Elizabeth, 76
McKeon, Michael, 110, 135–6, 138, 141, 180
Madrid, 131
magazines, 4
Mallett, Shelley, 132
Malthus, Thomas, 13
Manchester, 141
Mandeville, Bernard, 12
Marie Antoinette, 68, 150
marital status, 14
Marlborough, Duke of, 74
Marot, Daniel, 95

marriage, 39–40, 41, 60, 134, 147, 164–5
masculinity, 34–5, 48, 55, 112, 131, 142, 143, 145, 152, 152–3
material wealth, 32–3
Mayhew, John, 95, 98
mechanization, 10–1
Meldrum, Tim, 111
men
    authority, 34
    and consumption, 149
    and domestic space, 33–5
    and domesticity, 142–3
    fictional references, 33–5
    household leadership, 191–2
    households, 47–50
    relationships with female relatives, 48
    role of, 14
Merlin, John Joseph, 103
Metcalfe, Helen, 14
Millar, John, 139
Millon, Henry A., 73
mixed-sex socializing, 143–4, **144**
moderation, 176
modernity, 109
modernization, 65
Montagu, Elizabeth, 113
Montesquieu, Charles de Secondat, Baron de, 145
moral competence, 160, 167, 171
moral hierarchy, 167–8
moral inconsistency, 197–200
More, Hannah, 169
Morland, George, 4
motherhood, 134
Muldrew, Craig, 54–5
multi-use spaces, 15
musical performances, 168–9

National Style, 24
Neal, Matthew, 18
neighbourliness, 188–90, 203
Nenadic, Stana, 100, 107
Neoclassicism, 9, 78, 83
Netherlands, the, 95
newspapers, 4
Newton, Isaac, 2
noise, 82
North, Roger, 78

novelists, use of houses and interiors, 13–4
novels, 6–7

occupational relationships, 3
oeconomy, 50, 56
organization, arrangement and decorative style, fictional references, 23–30, **28**
Ottoman empire, 135
Ottoway, Susannah, 48
over-consumption, 4

Palladianism, 24
Palling, William, 81
parenting, 38
Paris, 68, 72, 73, 75, 133
Parker, Rozsika, 151
parlours, 80, 81
paternalism, 61
pattern books, 77, 87, 88, 95–6
Pearsall, Sarah, 37, 48
Pennell, Sara, 91
periodicals, 139
Perry, Ruth, 22–3, 40, 57
Philadelphia, 69
Pitt, William, the Younger, 160–1
place
    types of, 25–6
    woman's need for, 24–30
Platt, Colin, 75–6, 77
polite buildings, 65–6
polite threshold, the, 15, 66, 77
politeness, 13, 65–6, 90, 143–7, **144, 146,** 152–3, 176, 202
political economy, 87
Pombaline style, 71
Ponsonby, Margaret, 39
population growth, 68
possessions, accumulation of, 3
power structures, 40
Prague, 72
Prendergast, Amy, 113
press beds, 104–5
Primrose, Charles, 33
print culture, 4
privacy, 3, 13, 14, 23, 80, 81, 83, 87, 110, 134
    protection of
private domestic spaces, fictional references, 30–2

private space, 27
propriety, 27
public-private division, 3–4, 109–10, 111–2, 132–8, **137,** 176–7

Quakers, 143

Rabelais, François, 19
Read, George, I, 69
religion, 18, 175–202
    Christian revivalism, 177
    concept of home, 180–2
    and domesticity, 183–8, **187,** 202
    and faith, 195–7, **198**
    and harmony, 193–6
    and hospitality, 188–91
    and household leadership, 191–2
    and hypocrisy, 199–200
    moral vision, 200–2
    women's roles, 192–3
Repton, Humphrey, 102
respectability, 13, 17–8, 158, 159–62, **159,** 162–6, **163**
    and class, 169–73
    representations of respectable, **163, 164,** 166–73, **167**
Retford, Kate, 44
Reynolds, Joshua, 44, 48, 85
Richardson, Catherine, 40
Richardson, Samuel, 4, 19–20, 23, 30, 30–1, 35, 82
    Clarissa, 24–5, 32
    Pamela; or, Virtue Rewarded, 6–7, **6,** 13–4, 21, **22,** 25–6, 31–2, 61
    Sir Charles Grandison, 14, 34–5
rococo, 71, 72, 96, 100
rooms, 3, 15, 24, 79–83
    differentiation, 12–3
    gendered, 25–6
    spatial diversification, 79–80
    specialization, 80
Rousseau, Jean Jacques, 145
Royal Society of Arts, 123–8, **127**
Ryder, Dudley, 144

Sambrook, Pamela, 121
Saunders, Peter, 131
scientific experiment, 113–5, **114,** 128–9
Scotland, 66, 100, 107

sculleries, 122
Second Great Rebuilding, 75–6
self, representation of the, 3
self-consciousness, 16
self-image, 8, 12
self-respect, 160
sensibility, 145, 147, 149, 152–3
sentimentality, 145
Sermons to Young Women (Fordyce), 182
servants, 4, 25, 38, 55–6, 61, 79, 81, 109, 110–1, 187–8
Shaftesbury, Earl of, 7
Shagan, Ethan, 176
Shammas, Carole, 131, 144
Shapin, Steven, 114–5
shell-work, 8
Sheraton, Thomas, 97–8, 98–9, 101, 103
   Cabinet Dictionary, 94
   The CabinetMaker and Upholsterer's Drawing Book, 88
Sheridan, Frances, 23
   Memoirs of Miss Sidney Bidulph, 26–30, 28
Shevelow, Kathryn, 141
Shipley, William, 123
Shorter, Edward, 139
Shove, Elizabeth, 110
Shugborough Hall, 121
Smith, Charles Saumarez, 149
Smith, Elizabeth, 133
Smith, Thomas, 119
Smith, Woodruff, 17–8
sociability, 4, 23, 51, 143–7, **144**, **146**
social cohesiveness, 14
social communications, 7
social domestic spaces, fictional references, 24–30
social mobility, 7
social ordering, 82
social performance, 16
socialization, 176, 191
Society for the Encouragement of Arts, Manufactures and Commerce, 123–8, **127**, 129
space
   gendered, 136–8
   hierarchy of, 24
   see also domestic space
Spershott, James, 88
stairs, 80–1

status, 7, 12, 24, 25, 76, 77–8, 91
Steedman, Carolyn, 21–2, 110, 111
Stennett, Samuel, 180, 180–1, 183–6, 188–90, 191–2, 195, 196, 199–200
Stevens, William Bagshaw, 48
Stillingfleet, Edward, 195
stillroom, the, 119
Stone, Lawrence, 37, 38
Stranks, Charles, 178
Summerson, John, 68
Swan, Abraham, 77
Sweet, Rosemary, 113
Swift, Jonathan, 14, 23, 32–3
   A Lady's Dressing Room, 33
Syon House, Middlesex, **9**, 137

Tadmor, Naomi, 37–8, 38, 49
taste, 12–3, 75, 83, 87–8, 92, 149
tea, taking of, 18, 162–6, **163**, **164**
Thomson, Alexander, 127–8
Tillotson, John, 195
toilets, 81–2
tolerance, 55, 176–80, 182, 184, 186–8, 190–1, 193, 195–7, 200–2
Tomaselli, Sylvanna, 134
town houses, internal layouts, 13
town planning, 15
transportation networks, 76
Trumbach, Randolph, 37
Trussler, John, 42, 43
Tryon, Thomas, 104

upholstery, 94
urbanization, 3, 9–11, 15, 68–72, **70**

Vauxhall pleasure gardens, London, 19
vernacular buildings, 66
Versailles, Palace of, 63, 68, **72**, 73
Vickery, Amanda, 40, 86, 110, 138, 139, 141, 148, 176, 180, 186
villas, 78, **79**
virtue, 21, **22**, 30, 141–2
Virtue in a Cottage; or, A Mirror for Children in Humble Life, 141
visual and material culture, 4–9, **5**, **6**, **7**, **8**, **9**
Voltaire, 139

Walker, Lynne, 136
wallpaper, 82, 92, **93**

Walpole, Sir Robert, 74
Ware, Isaac, 77, 95, 97, 101
Warriner, the Reverend Enoch, 141
Washington, George, 162
Watt, Ian, 6
Weatherill, Lorna, 102
Wedgwood, Josiah, 11
Werrett, Simon, 115
Whatman, Susanna, 122
Whole Duty of Man, The (Allestree), 18, 41, 177–8, **178**, 181, 185–6, 192, 194, 196, 197–9
Whole Duty of Woman, The, 18 178–9, **179**, 184–5, 186–8, 190–1, 199
Wilberforce, William, 160–2
Wilkes, Wetenhall, 179, 181, 182, 190, 196–7
Williams, Abigail, 138
Williams, Peter, 131
Wills, Abigail, 133
windows, 82
withdrawing rooms, 136–7, 138
Wollstonecraft, Mary, 134
women, 79, 131–53
    in bachelors' households, 57–9, 61
    Bluestockings, 113
    and consumption, 14, 32–3, 148–9
    craft and production, 150–1, **151**

    domestic duties, 33
    domesticity, 138–9, **140**, 141–3
    dressing rooms, 97–8
    and duty, 141
    education, 152, 168–9
    elderly, 48
    and homemaking, 86–7
    and household management, 147–51, **151**
    musical performances, 168–9
    need for place, 24–30
    and politeness, 143–7, **144**, **146**
    private domestic spaces, 31–2
    and the public-private division, 132–8, **137**
    roles, 111, 131, 139, 182, 192–3
    seclusion, 134
Wood, John, 91
wood panelling, 92, **93**
Woodforde, James, 48, 48–9, 51–7, 59–60, 107
Wootton, Sir Henry, *Elements of Architecture*, 7
Wordsworth, Dorothy, 58
worldview, 64
Wrightson, Keith, 37
Wyndham, Elizabeth, 126–7, **127**

Zoffany, Johann, 44, 146